My Favourite Restaurants

in Calgary & Banff

4th Edition

JOHN GILCHRIST

Edited by Catherine Caldwell

Escurial Incorporated

Calgary, Alberta

Published by
Escurial Incorporated
9519 Assiniboine Road SE
Calgary, Alberta
Canada T2J 0Z5
Phone: (403) 255·7560
E-mail: escurial@cadvision.com

National Library of Canada Cataloguing in Publication Data

Gilchrist, John, 1953–
My favourite restaurants in Calgary & Banff

Includes index.
ISBN: 0 – 9693106 – 3 – 3

1. Restaurants—Alberta—Calgary—Guidebooks. 2. Restaurants—Alberta—Banff—Guidebooks. 3. Calgary (Alta.)—Guidebooks. 4. Banff (Alta.)—Guidebooks. I. Caldwell, Catherine, 1956 – II. Title. III. Title: My favourite restaurants in Calgary and Banff.

TX910.C2G54 2001   647.957123'38   C2001-911282-3

CREDITS:
Interior & Cover Design: Jeremy Drought, Last Impression Publishing Service, Calgary, Alberta
Cover Illustration: Kari Lehr, Mosaic Artworks, Calgary, Alberta
Printing: Friesens Corporation, Altona, Manitoba

Printed and bound in Canada

Table of Contents

Acknowledgements

I am constantly amazed at how my charming wife and editor Catherine Caldwell can convert my ramblings into something readable. Her skill with the comma remains unparalleled. She has committed an immense amount of effort to this and all our books and I can't thank her enough. I've offered to take her out to dinner but...

I owe a bottomless mug of Planet high-test coffee to James Martin. I am honoured once again to have his words kick off this book in the Foreword. James is both a great writer and a great friend, and I thank him for taking the time from work on the second edition of his own book, *Calgary: Secrets of the City*, to contribute to mine.

I'll be taking Richard White and Maureen Healey of the Calgary Downtown Association out for a nice lunch—probably somewhere in the downtown—to thank them for joining us on this project.

A big bag of baguettes from the Eiffel Tower Bakery goes to Jeremy Drought of Last Impression Publishing Service. His calm and creative mind has given us the "look" of the book, from the shape of the page to the distance between the letters.

And I've got some boxes of donuts for Dougall Cameron as well as the good folks at Knight Enterprises who help us out in the computer department. Plus, Catherine will be taking a big whack of Callebaut chocolates to the staff of the Education Resource Centre for Continuing Care for their support during this project.

I'd also like to thank all those committed souls in the food industry who put food on the table at all times of the day for all sorts of customers in all kinds of weather. It takes a particular type to thrive in the food biz. I have tremendous respect for them all.

Foreword

by James Martin

WHEN John Gilchrist steps into a restaurant, he's looking for more than just chow. (Or a washroom.) He's looking for a story. Yes, the food is important, but what John really writes about is the *experience*. Reading one of his reviews puts you right there at his table—in spirit, if not stomach.

Right now, please indulge a little story of my own.

At the behest of my guidance counsellor, I once job-shadowed John Gilchrist as he made his Friday morning rounds. Sitting in a CBC Radio broadcast booth at an hour when many Calgarians are contemplating caffeine IV-drips (me, I didn't even know there were *two* seven o'clocks in any given day), I watched John deliver his latest restaurant review. He was sharp, eloquent, informed, and completely "on." Glimpsing my bleary mug reflected in the soundproof glass, I had a revelation: "Oh, how I despise this chipper fellow." John later bought me a potent espresso-and-French-roast elixir (it jacked me up like a greased chimp on rollerblades) and all was forgiven.

I turned the whole experience into a magazine article entitled "The Man Who Ate Calgary, and Asked for Seconds." My opus was chockablock with hard-hitting journalistic insights, including:

John Gilchrist started eating at a young age.

John Gilchrist has eaten everything from saffron risotto to locusts.

John Gilchrist firmly believes every meal (not just those traditionally associated with Biblical plagues) should be fun.

An unrepentant moocher who's never passed up a free meal (insect or otherwise), I've shared many a repast with John Gilchrist. Sometimes I've even been invited. John brings to the table impeccable manners and an immaculate expense account—plus all the verve, wit, insight, and encyclopedic know-how you've come to expect from his reviews. He knows, for example, why Thai food is supposed to be eaten with a fork (something to do with Yul Brynner) and why fondue is not a toy (nothing to do with Yul Brynner).

Once, between mouthfuls of spicy tuna roll, I posed what I naively believed to be a blue-ribbon stumper: "Why do the mac'n'cheese instructions recommend boiling *cold* water? Wouldn't it be quicker to boil warm stuff from the tap?" Wielding an oversized pepper mill as an educational prop, John launched into the molecular explanation of how warm tap water contains less oxygen than cold tap water. "Oxygen makes food taste better," he concluded. "If you don't believe me, try eating without breathing." Always the contrarian, I took up his challenge. Later, upon being resuscitated by the sweet scrape of a paramedic's endotracheal tube, I thought to myself, "By gum, John's right again!"

In short, you can trust John Gilchrist. Moreover, you now hold before you 200-plus nuggets of his taste-tested advice. (No locusts, but you can't have everything.)

As they say in Antarctica, dig in.

James Martin is the author of Calgary: Secrets of the City—*now available in a revised and expanded 2nd edition—and writes the "Mr. Smutty" column for* FFWD Weekly.

Introduction

WELCOME to book number four. Wait a minute. Already? How can that be? It's been just two years since my last guide. But the food and restaurant industry is so dynamic that there have been immense changes—fully seventy-five of the over 200 recommended places here are new. It's hard to keep up. And it just gets better. In this book, we see the return of Cajun, Turkish, and Hungarian cuisines and the arrival of Syrian, Southern barbecue, tapas, and Euro-Asian Fusion. Plus the continuing increase of noodle shops, sushi bars, and Irish pubs.

I've created a new chapter called "Purveyors" which contains places where the focus is not necessarily meals but is still good food in some form. These entries could be coffee houses, butcher shops, bakeries, ice cream parlours, grocery stores, or chocolate shops.

So here's what you need to know. No one has paid to be in this book. The reviews are compiled from the work I do for CBC Radio One, the *Calgary Herald*, and *WHERE Calgary* and *Avenue* magazines, and they simply reflect the spots I like the best. When I review a restaurant, I go as a regular customer—albeit under an assumed name—and I pay for my meal. On the surprisingly few occasions when I am recognized, I try to assess whether I am receiving any special treatment. (I actually find that it can throw staff off if they know I am a restaurant reviewer.) And though the information collected for this book is as current as possible, remember that staff move around, hours change, and some places will inevitably close.

Here's some other pertinent information:

• The "Restaurant Reviews" section as well as the "Purveyors" section are each arranged alphabetically.

• While I was working on this book, the City of Calgary was in the process of redefining the smoking bylaw. Hopefully by the next edition I can dispense with references to non-smoking sections altogether, at least for Calgary entries.

• If you're calling long distance, all phone numbers in the book are preceded by the area code 403.

• The presence of the "Downtown That's the Spot" logo indicates that a restaurant or food outlet is located within Calgary's downtown.

- Credit card abbreviations are pretty straightforward: **V** for VISA, **MC** for MasterCard, **AE** for American Express, **DC** for Diners Club, and **JCB** for Japan Credit Bureau.

- Cost categories are based on a dinner for two with appetizers, main courses, and desserts (or equivalents) and include tax but not drinks or gratuity: **$** means under $30, **$$** ranges from $30 to $60, and **$$$** pushes it over $60.

There is an amazing amount of quality out there and a lot of chefs and other food purveyors who really care about their products and customers. This is a collection of my favourite places, and I hope it guides you to some new ones of your own. In the meantime, I'll just keep on eating and letting you know what's cooking in Calgary and Banff.

John Gilchrist
Calgary, Alberta

Aida's

Lebanese

2208 – 4 Street SW
Phone: 541 · 1189
Monday 11 am – 9 pm, Tuesday – Thursday 11 am – 10 pm
Friday & Saturday 11 am – 11 pm, Sunday 4 pm – 9 pm
Reservations recommended — Fully licensed — Non-smoking
V, MC, AE, Debit — $ – $$

ALTHOUGH AIDA's is on a busy stretch of 4th Street, it can be hard to find. Its street presence is minimal, but once you're inside, it is more open and airy than is initially obvious. Seating forty-four under a gold-painted tin ceiling, the room is pretty with its dark purple tones.

And yes, there is an Aida. She's not new to 4th Street. She ran Cafe Med (where Sushi Kawa now resides) almost next door for a few years. She left the business for a while, but we—and her many fans—are glad to see her, her family, and her food back. Aida sets the tone for her staff, who are earnest and willing to please.

Her food is very, very good. Lebanese cuisine is fresh and totally in tune with the market's move to lighter, healthier, and tastier foods. Incorporating spices like sumak (a dried, ground Middle Eastern berry that imparts a sour, almost lemony taste) and grains such as ferik (a lightly smoked wheat), Aida creates delicate, savoury flavours that meld dishes together.

The fattoush is a crunchy salad of romaine, cucumbers, tomatoes, radishes, and pita chips in a sumak and olive oil dressing. It is such a simple yet tasty dish and is reasonably priced, with a small portion costing only $3.95 and a large, only $4.95. The platters of things like lamb kebabs or falafel or shawarma include fattoush or tabouleh (the parsley and bulgar salad) and hommous or baba ghannouj dips. These plates are also a great bargain. A salad, a dip, and a pile of falafel for $7.95 is outstanding value. As are strips of warm, marinated chicken with diced vegetables and tahini, with salad and dip, for $8.95. And presentation is beautiful with all those fresh vegetables.

Vegetables and grains play as important a part in Lebanese cuisine as meats, making it a great cuisine for vegetarians. The lentil and spinach soup, for example, is lovely. It demonstrates more subtle flavours blended with skill and is a staple for us through the winter.

We thought we had enjoyed all of Aida's menu until we discovered her mouhammara. This dip of roasted peppers, walnuts, and bread crumbs—which we had never tasted before—wowed us with its depth and richness and now is a must every time we go.

I like Aida's. In fact, I like it so much—the combination of food, service, and value—that I named it the best new restaurant of 2000.

Ali Baba

Syrian

3745 Memorial Drive SE (Glencrest Centre)
Phone: 273·4417
Monday–Thursday 11 am – 11 pm, Friday & Saturday 11 am – 1 am
Sunday noon – 10 pm
Reservations accepted — Fully licensed — Small non-smoking section
V, MC, AE, Debit — $ – $$

YOU won't find forty thieves lurking in the parking lot, but a simple "Open Sesame!" will bring you to Ali Baba, the only Syrian restaurant in town. It's a family-run cafe in a strip-mall bay that has been spruced up recently. The walls are painted with murals from the *Arabian Nights*, there's new carpet, and the tables are topped with delicately embroidered cloths.

Syrian cuisine is similar to Lebanese—there are the hommous and baba ghannouj dips, the tabouleh and fattoush salads, and the various meat kebabs. But most dishes are prepared a bit differently.

We tried a lentil soup, which most Middle Eastern cafes do in a rich, dark, hearty style. Ali Baba's is a light, lemony broth filled with yellow lentils and spiked with freshly ground cinnamon and more lemon. This unusual blend of flavours is at once satisfying and appetizing: the lemon opens the appetite while the cinnamon soothes the palate.

Then we had some mouhammara, a creamy purée of roasted red peppers, walnuts, and bread crumbs. Ali Baba's is robust, the grind is coarse, and the bite of the peppers is strong. They serve it with pita chips, an excellent way to scoop it up.

Next in our mezza-style dinner was a plate of b'storma. Much of Middle Eastern food is vegetarian friendly. This is not. B'storma is raw, air-dried beef that has been rolled in fragrant yellow and red spices and thinly sliced. Lemon is then squeezed over it, bringing out more flavours. This will be popular with carpaccio fans out there. (The yellow and red coatings are secret blends of Syrian spices.)

We also had a plate of falafel with a pile of fresh greens, lightly pickled beets, chopped parsley, and tahini sauce. The flavours were excellent, but the crust on the falafel was a little thick for our taste. And the house-made pita was a bit dry. But those are minor criticisms.

Ali Baba's owners are hoping to receive a license to operate a tobacco-filled water pipe on the premises. Customers will be able to purchase a bowl of natural Turkish tobacco to smoke, so though it certainly is a Middle Eastern tradition, be forewarned. If tobacco isn't your dessert of choice, try out the crème caramel. It's dense and rich, one of the best in the city.

All round, Ali Baba is one fine little cafe. And cheap too. Our bill for all that food with a glass of wine was about $35. You can't beat that for the quality.

Annie's
Bakery Cafe

Bow Valley Ranch, south end of Bow Bottom Trail SE
Phone: 225 • 3920
Easter weekend – Labour Day: Daily 9 am – 6 pm
Reservations not accepted — No alcoholic beverages — Porches — Non-smoking
V, MC, AE, DC, Debit — $

THERE aren't a lot of restaurants inside the city limits that provide a view of a grassy valley with a beaver-filled stream winding through it. And, although the numbers are growing, there aren't too many cafes in historic buildings. But you get both at Annie's, with good food to boot.

Annie's resides in the old foreman's house at the Bow Valley Ranch in Fish Creek Provincial Park. It is a simple wood-frame building with south- and west-facing porches and three rooms inside for dining. Perhaps "dining" is too serious a word for a small cafe that services cyclists, bladers, strollers, and their dogs. With a hodgepodge collection of old furniture and a decor that spares us trendy upgrades, Annie's is casual and comfortable. Families chow down on wraps and bowls of soup after hiking the trails, groups of ladies enjoy muffins with tea, and helmeted bikers rehydrate with fresh lemonade and iced tea. Underlying it all is the parched Prairie smell of an old house, the scent of century-old wallpaper, and the clatter of heels on hardwood. Annie's exudes undeniable atmosphere, the history of ranching Alberta.

In 1899, ranch foreman Billy Bannister married Annie Birney, the cafe's namesake, and the couple moved into the loft of the main ranch house. By the time Annie was expecting her fourth child, the loft just wouldn't do, so a separate residence was moved to the property for the Bannisters and their growing family. This is the building that houses Annie's today.

The menu is simple, comprised of fresh-baked muffins and cookies, tuna and veggie wraps, daily soups and quiches, ice cream and drinks. Items are scrawled on an overhead chalkboard and you order at the counter. Service is always pleasant, but this style is a bit confusing—I'm not quite sure if I should wait at the counter for my food or sit down and wait for someone to bring it to me.

A few other good things about Annie's. First, it's non-smoking both inside and out. It is, after all, an old wood-frame building. And second, it has the best view of Prairie sunsets going. Sitting in a rocking chair on the west porch with a cup of coffee and a chewy brownie, watching a summer sunset while the grasses rustle, is just about as good as life gets. It's one of those things that reminds me of why our forefathers stayed here and toughed out those cold winter days.

Anpurna

Indian (Vegetarian Gujarati)

175 – 52 Street SE
Phone: 235 • 6028
Tuesday – Friday 11 am – 2:30 pm, 5 pm – 8:30 pm
Saturday & Sunday 11 am – 8:30 pm
Reservations accepted — Beer & wine only — Non-smoking
V — $

WAY east on Memorial Drive, there is a little vegetarian Gujarati restaurant called the Anpurna. Named after the Anpurna mountain range, it features the vegetarian cuisine of Gujarat, a western province of India. Not all Gujarati food is vegetarian, but it is the preferred style of this region.

The menu here offers only about twenty choices—all are totally non-meat, non-fish, and non-egg, though you will find dairy products used. There are a number of chickpea and lentil dishes as well as samosas and rasmalai, but they are done Gujarati style. One of the most expensive items is the $4.95 combo plate of masala dossa—that's a potato- and onion-filled crepe served with a lentil dhal and a coconut chutney. It makes an excellent, filling meal. A plate of three large samosas is $3.75, the chole puri (a chickpea curry) is $4.25, and the gulab jamun dessert is $2.50. This is cheap food.

We ordered the thali, a combination plate of two vegetable curries, dhal, rice, paratha, pickle, pappadam, and dessert for $8.95 per person. The two curries were quite distinct: one was prepared with string beans and lima beans, the other, with black-eyed peas. Neither was overly complex but they were very different from each other. And the beans were all expertly cooked. The dhal came in a different form from what I am used to: the lentils appeared sparingly in a thick soup rather than in a tasty pile. Both the carrot-mustard pickle and the fresh paratha (a flat, whole wheat bread) were excellent, and the rice pudding was rich and flavourful.

The biggest treat I've had here is the kachori, something I've not seen anywhere else in the city. Kachori are about the size of billiard balls and are made by rolling dough around a lentil-coconut combo. They are rich with Indian spices and a fresh mint dipping sauce.

To say that the decor at the Anpurna is plain would be a compliment. It is a homely little room that was once a fish and chip shop. It seats about forty under glaring fluorescents in an industrial setting. Do not dress up for the Anpurna. The staff, however, are very pleasant. It is a family operation, so you get the friendly feeling of being invited into someone's home.

Good luck finding it. It's at the southwest corner of Memorial Drive and 52nd Street SE. A more obscure location would be difficult to imagine. Perhaps that is appropriate for a cuisine as unique to Calgary as vegetarian Gujarati.

Banffshire Club

Continental

Fairmont Banff Springs Hotel, Banff
Phone: 762·6860
Daily 6 pm – 10 pm
Reservations recommended — Fully licensed — Non-smoking
V, MC, AE, DC, JCB — $$$

THE harp player and the kilted hostess at a gated entrance to the Banffshire Club are the first indication that there's important stuff going on here. This is the formal dining room at the Banff Springs Hotel, and the message given is to be prepared and dress well.

Which is not to intone that the Banffshire is snooty. It is very comfortable—"understated extravagance" is how they describe it. High-backed chairs, tables discreetly placed around the room, fireplaces glowing in the upholstered light, more friendly staff in kilts.

Anthony Chalmers is the maître d' and sommelier, a fellow with an encyclopedic knowledge of wine and an encyclopedia to back it up: He's created a sixty-page wine menu that ranges from tasty Spaniards and Canadians in the low $40s to hilariously priced bottles of Bordeaux in the thousands. Daniel Buss is the chef, a talented lad with a flare for local ingredients and Swiss preparations. They and their staff are justifiably proud of their room and their menu.

And a good read the menu is. Butter-poached lobster with an asparagus ragout and a foie gras and potato purée. Or pecan-crusted caribou with turnip flan. Or Alberta lamb in a black trumpet mushroom rub. All with commensurate prices. A two-course meal runs $75, three courses are $85, and four courses are $95.

But why equivocate. We opted for the nine-course blowout at $110, paired with six wines to bring it up to $175. Per person.

And it was a gustatory workout, starting with a white asparagus soup infused with lemon essence and topped with chive foam, bits of foie gras, and Oregon truffles. Stunning. Then a zucchini flower stuffed with a salmon mousse and drizzled with a clam-tomato vinaigrette. A terrine of squab, partridge, and rabbit. A lemon grass and sake granita. A buttery bison tenderloin in a Madeira-walnut sauce. Some Oka cheese and on to a cloud-like chocolate cake with macadamia nut ice cream and a passion fruit beurre blanc.

Execution was flawless in both service and preparation—every dish, a work of art on the plate and a burst of flavour on the palate. And the wines—from a Gray Monk Pinot Auxerrois to the heavy hitting 1997 Dominus and a finishing Oloroso sherry, the wines were perfectly paired with each course. And served in demurely consumable quantities.

The Springs cast a golden glow as we strolled through the halls after our meal. We were full, but not overly so. We had just eaten one of the best meals of our lives.

Barpa Bill's Souvlaki
Greek Fast Food

223 Bear Street, Banff
Phone: 762·0377
Daily 11 am−9 pm
Reservations not accepted — No alcoholic beverages — Non-smoking
V — $

WHOOEE! I have waited almost three decades to find a souvlaki to match the one I had at a little hole in the wall in Athens on a rainy Christmas Eve many years ago. Standing under a ripped awning as the souvlaki chef charred the lamb and rolled it into a warm pita with tomatoes and cucumber and tzatziki sauce, I was bathed not only in the heavy rain but in the smells of robust Greek cooking. I enjoyed the juicy, garlicky bite of the souvlaki so much that I went back five times before leaving the city three days later. And over the next twenty-seven years, I tried souvlaki from the vendors on the Broadview in Toronto and at little alley cafes in New York City and Vancouver and from some very good restaurants in Calgary. Never was I able to find the full-bodied, garlic-to-the-hilt, tzatziki-dripping, grilled meats of my memory.

Then someone told me about Barpa Bill's in Banff, a tiny twelve-stool operation on Bear Street in a building with a combo laundromat-video store. I had to go.

Entering Bill's, the smells were promising and the level of confusion reassuring. Behind the counter, covered in hand-scrawled menus, are coolers filled with drinks and a smoking grill. The menu is fattened by burgers, fabulous spanakopita, and stuffed grape leaves, but the essence lies in the souvlakia—chicken, pork, beef, and recently, lamb too.

In a few moments, I was holding a foil-wrapped pita oozing sauce, chicken, tomatoes, and onions. Good chicken and greens. Soft, dense pita that is shipped in from Chicago and is good enough to go that far to get. But the sauce. Creamy yogurt and garlic and garlic and garlic. This was the souvlaki of my memory. Actually, this pita was a little better and the sauce, a little creamier. And more garlicky. No one came near me for days.

This was exacerbated by the Caesar salad, which was also loaded with garlic, but was balanced with excellent cheese and fine, fine croutons. With crisp romaine, this was one of the best and most forceful Caesars I have had.

Bill's is a great place—if you love garlic. The prices won't kill you: the souvlaki was $5 and the side salad was $4.50. It is not the most elegant place to dine, but Bill's is the kind of place that will keep me coming back. And more than once in the next twenty-seven years.

The Belvedere

Contemporary Continental

107 Stephen Avenue Walk SW
Phone: 265·9595
Monday – Friday 11:30 am – 2 pm, 5 pm – 10 pm, Saturday 5 pm – 11 pm
Reservations recommended — Fully licensed — Patio
Non-smoking dining room, smoking in lounge
V, MC, AE, DC — $$$

Rack of lamb crusted in black olives with fig vinegar and mint reduction, a compote of peas and lettuce, and pommes fondant on the side. Oven-roasted venison chops with bashed neeps, Stilton apples, and pomegranate jus. Buckwheat blinis. Barolo gravy. Sea urchin dressing. Langoustine risotto.

Outstanding flavours. Amazing balance of textures. Beautiful plates. Intense cuisine. The Belvedere.

Packed into yet another revived bank building, The Belvedere features a sixty-seat, non-smoking dining room and a smoker-friendly, forty-seat lounge. The dining room is a lovely, compact space that is part historic with exposed beams and a big skylight, part contemporary with backlit, mirrored panels, and part '50s dinner club with plush accoutrements. The dining room is separated from the lounge by a velvety floor-to-ceiling curtain, accentuating the sumptuous feel. They could have gone a little more comfy with the chairs however. They are hard, unpadded wood, fine for a quick lunch but uncomfortable after a few hours.

And a few hours you will need. The Belvedere falls into the "dining experience" category, with dinner becoming a two- to three-hour event, and lunch feels rushed at an hour. But it is time well spent.

The food here is stellar. The menu features a Contemporary-Continental style that uses fresh local ingredients, a certain amount of Asian sensibilities, and striking combinations like ahi tuna with foie gras or anchovy bread crumbs or a Madeira-fennel glaze. They have never been shy about putting flavour on the plate. The beef short ribs melt off the bone, shining in their Sylvaner-horseradish sauce, and a Manchego-mushroom risotto satisfies every corner of our appetites.

And they don't skimp either. The servings are hearty. As are the prices. The white asparagus vichyssoise with smoked salmon and caviar is $13, a Hotchkiss tomato salad with a Shropshire blue soufflé is $12. Dinner entrees start with a potato rösti torte with spinach and paneer at $22, pass through some seared scallops at $28 and the ahi tuna at $33, and top out at a tenderloin for $38. Add a little wine, desserts, tax, and tip, and a dinner for two will be in the $125 to $150 range. It is at the high end, but Calgarians are willing to pay for quality cuisine served with skill in a lovely setting.

The Belvedere pushes the boundaries of Contemporary cuisine, giving diners a chance to taste some of the best food anywhere. It is worth the experience.

Big Rock Grill
Contemporary Grill

5555 – 76 Avenue SE
Phone: 236 • 1606
Monday – Friday 11:30 am – 2:30 pm
Reservations recommended — Fully licensed — Patio — Non-smoking section
V, MC, AE, DC, Debit — $$

Big Rock Brewery is quite spiffy—it is a green-roofed complex with a huge brewery building and a restaurant called the Big Rock Grill. The Grill reminds me of the winery-restaurant combos in California and the Okanagan, where restaurants attached to wine-making facilities prepare food to match the drink. At Big Rock, the beverage of choice is their fine beer.

The Grill seats over 100 in a sunny room with high ceilings. A cobblestone fireplace, a terra-cotta tile floor, and the dark green walls give it a lodge feel, and a big bar along one end serves all of Big Rock's beers. (Do not order a Labatt Lite here.) It is set up for lunch, a relaxing brew, and evening functions. The space is flexible, but it has a tendency to become smoky—beer and tobacco still seem to go together for a lot of people.

One key asset of the Grill is the team of Klaus Wöckinger and Klaus Wöckinger. Senior and Junior that is. Klaus Senior spent a decade as executive chef at La Chaumière and owns Dante's downtown. Junior learned the ropes in his father's kitchen and serves as manager at the Grill. Their food is simple, fairly natural, even moderately healthy, but with lots of taste. And it goes great with beer.

I've had a velvety mushroom soup that was lightly thickened, filled with various mushrooms, and exuded a gentle, clean flavour. It went perfectly with a Big Rock Traditional Ale. (Beers are available in six-ounce taster glasses—a decent size, especially if you are going back to work.)

They use a rotisserie oven, cooking poultry and roasts and even the odd suckling pig. I have tried a tasty chicken and cashew salad, with chunks of tender chicken and roasted cashews piled onto fresh greens. And a lunch special of roast suckling pig with garlic mashed potatoes was a rich and crunchy meal. Other items include house-smoked salmon on rye bread served with potato salad, pork medallions served with caramelized apple salsa, and a roast beef sandwich grilled to a perfect medium rare.

For more perfection, check out the daily sherbet. I had their champagne version with fresh blueberries, oranges, kiwi, and strawberries, with a cherry and mint sprig on top. Excellent all around.

The Big Rock Grill is one of the few places in the deep southeast section of Calgary, so call ahead for a reservation. It is very popular, and deservedly so.

Blonde

Contemporary Global

160 Stephen Avenue Walk SE
Phone: 269·1600
Monday – Friday 11:30 am – 2:30 pm, Monday – Saturday 5 pm – midnight
Reservations recommended — Fully licensed — Non-smoking
V, MC, AE, DC, Debit — $$ – $$$

WHEN BLONDE splashed onto the dining scene in December 2000, it generated more discussion than any restaurant I have ever known. People were interested in the look, the food, the prices, and practically anything else about Blonde.

And rightly so. Blonde is a gorgeous 100-seat space with three distinct areas, plus bar seating. The room holds more shades and textures of blonde—in the paint, the wall coverings, and the floor—than I would have thought possible. It has a minimalist sparseness that would drive my clutter-loving sister crazy but that others find airy and fresh. Blonde also features an open kitchen that sparkles with new equipment. The staff work studiously on the Contemporary menu of lobster perogies, panko-crusted tuna, and venison loin with rhubarb-kumquat marmalade.

It's an adventurous list that glazes baby hens in truffle honey and coats lamb loins with cinnamon and star anise. This is one of those several-descriptive-lines-per-entree places with dinner prices in the $20s and $30s to match. The lunch menu is less pricey, topping out at $17 for the combo of cured and smoked salmon with wild rice blinis. But there are more familiar items like a steak sandwich with fries and a six-cheese macaroni with rosemary ham.

I've had both a steak and a plate of fish and chips, and they were not bad. Not fabulous, but quite decent. Blonde put their own spin on these classics: a foie gras hollandaise added a silky richness to the steak, and a sauce Vincent replaced the tartar sauce on the fish. The hollandaise elevated the dish to decadence. The sauce Vincent was dull. I would have been happier with a good tartar sauce.

Blonde is attempting a few things that have people talking. First, they do not serve bread. This draws focus to the food, but can disturb our cultural sense of a meal. Though not Blonde's intent, it also sets up the feeling with some that the restaurant knows better than the customer just how to eat. Second, the staff do not wear uniforms, but rather, dress in what they see as suitable. Some staff are better than others at pulling this off.

In all, I applaud Blonde for making some statements and taking a few chances. I'll take that over all the safe and dumbed-down places inhabiting the food world. Blonde is definitely not for everyone, but if they can keep their food quality high and their service consistent, they may well become one of the best restaurants in the city.

Blue Rock

California, Wine & Cigar Bar

512 – 23 Avenue SW
Phone: 229·9366
Monday – Saturday 11 am – midnight
Reservations recommended — Fully licensed — Patios — No non-smoking section
V, MC, AE, DC, Debit — $$

THE BLUE ROCK is named after a last-chance saloon that sat near the banks of the Elbow in the old Mission district many years ago. It's nice to see the historic name live on in this restaurant.

The Blue Rock bills itself as a cigar bar. Personally, I can't handle dining in a place where there is active cigar smoking. But a couple of friends convinced me to join them for lunch, which is not a big cigar time. And since the Blue Rock has huge doors opening onto an airy patio, I was pleasantly surprised: I was expecting a stale, stinky place, but found it quite fresh, with only a hint of past indulgences.

The menu is a Contemporary blend of tuna wraps, sausage rotini, spinach salads, and grilled salmon. The dishes have some force of flavour behind them, perhaps in deference to the reduced taste bud capacity of cigar smokers. More flavour for the flavour challenged. They carry a decent wine list too.

The soup of the day was a chilled raspberry and white wine concoction that sounded unusual enough to try. Raspberry and white wine is a combination usually found as dessert, not often as soup. But I enjoyed the broth of clear raspberry-red liquid with large berries floating in it. It felt like soup and dessert at the same time. One of my lunch partners commented that it was like eating your grandma's preserves.

We shared a chunk of brie baked in phyllo and served with a Cranberland sauce, a cranberry variation on a Cumberland sauce. Both sweet and tart, it was a nice dish.

Then I had the warm seafood salad—a mixed grill of prawns, scallops, and salmon on mesclun greens. Nicely spiced, grilled seafood, fresh greens, a light vinaigrette— very well prepared.

We also shared a crème brûlée that was huge. But the crème was too much of a custard rather than a true crème. It was tempting to go for another bowl of the raspberries and white wine, but we declined.

In all, I would certainly return to the Blue Rock. I'm still leery about their predilection towards cigars, so I would probably stick to the lunch hour. But if you like the smell of a good stogie, the sound of live jazz (that's on Wednesday, Friday, and Saturday evenings), and the taste of good food, the Blue Rock is definitely worth a visit.

Bodega
Tapas & Spanish

720 – 11 Avenue SW
Phone: 262·8966
Monday – Friday 11:30 am – 2 pm, Monday – Thursday 5 pm – 10 pm
Friday & Saturday 5 pm – 10:30 pm
Reservations recommended — Fully licensed — Non-smoking section
V, MC, AE, DC, Debit — $$ – $$$

JESSICA BATTISTESSA and Mario Djordjilov have worked wonders with the cool basement space that once was Celadon. They hauled in some wine barrels and candles, installed a fireplace and some stonework, darkened the walls, and created a cozy cavern. And they named it Bodega after the wine cellars of Spain.

Bodega has settled comfortably into the room, and on many nights, they turn away hungry souls looking for a taste of the Iberian peninsula. The look, the sound, the taste, and the overall style of Bodega exude the crowded, zesty essence of Spanish tapas bars. It may not be as smoky and hot as those we have visited in Spain, but it has the requisite grotto feel.

Bodega succeeds with an extensive list of forty tapas. Both traditional Spanish tapas (items like steamed mussels or potato omelette) as well as New World tapas (snacks like chicken with mole adobo glaze or shrimp and crab cakes with coconut, lime, and curry) are served. Bodega has divided their tapas menu into price categories ranging from $7 to $12 per plate. About half are vegetarian, making this truly a menu with something for everyone.

The tapas offer both subtlety and intensity of flavour, bold combinations of tastes and textures, and colourful presentations. A crock of marinated vegetables sprouts shards of Sardinian parchment bread while a small cast-iron pot spits aromas of olive oil, garlic, chilies, and prawns. The chicken liver, currant, and mushroom terrine is one of our favourites. It's all mighty fine food. And expertly served too.

Common practice at Bodega is to order a couple of tapas per person for a meal. This is usually enough and still leaves room for dessert. (We, however, always add an extra dish for the two of us.) In addition to the tapas, they offer full lunch and dinner menus that cruise beyond the shores of Spain and a tasteful liquid list featuring Spanish wines and sherries. Either is great with a few tapas.

If you aren't tapa-ed out, desserts, which change daily, are worth a look. No small plates these. An almond cake with preserved fruit was a delight, while a crème brûlée was one of the best in town. It had a crusty "tapa" lid, velvety cream, and sides of fresh fruit and strawberry compote. A fine way to end a meal.

And to get you dancing a little flamenco on the steps up to 11th Avenue.

Bonterra

Contemporary Italian

1016 – 8 Street SW
Phone: 262 • 8480
Monday – Friday 11 am – 2 pm, Monday – Thursday & Sunday 5 pm – 10 pm
Friday & Saturday 5 pm – 11 pm
Reservations recommended —Fully licensed — Patio — Non-smoking section
V, MC, AE, DC — $$ – $$$

GOOD restaurant space never sits idle for long, so when Virginia's ceased operations, the Wildwood Restaurant Group swept up the spot quickly. This is the group that owns North, Wildwood, and the two 4 St. Roses. Following a much-needed makeover, they reopened it as Bonterra, another Italian restaurant—quite possibly something we don't need more of these days. But it does have a unique look and menu. They have used the high-ceilinged room well (it was formerly the press room for the *Albertan* newspaper), creating a cozy Euro-style cavern. Large glass-and-iron lamps cast a golden glow over the table linens, while big candles illuminate the walls. With a cobblestone fireplace and an open kitchen, Bonterra has an elegant look, yet one that is not imposing. On the contrary, it feels quite warm and inviting.

The food here is full bodied and rustic, yet light and fresh. A salad of oven-roasted prawns over greens and white beans in a tarragon vinaigrette created a delicate balance of flavours and textures. And a beef carpaccio was highlighted by a crisp Parmesan basket filled with greens. Nice touch.

We each had a bowl of pasta—the spaghetti amatriciana and the linguine con pollo. Both fairly common dishes, but both spiked with interesting ideas. The amatriciana included chunks of wild-boar bacon along with the Parmesan and chili flakes. Not enough wild boar according to Catherine, but a tasty pasta nonetheless. My linguine had a great mix of roasted peppers, mango, and toasted cashews along with the chicken, all in a cream sauce. One fine plate of pasta and an unusual blend of ingredients that really worked.

Our food was enhanced by skilled service: there when it needed to be, absent when not. One nice touch was not removing the plates until both of us were finished. I am a fairly quick eater, while my darling wife can be painstakingly slow. Etiquette says that empty plates should stay on the table until everyone is done, but this is seldom the case these days. In fact, I have been told that some diners demand that their plates be taken away immediately upon finishing, whether everyone is done or not. Suffice it to say that Catherine appreciated this service style, enough to forgive them for serving her a too-warm glass of Sauvignon Blanc.

Bonterra is one fine, well-run restaurant. And it has a great patio in summer, making it an all-season destination.

www.bonterra@wildwoodgroup.net

Boogie's Burgers
Hamburgers

908 Edmonton Trail NE
Phone: 230·7070
Monday – Saturday 10 am – 10 pm
Reservations accepted — Beer & wine only — 1 table outside — Non-smoking section
Cash only — $

BACK in 1969, Faye and Sam Attala bought a little burger stand on Edmonton Trail and started one of the longest-running food businesses in Calgary. For thirty-one years they ran Boogie's Burgers, building a loyal clientele and serving excellent burgers, fine espresso, and unbeatable character.

The young couple—he was from Lebanon, she was from France—settled into their new Calgary home in the '70s, raised a son, and sold more burgers. By 1999, they were busy enough to expand next door, creating their first non-smoking section and a more comfortable seating arrangement.

Faye was famous for her ability to sell almost anything to anyone. She was very convincing in telling customers what they wanted, seldom taking no for an answer. Meanwhile, Sam would quietly prepare the food. His burgers were always the best.

But in 2000, the Attalas decided to retire and passed the spatula to the Odendaal family, recent arrivals from South Africa. John Odendaal now runs the grill while son Keith and daughter Noelle take care of the front end. They have a more subtle approach to service than Faye, but they are nonetheless committed to their customers.

And to making good fast food the way the Attalas did for so many years. The double mushroom burger features two freshly grilled patties on a toasted sesame bun and a light mushroom sauce. That doesn't sound much different than most burger joints, but the patties and buns are made to Boogie's specifications, creating a hamburger with a difference. It reminds me of what a good independent fast food place—that is, one without corporate portion control and formula preparations—can do.

The espresso remains popular—it's the closest taste to the bistro bite of a French cafe—and nowadays they have a license to serve wine and beer. So a little Bordeaux with a tray of spicy fries and a Super Faye burger is quite possible.

The Odendaals have brought a different tone to Boogie's, but have kept the same flavour. They are very respectful of the history and the clientele that the Attalas built. They have added a vegetarian burger and a steak burger to the menu (I'd like to see the addition of a boboti, a South African stew), but they are committed to continuing the legacy.

Boyd's

Seafood

5211 Macleod Trail S
Phone: 235·7575
Monday – Wednesday 11 am – 9 pm, Thursday – Saturday 11 am – 10 pm
Sunday noon – 9 pm
Reservations recommended for 6 or more — Fully licensed — Non-smoking section
V, MC, Debit — $ – $$

I always like a restaurant that does what it says. Boyd's Seafood Restaurant is one of these. A simple setting, straightforward service from golf-shirted staff on the move, and good old down-home seafood dishes without any fuss or pretense.

Boyd's sits on a knoll above Macleod Trail next to a homely asphalt and concrete strip mall, far from any coast. But their commitment is to fresh seafood done better than in most seaside cafes. They do fish and chips with four kinds of fish—halibut, cod, haddock, and pollock—plus calamari, clam chowder, and salmon filets. They stretch a bit with bouillabaisse ($22), king crab legs ($43 for a pound), and seafood gumbo ($19). There are numerous pastas, fish burgers, and popcorn seafood dishes as well. And there's even one beef and one chicken dish, plus a few salads and sandwiches.

But most of the menu goes unnoticed by the crowd that floods into the cafe for lunch each day. All 100 seats are usually taken before noon by a group who know they want the cod dinner or the halibut burger or the pound of mussels. They are served almost as quickly by a cadre of experienced staff who seem to enjoy the challenge of getting mega-food on the table in mere seconds. Many customers vacate their tables before 12:30 for the next batch of hungry lunchers.

It's not delicate food by any stretch, but it is fresh and good. The Atlantic cod in one of the two-piece fish and chip dinners is coated in a light and flavourful batter and deep-fried to a crispy oiliness. With a big whack of scorching-hot fries, it is a sizable feed for $12.50, one that has many groaning from the table but returning within days.

The clam chowder is genuine—lots of clams in a creamy base with some vegetables. And if clams are not to your liking, they do a fish chowder and a seafood chowder as well as a tomato-basil soup. They also do a lobster roll that has folks longing for the banks of the Miramichi.

Boyd's is a sunny space that is mostly utilitarian, appropriate for the menu and the clientele. It feels like the kind of place where it's OK to put your elbows on the table and eat with your fingers. How else can you truly enjoy fish and chips? Admittedly it's not like dangling your feet off the pier, but then again, there are no seagulls circling overhead either.

Brava Bistro
Canadian Provençal

723 – 17 Avenue SW
Phone: 228•1854
Monday – Saturday 11:30 am – 11 pm, Sunday 5 pm – 10 pm
Reservations recommended — Fully licensed — Patio — Non-smoking
V, MC, AE — $$ – $$$

A few years ago Figbelly's arrived on the scene with a fresh meals-to-go concept. Soon it sprouted a little cafe next door that became instantly popular. The owners upgraded the cafe into a sparkling bistro named Brava, and after a while, it consumed the Figbelly's section. It became even more popular for its quality, variety, and value, not to mention its trendy look and sweeping wine bar. But then the owners tried to upscale the menu and the prices to move it into the same category as Teatro, the River Café, and such. The market liked Brava as a more casual, less expensive place and quickly voted with their feet.

But things continue to change and now Brava is back. A bistro menu has been developed that places wild rice risotto, lamb sausage panini, and seared ahi tuna in the mid-teens. Creative combos, decent servings, and reasonable prices—just what the market wants. In the evening, they also offer a short, higher priced entree list with items such as rack of lamb for $29 and beef tenderloin for $32, but the main interest continues to be with the bistro side of the menu. And with the innovative wine list that includes about fifty offerings by the glass, mostly at $5 to $8 per serving. Dessert-wise, Brava rolls out a crème brûlée with a fig and star anise spin, a bread pudding hyped with chocolate chip and banana bread, and a cheesecake infused with espresso, each for $7.

I tried a daily soup of beef strip loin, wild rice, and porcini mushrooms that was a deep, beefy broth highlighted by the smoothness of the mushrooms and the soft texture of the rice. With strips of beef, this was one hearty bowl of soup. The flatbread, or pizza, that followed was a seasonal combo of double-smoked bacon, soft goat cheese, and grilled apricots. Interesting choices that worked well, the tartness of the fruit balancing the oils of the cheese and the bacon. The only downside was the skin on the pieces of apricot: without being peeled, they were a touch difficult to bite through. And frankly, these trendy Contemporary places never do a pizza crust as well as the old Italian joints, though Brava's wasn't too bad.

It's great to see Brava back doing what they do best. It is still one of the most stylish dining rooms in the city, and now they once again have a menu that fits the tone of the space and the attitude of their clientele.

Buchanan's

Chophouse

738 – 3 Avenue SW
Phone: 261•4646
Monday – Thursday 11:30 am – 10:30 pm, Friday 11:30 am – 11 pm
Saturday 5 pm – 11 pm
Reservations recommended — Fully licensed — Patio
Non-smoking section, no cigars
V, MC, AE, DC — $$ – $$$

EARLY in the twentieth century, chophouses started popping up on the American East Coast as a casual and economic alternative to the classic Continental restaurants that occupied most good hotels at the time. Called chophouses because of their dedication to red meat, particularly chops, they became popular with travellers of the day.

Here in Calgary, the oldest chophouse is Buchanan's, with its masculine decor splashed in blues and deep yellows. Open since 1988, paper covers the tables at lunch, old photos warm a largely wood decor, and sporting memorabilia dot the walls.

Buchanan's lunches are slick, professional, and fast. The room fills automatically at noon and empties at 12:55. A clientele almost exclusively of guys in suits piles in, eats, and leaves. The staff buzz through the room delivering food impossibly fast, tailored to the market that they serve. At dinner, things are much quieter and more relaxed with as many jeans as suits.

The menu goes beyond the usual chophouse choices of various red meat cuts to include seafood, chicken, and pasta. And there are even some tasty green things on the menu, such as a salad of field greens with a roasted tomato and ginger vinaigrette that can stand up to any red meat. The influence of other cultures can be seen, for example, in a duck-stuffed pancake served with a black muscat-plum sauce, which is quite similar to a good Peking duck.

For a recent main course, I went for the red meat with a mixed grill of lamb, smoked pork loin, and a beef filet with a foie gras butter. All were outstanding. The beef was as good a piece of tenderloin as I've had anywhere. And sides of a sweet potato pancake, grilled vegetables, and a corn, spinach, and pepper ragout made for a lot of colour as well as flavour. With a blueberry mousse for dessert, it was a fabulous meal.

Buchanan's is not cheap. A nice dinner for two, with a couple of glasses of wine, will run you about $80. But it's good value. And you get sizeable platefuls of food— another chophouse tradition.

So in spite of the sign at the front door that says "No Restaurant Critics," I have returned. Buchanan's continues to be one fine restaurant.

Buddha's Veggie
Chinese Vegetarian

9737 Macleod Trail S (Southland Crossing)
Phone: 252·8830
Wednesday – Monday 11 am – 1:30 pm, 4:30 pm – 9 pm
Reservations recommended — No alcoholic beverages — Non-smoking
V, MC, AE — $ – $$

BUDDHA'S VEGGIE is the only out-and-out vegetarian restaurant that I know of in Calgary. Elevating fake meats to a new level, they offer deep-fried duck, spicy eel, Szechwan squid, and smoked goose, all made without any meat or seafood. Instead, it could be tofu or mushrooms or gluten.

They have expanded their list of vegetable dishes that aren't trying to imitate meat, but there are still only ten of these offerings. Like oyster mushrooms with broccoli, enoki mushrooms with spinach, and snow peas and celery. Most dishes are the other style: crispy lemon chicken, veggie scallops, and so on.

We ordered the crispy eel in spicy salt made from black mushrooms. Even knowing the concept, Catherine's first reaction was, "Eel, hmm, I don't know." It took a little mental work to get around the fact that we were not eating eel. Sure it was breaded and deep-fried, but it looked like eel with its long, thin, slightly curly pieces. In the end though, it still tasted like mushrooms.

We also tried the Kung-po chicken and the ginger beef—again, totally vegetarian. I was surprised by the ginger beef. Looking at the dish with its slivered carrots and chilies, it was indistinguishable from any other ginger beef. The soy "beef" strips had a light crunchiness outside and some chewiness inside and were distinctly more tender than the meat in many ginger beefs. The key to any ginger beef is the sauce, and this one was good, albeit a little sweeter than I would have liked.

The Kung-po chicken sauce was also good, but also a little sweet and could have used more spice. With lots of fresh vegetables in the dish though, it was tasty. Less successful were the chunks of soy curd that were meant to double as chicken. They just tasted like soy curd. Not that there is anything wrong with soy curd, but I would have been just as happy with a straight vegetable Kung-po dish.

Volume-wise, you get a lot of food here. With the ginger beef, the Kung-po chicken, and the small dish of spicy eel, we had enough for two extra dinners for the two of us. And price-wise, there are only a few dishes over $12, so it is great value.

Service is top-notch—quick, happy, and helpful. It doesn't hurt that they bring a bowl of freshly brined pickles to the table to start and a bowl of fruit to finish, all on the house. And neither is disguised as meat.

Buffalo Mountain Lodge
Rocky Mountain Cuisine

Tunnel Mountain Road, Banff
Phone: 762·2400
Daily 7 am – 10 pm
Reservations recommended — Fully licensed — Non-smoking
V, MC, AE, DC — $$ – $$$

BUFFALO MOUNTAIN LODGE is one of Banff's most discreet hotels, located away from downtown up Tunnel Mountain Road. The entrance lounge features a chandelier made of elk antlers, a fireplace, and a rustically sumptuous feel. The dining room itself is not huge. It seats about sixty at comfortable wooden tables and chairs, but a vaulted ceiling lends a feeling of space and quiet. Forest green walls match the trees outside, while large windows showcase the wildlife that frequently grazes just a few metres away.

The Buffalo Mountain breakfast menu is simple but stylish, in keeping with the surroundings. There are multi-grain pancakes with sautéed apples and blueberries, house-made granola with yogurt and berries, a great eggs Benedict with smoked salmon, and carrot-zucchini French toast. Nothing terribly fancy, just good stuff done well.

I tried an outstanding ham and cheese omelette—light and fluffy, with thin slices of Westphalian ham layered with melted cheddar. With a few hash browns, some fresh fruit, and some whole wheat toast, it was a lovely meal. The toast was great, not just because it was made with house-baked bread, but because it came with two pots of very good preserves. First, there was the marmalade, something I do not usually like, and second, there was the bumbleberry, a mix of raspberries, strawberries, blueberries, and more. Both had a homemade yet professional quality, with lots of fruit and not too much sugar. Great preserves.

If breakfast is not your style, they roll out their Rocky Mountain game platter at lunch, which includes air-dried buffalo, venison ham, smoked pepper duck, and game pâté along with tangy mustard melons and cranberry relish. And there are plenty of other good things, like the burger with double-smoked bacon and onion marmalade or the capicollo, cheddar, and roasted peppers on sourdough. Dinner kicks it up a notch with the likes of elk in a sour cherry compote, hazelnut-crusted pork tenderloin, and medallions of caribou with a sweet potato gratin.

Service is among the most consistent to be found in Banff. Buffalo Mountain is one of the few places in the area that we trust. We know that we will always get good value, great food, and an excellent view.

Also of note is Cilantro Mountain Café, a seasonal outlet at the lodge that serves lighter, cheaper, wood-fired fare. Their pizzas are always worth a look. And it has one of the best patios in the Rockies for those few days when we can sit outside.

www.buffalomountainlodge.com

Buzzards

Steaks & Burgers

140 – 10 Avenue SW
Phone: 263·7900
Monday–Saturday 11:30 am – 10:30 pm, Sunday 4 pm – 10:30 pm
Reservations recommended — Fully licensed — Patio — Non-smoking
V, MC, AE, DC, Debit — $$

CATCHING the trend of "cowboyism," Buzzards' owner Stuart Allan turned his aptly named restaurant into a full-tilt Western eatery in 1997. The room is done in dusty Prairie colours, filled with saddles, branding irons, lamps, and other cowboy memorabilia. The look extends to the deck with its campfire and range-corral feel.

They've softened of late on the pure cowboy theme when it comes to the menu however—the concept is now a combination of century-old recipes from chuckwagon cooks with more recent red meat variations.

Steaks are served in abundance, from a simple six-ounce steak sandwich at $10 to a one-pound T-bone at $30. In between, there are buffalo sirloins, ribs, meatloaf, and burgers. A lunchtime buffalo burger done steak-house style with mushrooms, cheddar, and onion rings is a belly-filling plate of food. And at $9.50, it won't empty the wallet.

But beware. I've never left Buzzards feeling anything less than stuffed, which may have something to do with the saskatoon pie that always tempts me. A lunch at Buzzards can lull you to sleep in an afternoon office environment. What seems like a pleasant lunch at 11:45 a.m.—say the meatloaf with mashed potatoes or the bangers and mash—can weigh you down by 3 p.m.

But they have lightened up the menu with a few salads—such as the chicken Caesar—and wraps and quesadillas. And watch for Buzzards' now-famous annual Testicle Festival. This is a summer festival with lots of, er, chutzpah. So if you've ever wanted to partake of prairie oysters, this is your chance. (As the folks at Buzzards say, you'll have a ball.)

Beside Buzzards—and sharing the same deck and owner—is Bottlescrew Bill's, one of the oldest and best pubs in the city. They have more interesting beers here, ranging from Belgian micro-brewed ales to local brews, than anywhere else. The house beer—Buzzards Breath Ale—was the first custom-made beer produced by the local favourite, Big Rock. It remains popular not only at Buzzards but in the export market as well.

Buzzards is not high-tone dining—it's closer to the bunkhouse than the ranch house. And we'd never claim that this food is highly complex or intricate. It's good, hearty, red meat fare, great with a Big Rock brew or two, especially on the deck in the setting sun. So when you get the urge to round 'em up and head 'em out, Buzzards makes a tasty stop on the trail.

Cafe de Tokyo

Japanese

630 – 1 Avenue NE
Phone: 264·2027
Monday – Friday 11:30 am – 2:30 pm, 5 pm – 9 pm, Saturday noon – 9 pm
Reservations accepted — Beer, sake & wine only — Non-smoking sushi bar
Cash only — $

T HE movie *Tampopo* outlines the Japanese passion for noodles and the obsession with finding the quintessential noodle soup. Perfection is in the delicate blending of broth, seasonings, meats, vegetables, and ramen noodles, plus the efficient use of time and effort that goes into the preparation. Handmade noodles might be combined with a soya-tinged chicken broth, a pile of bean sprouts, chopped green onions, and thin slices of lean roast pork, all melded to maximize flavour and texture without overcooking anything. It takes a skilled ramen chef to achieve this pinnacle.

At Cafe de Tokyo, huge pots of broth simmer next to bowls of fresh vegetables and freshly made noodles. The soup here is excellent. Chef Ken Doshida is known among local Japanese cooks as a master of noodles.

Cafe de Tokyo also does sushi, with a tiny sushi bar tucked into the back, and it is available in combos with the noodles or just by itself. A lunch of five pieces of sushi is teamed with a bowl of ramen plus a green salad for a very reasonable $9.50. The sushi is well made too.

This is not the prettiest place. It qualifies as a hole in the wall. It's about sixteen-feet wide, with an open kitchen consuming half the room. A row of tables hooks around the kitchen, seating twenty-four in orange vinyl comfort. A few Japanese lanterns decorate the place; other than that, it is pretty minimal, but the good soya smell of Japanese fare fills the air.

One thing Cafe de Tokyo does not do is tempura, perhaps the most unusual of Japanese dishes. Tempura was unknown in Japan until Portuguese traders arrived about 450 years ago. The Japanese forbade the traders from coming ashore, preferring to deal with them on their ships or on small islands in the harbour. On the deck of each ship were pots of oil for deep-frying. The Portuguese would dip fish and other foods in a simple batter and toss them in the hot oil. Some of the Japanese thought this idea was good enough to refine into something more in keeping with their traditions. And so, tempura was born.

But since Cafe de Tokyo is mostly a noodle house and sushi bar, you can't get tempura there. You can, however, get a taste of what *Tampopo* is all about and how the sliced and simmered side of Japanese cuisine tastes. Rent the movie, drop into Cafe de Tokyo, and feel free to slurp your noodles.

Cafe Divine
Market-Fresh Cuisine

42 McRae Street, Okotoks
Phone: 938·0000
Monday – Saturday 9 am – 4 pm, Thursday – Saturday 5:30 pm – 9 pm
Reservations recommended — Fully licensed — Veranda & patio
Smoking on patio only
V, MC, Debit — $$

WITH all the development going on in Okotoks these days, it only makes sense that there will be some new restaurants popping up there. And some expansions to old ones. Cafe Divine has been around for a few years, but in early 2000 it relocated to a new and larger building on McRae Street, just east of downtown Okotoks. It's a large Victorian-style structure with a wraparound veranda, so it is hard to miss. It was built specifically for the cafe and has a large, open kitchen and a comfortable dining room. On a warm day, it's a pleasure to relax on the veranda and dine on fine food.

The menu at Cafe Divine is a Contemporary, market-fresh collection of things like smoked chicken sandwiches, seared salmon salads, thin-crusted pizzas, and mango-shrimp salad rolls. Nice ideas and great flavours.

The salad rolls we tried were huge. They lacked the tightness of Vietnamese salad rolls, tending to slide apart easily, but they were still tasty with their curried coconut-lime cream. And a soup of roasted squash with pumpkin seeds was rich, thick, and very squashy.

It was also huge. Whatever Cafe Divine does, they do in abundance and at reasonable prices. The soup was $4. The lamb shank braised in red wine—in other words, osso bucco—served with gnocchi and seasonal vegetables was $15.25. That's a pretty good deal, and considering you get two shanks, it's even better. Though it was not the most complex osso bucco I've had, any fan of this dish will be quite happy.

Catherine's daily special of skewered chicken with a pile of vegetables was also well received. By the end of dinner, we were too stuffed to have any dessert, but I understand that Cafe Divine's huge pieces of apple pie are popular.

We visited Cafe Divine in their early days at the new location and were impressed. There were a few rough edges, but the talent and potential were obvious; even with the rough edges, the food was pretty interesting. The two young chefs at Cafe Divine have good ideas, they are committed to market-fresh food, and they want to prepare as much as possible themselves.

Folks in Okotoks should be proud of these young people for bringing such a dynamic concept to town. And for those of us in the city, it is definitely worth the drive.

Café Metro
Montreal-Style Bistro

7400 Macleod Trail SW
Phone: 255·6537
Sunday – Thursday 11 am – 9 pm, Friday 11 am – 11 pm, Saturday 11 am – 10 pm
Reservations accepted for 6 or more — Fully licensed — Non-smoking section
V, MC, AE, Debit — $

MONTREALERS love the smoked meat sandwiches at Schwarze's, Ben's, and Dunn's. And here in Calgary, Café Metro comes closer to replicating that bit of Montreal than anyone else.

Metro's briskets are brought in from Delstar in Montreal, and the meat is quite good. It's fairly coarse, with a reasonable amount of pepper, but it's not too fatty, though they do fatty if you ask. They layer six ounces of thickly sliced brisket hot from the steamer onto locally baked rye bread. You get a slather of French's mustard— Dijon or Keane's on request, but none of that chi-chi coarse-grained New York stuff. Some fries, slaw, and a pickle and you have a meal for $8.25. If you are real serious, you can drop an extra $1.70 for the nine-ounce version. The menu also includes chicken club sandwiches, Thai chicken wraps, and vegetarian quesadillas, among other things, but we go here for the smoked meat.

The staff at Metro are quite nice, far too nice to replicate a real Montreal deli. They would have to be rude, or at the very least ignore you, to make it authentic. Plus, the tables are not crammed together—you can easily walk between them without bumping anyone. And the room has far too much fresh air in it to ever pass as a real deli. Thank heaven for those improvements.

Metro is packed into a strip mall where they have created a kind of outdoor cafe atmosphere indoors. The concrete floor resembles a brick road, and a fire hydrant and street lamps are planted on the floor. The walls are painted with street scenes that evoke the Prince Arthur section of Montreal. It's a distinctive look that is charmingly out of place on Macleod Trail.

For those of us who live in the south, it is a blessing. A quick, tasty lunch can be had for under $10, if you can stay away from the desserts. The maple sugar pie, New York-style cheesecake, and English gingerbread cake are all made in-house. The gingerbread with caramel sauce and Granny Smith apples is excellent if fresh, mouth-locking with dryness if stale.

So a little bit of Montreal exists on Macleod Trail. And an even smaller bit has been dropped into downtown—Café Metro Express has recently opened in Sun Life Plaza's food court at 112 – 4 Avenue SW. These two eateries are enough to kindle fond memories, but not enough to keep us from wanting to head east for the real thing.

Calzoni's
Pizza

825 – 12 Avenue SW
Phone: 216•0066
Monday – Wednesday 11 am – 8 pm, Thursday – Saturday 11 am – 9 pm
Reservations not accepted — No alcoholic beverages — Non-smoking
V, MC, AE, Debit — $

I have long complained about the lack of good pizza joints in the city. So the arrival of Calzoni's hand-rolled pizzas, folded calzoni, and Italian panini sandwiches has been long awaited.

Calzoni's shows creativity by working with ingredients like Gorgonzola and Asiago cheeses, prosciutto, and oyster mushrooms in what is primarily a takeout setting. It's a trendy glass, wood, and steel-cable place smack in the middle of the Beltline area. You can actually eat in at Calzoni's if one of the counter stools is open, but most of the room is taken up by a huge pizza oven. It's not a place for a candle-lit dinner for two.

In addition to fine pizzas, you'll find panini that are filled with things like roast chicken or capicollo, grilled peppers, and olive tapenade. We tried one of these and were impressed with the quality of the ingredients. Nicely put together with Asiago cheese and marinated tomatoes, it was a drippy delicacy.

Our pizza was tasty but suffered from an excess of dough. Although the crust was good, there was so much of it that a large ring was formed around the outside of the pie. Called Mass Exodus (there is an odd biblical theme, with pizzas named Moses and His Buds, the Seven Deadly Sins, and so on), it was vegetarian and very good, except for the extra dough.

But our favourite product here is the calzone itself. The word means "pant leg" and is supposedly named after the billowy pants of nineteenth century Neapolitans. It's basically a folded-over pizza with most of the same ingredients. We tried a vegetarian one with peppers, eggplant, tomatoes, Parmesan, and fontina—a perfect balance of taste and texture. A transportation note: if you are travelling a long distance, a calzone stays hotter much longer than a pizza.

Calzoni's also carries two salads and one dessert, a tiramisu. The tiramisu is too watery to draw me back for more, so I would advise sticking to the doughy dishes. Pizzas run $11 to $23, with panini at $6 to $7, and calzoni at $6 to $11.

Service-wise, the staff at Calzoni's are pleasant and not locked into the routine of the chain pizza parlours. They actually seem to have individual character here. But since service is largely limited to passing you the pizza box, it's hard to get a real read on this.

Calzoni's is a great concept in a great location. I only hope they can create a few more around the city.

Carver's
Steak House

2620 – 32 Avenue NE (Sheraton Cavalier)
Phone: 250·6327
Monday – Saturday 5:30 pm – 10:30 pm, Sunday 5 pm – 9 pm
Reservations recommended — Fully licensed — Non-smoking section
V, MC, AE, DC, Debit — $$$

S TEAK houses do not need to be the dark and overly upholstered rooms of yesteryear. They can be bright and hip and dedicated to big service as well as to big beef. And one place that uses this approach is Carver's in the Sheraton Cavalier.

The result of a huge hotel reno, Carver's has placed itself at the top end of the local restaurant scene with its sleek room, vested waiters, and pricey menu. Here a steak Diana is $34, a ten-ounce filet is $37, and the surf and turf is $43. Not delicate prices, but then Carver's is aimed more at the business traveller (read: expense account) than at the regular public.

Which is not to say that it is elitist. It has also gained standing with locals who just crave a good piece of beef. Carver's serves AAA Alberta beef well-aged, well-cut, and well-cooked. Catherine declared her tenderloin to be the best beef she had ever eaten. She discouragingly added that it surpassed all my own backyard efforts. Just see if I cook for her again!

But I have to agree. The AAA is so good that it barely needs to be dunked into the demi-glace sauce they serve on the side. They could improve on the swirl of whipped potatoes that comes with the beef (they were a bit dry), but then, beef is definitely the thing here.

We also tried a Caesar salad prepared tableside, a bowl of lobster bisque (at a mouth-dropping $13), and some bruschetta. All were done well, and the bisque justified its price with a big whack of lobster in the bowl. For dessert, which we were barely able to consume after all this food, we had the peppered strawberry crepes, again prepared tableside. Excellent. And $19 for two. (Did I mention that Carver's is pricey?)

The service here is as outstanding as the food – professional and not the least bit pretentious. The staff are well trained and a pleasure to be around. Carver's also has an excellent wine list and more professional staff to assist in selecting the right wine for the cut and preparation of beef you are having. These people know their stuff.

It is impressive that the Sheraton committed to running a high-end steak house in their hotel. It is even more impressive that after three years, they have stuck to that commitment and, in doing so, have created a landmark restaurant not only for the northeast hotel strip, but for the city.

Casa de la Salsa

Mexican

221 Stephen Avenue Walk SW
Phone: 264·4777
Monday – Wednesday 11 am – 9 pm, Thursday 11 am – 10 pm
Friday & Saturday 11 am – 2 am, Sunday 5 pm – 10 pm
Reservations recommended — Fully licensed — Patio — Non-smoking section
V, MC, AE, DC, Debit — $ – $$

Perhaps the most obscure restaurant on the Stephen Avenue Walk is the Casa de la Salsa, an underground restaurant that thousands of people walk by each day. Overshadowed by its active neighbour The Palace, the Casa goes quietly about its business of serving some of the best Mexican food in the city. A doorway with a small sign and a tiny patio that appears on sunny days are the only things from the outside that indicate the Casa even exists. There is no storefront, no windows. Instead, there is a set of stairs leading down to a large and comfortable room.

The excavated sandstone foundations of the building create a sandy, Mexican cantina look, and with some colourful table coverings and various south-of-the-border paraphernalia, it feels like a vacation hideaway. It's a quiet lunch place—a good location for work groups to get together—and it's a raucous evening place when the Latino music gets fired up. A huge dance floor bustles with weekend salsa dance events. (We were once called upon to judge a *merengue* contest at the last moment—extremely difficult since we didn't know a good *merengue* from a lemon meringue.) And in spite of its confines, it is surprisingly non-smoky.

The food here is good and as adventurous as any Mexican fare you will find around town. There is the usual selection of burritos and enchiladas and flans, but there are also tamales, chiles en nogada (poblanos stuffed with ground pork and beef in a sweet, creamy, cold salsa), and pollo en mole de ciruela (chicken breast in a spicy prune salsa). This last dish is rich, creamy, and filled with prunes, and though it is not terribly spicy, it is of good value for the $10.95 price tag. I have always enjoyed the bite of the tomatillo-serrano salsa that comes with the enchiladas for $8.95. And the chicken quesadillas drip with cheese and chicken for a reasonable $5.75. There is also an interesting ground pork lasagna, fettuccine with cactus paddles, and shrimp in a chipotle sauce.

The salsas are always fresh and creative and never quite the same. They are filled with whatever ingredients the chef happens to have on hand that day. With their fresh taco chips and a margarita, I could sit there all day. If only they had a pool.

Cedars Deli Cafe
Lebanese

225 Stephen Avenue Walk SW
Phone: 263·0285
Monday – Friday 10 am – 7 pm, Saturday 10 am – 4 pm
Reservations accepted — Fully licensed — Patio — Non-smoking section
V, MC, AE, Debit — $

CEDARS DELI CAFE, the only sit-down restaurant of the Cedars outlets, seats ninety in its long, narrow storefront on Stephen Avenue. It's easy to miss, with its slim face squeezed between the Treasury Branch and that crucial downtown landmark, Arnold Churgin's Shoes. They have primped the space nicely by exposing old brick walls and mosaic tile floors and by elevating the ceiling to give it a bright, open look.

You line up at the counter, order your food, pay for it, and pick it up or have it delivered when it is ready. The cafeteria process is hindered by the narrowness of the room: it tends to clog up, but they are efficient and the line does move quickly.

Part of Cedars' secret to success is their quality control. Most of the food – like the falafel, the kibbeh, the baklava—is made at the Eau Claire retail and production location and then shipped quickly to the other ones. But meats are spit-roasted on-site to create fresh shawarma and shish tawouk sandwiches, and there is always an appealing immediacy to the food.

This is Lebanese fare at its purest and simplest, which is still pretty complex. Cedars' tabouleh salad of chopped parsley, bulgar, tomato, and onion is always a treat—tart with lemon, nutty with cracked wheat. I had it in a combination with the shish tawouk, a sandwich of stacked, spit-roasted chicken layered with tomatoes, lettuce, and a garlic-mayo sauce. Messy as all get out and very garlicky. Guaranteed to keep people at a distance for a good twelve hours.

Cedars also makes a fattoush salad of lettuce, vegetables, and pita chips in a lemon dressing and a spinach fatayer with parsley, onions, and pinenuts baked in a pastry shell. Tasty eating. And they do the phyllo pastry treat of baklava in many different ways—with pistachios, almonds, cheese, or cherries. It is comparatively light for baklava—still very sweet, but not as sticky as some.

Most things at Cedars remain under $6. It is well worth putting up with the lineups for this food at these prices. The Salloum family runs Cedars and pride themselves in offering a good meal of homemade Lebanese food for a reasonable price. They have built a huge throng of loyal followers with this concept.

The other two Cedar locations are kiosks, with one in Eau Claire Market (264·2532) and the other, Cedars Falafel Hut, in MacEwan Hall at the University (282·0713).

Chez François
French

Bow Valley Trail (Green Gables Inn), Canmore
Phone: 678·6111
Daily 6:30 am – 2 pm, 5 pm – 11 pm
Reservations recommended — Fully licensed — Non-smoking section
V, MC, AE, DC, Debit — $$ – $$$

T HE simple facade of the Green Gables Inn hides the fact that Chez François is much more than a motor lodge cafe. It is a fine French restaurant with some rare talent in the kitchen.

Chez François is the resident dining room for the hotel and therefore serves breakfast, lunch, and dinner daily. Here you will find one of the best eggs Benedict for many miles around. The chef, Jean-François Gouin, uses the free-form method to poach the eggs perfectly before placing them on Valbella back bacon or smoked salmon. The key is a perfect hollandaise that is draped over the dish and then lightly browned before serving. Each element of the Benedict, including the English muffins, comes together into a superlative dish. (And a real plus is that the breakfast menu is available until 2 p.m., a bonus for Calgarians who sleep in.)

The culinary skill continues through to lunch when I have had a beautifully flavoured and clarified consommé Célestine. This soup looks much simpler than it is. The chef builds outstanding flavour intensity into his broth and then serves it with crisp vegetables floating in it.

At lunch Chez François offers a table d'hôte that, at $13, represents exceptional value. In addition to the consommé, a recent table d'hôte included a tasty beef stroganoff that was packed with tender chunks of beef in a rich gravy finished with cream. And dessert was a simple yet pleasant vanilla ice cream topped with pears and a blueberry compote.

Dinner at Chez François can become more elaborate and elegant as they lay out the linens. Six course table d'hôtes are offered, starting with a consommé or daily soup (the chef does a fabulous lobster bisque) and followed by a choice of appetizers such as a prawn and scallop salad or smoked goose, prosciutto, and veal pâté. Then there is a granita palate cleanser and main course choices such as lamb loin with a peppercorn-mango chutney or pork tenderloin with a Calvados sauce. It all finishes off with a cheese plate and dessert. More outstanding value ranging from the high $30s to the low $40s, depending on the entree you choose.

Chez François offers a wealth of other dishes and service that is both friendly and professional. They can refuel conference groups quickly or provide a romantic evening for two. It's a great stop in Canmore, and the view out the big windows isn't bad either.

Chili Club
Thai

555 – 11 Avenue SW
Phone: 237·8828
Monday – Friday 11 am – 2 pm, Daily 5 pm – 10 pm
Reservations recommended — Fully licensed — Non-smoking
V, MC, AE, Debit — $$

THESE days Electric Avenue looks like someone has pulled the plug. The old watering holes have pretty much closed up, but we may be seeing the slow revitalization of the area as a restaurant strip.

One of the newcomers is the Chili Club. Actually, it's the return of the restaurant. The Chili Club on Centre Street was one of the first Thai eateries in the city and the hottest place in town in 1991, both for spice levels and popularity. The owners opened a second outlet on 17th Avenue SW, but by 1994 they had sold both locations and were focusing on their Singapore Sam's operation.

But the Chili Club has returned to a pretty space that seats thirty-six. It's small, with the deep red-sponged walls adding a coziness to the room. The original Chili Club chef is back, and he is preparing both old favourites and new dishes.

We started our meal with fried rice paper rolls filled with prawns and vegetables. This was the only disappointing dish of the night. Although there were lots of prawns, the overall impression was that of fried food; none of the delicate, light flavours that usually accompany Thai cuisine were there.

Fortunately, the rest of our dinner was better. We tried the panang duck curry, the chicken with basil and chili, and a dish called Evil Jungle Prince. I just had to order a dish called Evil Jungle Prince. And it was pretty good, if a little over-named. Basically it was a pile of stir-fried vegetables in a very hot sauce. Our panang duck was rich with smoky eggplant and roast duck and not overly heavy on the curry. It was a little oilier than I remember from the old days though. Another dish that we used to order was the chicken with basil—the basil leaves are now fried to crispiness, bringing an unusual but pleasant texture to the dish.

The food at the Chili Club is similar to its fare of almost a decade ago, but in that time, we have seen Thai cuisine in Calgary become more sophisticated. Some places, notably Thai Sa-On, offer more complexity in the spicing.

But it is still nice to see the return of the Chili Club. If you like Thai food hot, the Chili Club satisfies, and if you like it mild, it works equally well. It is a well-run restaurant with great service and a good menu, with prices ranging from $5 to $17. It may well help Electric Avenue shine again.

Cilantro

California Fusion

338 – 17 Avenue SW
Phone: 229·1177
Monday – Friday 11 am – 11 pm, Saturday 5 pm – midnight, Sunday 5 pm – 10 pm
Reservations recommended — Fully licensed — Patio — Non-smoking section
V, MC, AE, DC — $$ – $$$

WHEN patio season rolls around, we always like to spend a few hours at Cilantro in the cozy confines of its lush courtyard. Walled into a corner created by an odd juncture of two old buildings, the patio creeps with ivy and warms under the heat of the Calgary summer sun. We kick back and enjoy a pear and Gorgonzola pizza or slices of seared tenderloin with a Dijonnaise dressing. With a glass from one of the best wine lists in the city, 17th Avenue seems much farther away than the few feet that it is.

Cilantro has had its ups and downs in the past, but that seems left behind. They are definitely on a roll now. The menu has been reconceived, the kitchen is tight, and the service is crisp. The new list fits the old format, but the ideas seem refreshed— the food is rich and interesting and abundant.

A soup of roasted poblanos and potatoes ($6) with caramelized onions and goat cheese is a creamy-rich bowl of dark green liquid. The cheese adds an edge that takes the soup to a new depth, accenting the smooth chili taste. And a pizza of chicken and pancetta ($12) on an ancho pesto with a lime sour cream and pickled chilies is a vivid combination of tastes. All the flavours on the pizza are excellent, each mouthful a treat. As is the thin crust—neither too doughy nor too cracker-like.

A burger made with elk ($15) from their own ranch provides a gamey tone to the menu. Served with a mustard aïoli and a cherry compote, it is an unusual alternative to regular burgers. The cherry compote is very good, but the meat is almost too elky. If you're a game fan, this is a good choice; if you're not, it may be too strong for you.

On the dessert menu, Cilantro continues its tradition of quality. The fallen chocolate soufflé with white-chocolate ice cream and peach-strawberry compote ($6) is as decadent as it sounds. Maybe even a little more so. The soufflé is almost like a fudge cake—there is nothing airy about it. And the sauce is lovely. Even the white-chocolate ice cream is OK, even though I have yet to have a white-chocolate ice cream that is anywhere near as successful as its regular chocolate counterparts.

Cilantro remains a reliable classic with quality throughout and pretty good prices. And that vine-covered patio guarantees satisfaction every time.

Clay Oven

Indian (Punjabi)

3132 – 26 Street NE (Interpacific Business Park)
Phone: 250·2161
Monday – Friday 11:30 am – 2 pm, 5 pm – 9 pm, Saturday 5 pm – 10 pm
Reservations recommended — Fully licensed — Non-smoking
V, AE, Debit — $ – $$

THE CLAY OVEN is an exception to the chain restaurants of the northeast light industrial area. Tucked into a business park behind the huge Husky truckstop, it is a fine Indian restaurant.

It is much nicer inside than one might expect from the dark exterior. Seating about thirty, it is elegantly wallpapered and appointed with linened tabletops and comfortable chairs. This is not a high-tone dining room by any stretch, but considering that it is in a strip mall, it is quite pleasant and very clean.

The Clay Oven is a solid Northern Indian, Punjabi-style restaurant with a full menu that includes tandoori chicken, lamb vindaloo, and saag paneer. In keeping with their name, they use a ceramic-sided tandoor oven to cook many of the dishes.

On our latest visit, we had an all-vegetarian meal and were impressed with the tastes. We typically like bhindi tori, a mix of okra, potatoes, and tomatoes in various spices. Often this dish is reduced to a uniform mush with a single flavour. But at the Clay Oven, the potatoes had a distinct taste, as did the okra. That is a subtle but important difference. And the mild cheese in the shahi mutter paneer stood out against the backdrop of the butter sauce. This is the same sauce that is used on the butter chicken, so it is very rich. Then there was the dhal pachrangi, a rich blend of four kinds of lentils that was deep and dense. We also enjoyed the mango lassi made with buttermilk and the plain mango shake with lots of good fruit taste.

One of the biggest reasons to go to the Clay Oven is their naan, which I have considered to be the best in the city since they opened. It's huge, stretched into a rounded triangle and cooked on the side of the tandoor oven. Fluffy and light, crisp on the outside, chewy on the inside, it's very tasty. The whole wheat roti—a rich, round bread—is just as good.

They put out a weekday lunch buffet that is excellent value at $9, and most dishes on the menu range from $8 to $14. If you need another reason to go, we have always found the service to be pleasant, helpful, and professional. It is family run and the owners are a diligent bunch who strive for consistency and quality and take great pride in their food.

Coyotes

Contemporary Southwestern

206 Caribou Street, Banff
Phone: 762·3963
Daily 7:30 am – 11 pm
Reservations recommended — Fully licensed — Non-smoking
V, MC, AE, DC, Debit — $ – $$

COYOTES is just off Banff Avenue in the heart of the townsite. It's a long, narrow room seating forty, with a single row of tables and a lineup of stools at the counter. Thankfully it is totally non-smoking, because it's pretty tight in here.

Coyotes has a Southwestern theme, so there's black bean chili, blue corn encrusted chicken, and orange-chipotle prawns on the menu. They are the only restaurant in our area to use real New Mexican chilies, and they are as good as those used in the restaurants of Santa Fe.

Just as interesting are the prices, especially for Banff. Lunches top out at $12 for a seared salmon with mango salsa, and the priciest dinner items are beef tenderloin in a porcini-chipotle sauce at $22 and a spice-crusted rack of lamb at $23.50. Not bad these days.

But we're here most often for breakfast, and it's a good one. Coyotes carries the requisite mountain-man breakfast of two eggs, two pancakes, bacon or sausage, and potatoes, plus healthier choices of honey-baked granola or fruit salad. But being of a Southwestern bent, we usually order the huevos rancheros and the breakfast burrito.

The huevos features a stack of blue corn tortillas with black beans, fried eggs, cheese, and red chili sauce. The single serving is a filling effort at $6.50, the double is a major meal at $8.50. It packs lots of flavours, there's a little bite to the sauce, and a pile of chopped green chilies sits on the side. The breakfast burrito is a big flour tortilla stuffed with scrambled eggs and cheese and draped in red chili sauce for $7.25 —add chorizo for an additional $1.25. They could pour on a bit more sauce for my taste, but that may just be me. Suffice it to say that these breakfasts, plus most of the others, are a perfect setup for a day of mountain hiking or skiing.

You'll also find some of the most pleasant and professional staff in Banff working here. I'm sure, with the way the tables turn, it's a great place to work for tips. That's really the only downside to Coyotes: it's very busy all the time and there can be a wait to get in if you didn't think to reserve ahead.

There will be nothing delicate or romantic about your meal at Coyotes. But there are other places in Banff for that. This is a place for good food, served quickly and priced reasonably.

Crazyweed Kitchen
Global Cuisine

626 – 8 Street, Canmore
Phone: 609·2530
Daily 11 am – 7 pm
Reservations not accepted — No alcoholic beverages — 4 tables outside — Non-smoking
V, MC, Debit — $ – $$

THE best food we have eaten over the past couple of years has been at Crazyweed Kitchen in Canmore. It's a little place with only four tables—and that is only in good weather when you can sit outside. Inside, there are fourteen stools pushed up against a couple of counters that are loaded down with gourmet chutneys, fig-infused balsamic vinegars, last week's *New York Times*, and the plates of excited diners.

Jan and Richard Hrabec, two tall and rangy Canmorians, run the aptly named Crazyweed as a full-tilt assault on the senses. Richard oversees a tiny but extremely well-conceived cheese counter and operates the front end of the business with the help of some very adept staff. Jan is a picture of calm and focus in her kitchen— bowls of curried seafood, platters of sliced beef and roasted eggplant, and steaming pizzas topped with balsamic-marinated cherry tomatoes, artichokes, and Taleggio cheese emerge effortlessly from her kitchen to be consumed immediately by the waiting throngs. The food here is exceptional and the experience is unparalleled (just don't think elegant setting).

I lost seven minutes of my life to a roast lamb sandwich dripping juices from a crusty loaf. It was a transcendent experience where nothing else mattered for those few minutes. And a pizza brought me close to tears with its intense and balanced flavours. That kind of food experience happens so seldom.

Customers crowd into the tiny space to order whatever looks good and to pick up foods for later meals. A couple of coolers hold the products of the day—there might be ancho-layered scalloped potatoes or Thai chicken wraps or tandoori salmon. Crazyweed carries fresh herbs and seafood and other ingredients, especially Asian ones, that are difficult to find in the Bow Valley. But most folks seem happy to carry out tubs of sun-dried tomato pasta salads and Asian rice noodles with chicken. Or to grab a very chocolatey chocolate chip cookie from the counter.

Crazyweed fits well into the new face of the Bow Valley. Canmore residents and tourists are demanding a broader, fresher, and easier range of foods. And they are willing to pay for it. The fare at Crazyweed is not cheap, but it is of amazing value, especially if you factor the time-savings into it. Their timing could not be better as Canmore explodes in popularity.

The Cross House
Contemporary French

1240 – 8 Avenue SE
Phone: 531·2767
Monday – Friday 11:30 am – 2 pm, Monday – Saturday 5:30 pm – last guest
Reservations recommended — Fully licensed — Patio — Non-smoking
V, MC, AE, Debit — $$ – $$$

THE historic home of A.E. Cross sits quietly by the Bow River, surrounded by a caragana hedge. It's a small but stately Victorian wood frame with a huge yard and garden, the river along the back adding to the pastoral charm. Cross—a major mover and shaker in the early 1900s—purchased the house in 1899, wisely choosing a residence that was just a few short, upwind blocks from his brewery. Other buildings and roads have encroached upon this scenic location over the years, but once you are inside the hedge, it's a quick trip to the early twentieth century. The yard rolls back from a patio to flower beds and shady elms. On a warm evening, there are few more private patios in which to enjoy a meal.

The site gained historic status in 1977 and has been a restaurant since 1991. In the summer of 2001, it was taken over by Paul Rogalski, a former head chef at La Chaumière, and Olivier Reynaud, an experienced restaurateur from Provence via Andorra. Together they are reshaping The Cross House into a delightful Contemporary French restaurant.

The Cross House looks like it should be serving high tea, but instead has an interesting menu of salmon and roasted pecan purée baked in pastry and veal sweetbreads in horseradish jus. We tried an outstanding soup of smoked crab and spinach that was rich and creamy, yet light at the same time. And the coquilles St. Jacques with a Cambozola soufflé and port syrup was a delicate blend of seafood, cheese, and wine swirled into a wave of taste. The chef really knows how to combine ingredients and he's not afraid to play with flavour. The vinaigrette for a tomato salad is infused by chunks of bacon. This is not a cheap trick—the bacon adds a depth and a unique texture.

I have few complaints about the cooking at The Cross House and the quality of service that goes along with it. The dishes are superb but can occasionally lean a little too strongly on the salt shaker for my taste. And the lemon tart brûlée was just not lemony enough for Catherine. (If you've read more of this book, I'm sure you know of her penchant for mouth-puckering citrus.)

Regardless, The Cross House is one fine restaurant, certainly one of the best new places to arrive (or at least change hands) in 2001. And Mrs. Cross's garden is great.

Da Paolo

Italian

121 – 17 Avenue SE
Phone: 228·5556
Monday – Friday 11:30 am – 2 pm, Monday – Saturday 5 pm – 11 pm
Reservations recommended — Fully licensed — Non-smoking
V, MC, AE, DC — $$ – $$$

A few years ago, Paolo De Minico and Claudio Carnali made a bold move. After opening Da Paolo Ristorante on 4th Street and 17th Avenue SW, these two seasoned restaurant veterans (they had worked for years at Mamma's) purchased the La Chaumière building when that popular restaurant moved down the street. They spent time converting the space into a lively Mediterranean eatery, replacing the dim Continental wallpaper with a soft, yellow, sponged treatment and installing two east-facing windows. The room is still cozy, but it feels much more alive. The result is a sumptuously comfortable room with excellent traditional Italian cuisine.

Claudio runs the front end of the operation while Paolo oversees the kitchen. This is an equal partnership that ensures quality from end to end.

The food is superb. If it is true that a chef's personality comes through in the food, then Paolo's dishes are happy and boisterous and confidently rich. Meeting Paolo, he immediately engulfs your hand in a grasp that tells you he works with his hands, he feels the food, he can tell by the touch that it will taste good. He cares about his food and his customers—he never wants to see anyone leave unhappy or hungry.

His carpaccio is the best in the city. Cured beef tenderloin, caper berries, shaved Parmesan, lemon, olive oil – top-quality ingredients perfectly constructed. The pasta alla Paolo is a free-form ravioli folded over a velvety blend of veal, ricotta, and herbs and then bathed in a light rosé sauce. Hard to resist. The veal dishes are wonderful too—we have enjoyed the veal with white wine and truffles as well as the saltimbocca with prosciutto and fresh sage. And a veal chop special we once had was memorably delicious. Da Paolo's menu includes various seafood dishes along with chicken, beef, lamb, and of course, desserts. Their tiramisu is excellent.

This quality does not come without a price. Pastas are fairly reasonable, in the range of $11 to $16 for dinner. Veals run $15.50 to $18 and other meats roll up to $27 for the rack of lamb. Seafoods vary from $19 to $35. Again, not cheap, but considering the quality, it is good value. At lunch the only dish over $15 is a beef filet done with brandy and cream, so the midday meal can be quite reasonable.

The food is excellent, the service is quietly professional, and the room is lovely. Da Paolo Ristorante remains my favourite Italian restaurant in Calgary.

Da Salvatore

Italian

9140 Macleod Trail S (Newport Village)
Phone: 255·6011
Monday – Friday 11:30 am – 2:30 pm, Monday – Saturday 5 pm – 11 pm
Reservations recommended — Fully licensed — Non-smoking section
V, MC, AE, Debit — $$

NUZZLED against the Macleod Trail border of Acadia is an awkward strip mall incongruously named Newport Village. It is packed with the delights of an A & W, the King's Head Pub, a discount golf shop, and a dry cleaner—the usual strip-mall suspects. It has cramped access and difficult parking. It is no one's idea of a well-executed piece of urban design. And stuffed almost invisibly behind the 7-Eleven is a little Italian market named Sal's.

And a restaurant connected to it called Da Salvatore. It's quite a lovely place. Well, a bit over the top perhaps, but not in an unpleasant way. The arched ceiling has been muralled and lit to create a Mediterranean sky, and the walls have been painted with beach views. The floor has a stone-terrace look, and wrought-iron furniture replicates a seaside cafe. If you ignore the windows onto the 7-Eleven parking lot, it has a soft, even elegant atmosphere. But all the lovely ambience in the world is for naught if the food is poor.

Fortunately, the food at Salvatore's is very, very good. It is a melding of traditional Italian fare with some Contemporary flare—in addition to the beef carpaccio, there is also a daily seafood version (sushi lovers must try the delicate blend of sliced fresh Atlantic salmon with olive oil and lemon on crusty buns). Another appetizer combines grilled scallops with a red-pepper purée, and house-made sausage is featured in a few dishes.

There is a lot of talent in Salvatore's kitchen. A simple dish of mushrooms sautéed in white wine, herbs, and garlic is beautifully balanced so that every forkful is worth savouring. A spaghetti with smoked pancetta and Gorgonzola plays with the forceful flavours to create a simple and sensational dish. Neither the bacon nor the cheese is allowed to overpower the pasta—they work together, a concept that seems a mystery to some chefs. And the rigatoni with vodka, pancetta, green onions, and peppercorns in a fresh tomato cream sauce is rich and dense, each bite filling your mouth with flavour. There is nothing subtle about this food.

Salvatore's has brought a different tone to Newport Village, one that is welcome among the chains of Macleod Trail. It's funny how quality and service can make an undesirable location successful.

Dante's
European Cafe & Wine Bar

513 – 8 Avenue SW (Penny Lane)
Phone: 237·5787
Monday, Tuesday & Saturday 11 am – 5 pm, Wednesday – Friday 11 am – 9 pm
Reservations recommended — Fully licensed — Non-smoking section
V, MC, AE, DC — $$

IT has always struck me as strange that Kites Dim Sum is in the basement of Penny Lane, while Dante's is on the top floor. Shouldn't it be the other way around?

Regardless, Dante's is on the second level of the mall, with big windows looking onto Eaton Centre and a skylight pouring sunshine into the middle of the room. When they opened over a decade ago, they uncovered brick walls, laid down hardwood floors, and created an open and airy bi-level room. A ground-level entrance and wine bar have since been added to give some street presence; the wine bar also acts as the main food service area in the evenings. It's a tighter, darker space than the room upstairs, but it does allow street access for the once mall-locked eatery.

The menu at Dante's includes pastas topped with seafood ragout or venison medallions, salads with honey-lime chicken or grilled tiger prawns, and desserts of apple strudel or quark cheesecake. It is an elegant list that benefits from skillful presentation—the dishes are as pretty as you will find anywhere. And for the most part, the flavours come through nicely. A seafood chowder was enhanced by the presence of smoky bacon, creating a complex and silky soup. A daily special of Szechwan chicken, though delicately spiced, still had lots to taste.

The food seems geared to light flavours and low fat, which fits perfectly with the needs of the noon crowd that frequents Dante's. The heavily suited power-lunchers hunch over their salads while continuing the morning's meetings. This is the home of the working lunch, a place where deals are being made. But instead of the steak sandwich with a rye and coke of a few decades ago, it is a roasted, skinless chicken breast, perhaps with a glass of Chardonnay or just a Naya water.

Service at Dante's is punctual, again fitting with the needs of their customers. It is discreet, pleasant, and quick. Prices lean towards a tonier clientele—at $13.50 for the seafood ragout and $14.50 for a salmon steak, it is not a frequent stop for the brown-bag crowd.

Still, Dante's makes for a pleasant lunch alternative in the downtown. The room is bright, the food is good, and the service is professional. Just remember to go *up* the escalator to get to Dante's. No descent into the Inferno is required to visit here.

Deer Lodge
Rocky Mountain Cuisine

109 Lake Louise Drive, Lake Louise
Phone: 522·3747
Dining room: Daily 7 am – 11:30 am, 6 pm – 10 pm; Lounge: Daily 11:30 am – 10 pm
Reservations recommended — Fully licensed — Patio
Non-smoking dining room, smoking in lounges
V, MC, AE, DC — $$ – $$$

LAKE LOUISE is one of the few places in the world that actually lives up to its postcards. Millions of tourists throng to the lake every year, charging up the twisty road from the townsite to the Chateau and lakefront. Most folks head straight to the shoreline, drinking in the view. Afterwards, some of them stroll back downhill a few hundred metres for refreshments at Deer Lodge.

This is a vintage hotel serving Rocky Mountain cuisine along with its history. They have carefully renovated both the dining room and the lounge, retaining the rustic, hewn-wood feel and creating a more relaxed atmosphere than that of its bustling neighbour up the road.

Deer Lodge is not huge, but it is roomy. They offer breakfast and dinner in the lovely sixty-five seat Mount Fairview Dining Room and lunch as well as dinner in the smoker-friendly Caribou Lounge. They have a great patio and a spacious fireplace lounge for coffee and paper reading.

The lunch menu features a meaty platter with some Bow Valley delicacies such as air-dried buffalo, venison ham, and smoked duck. Served with mustard-marinated melons and house-made cranberry relish, these will take the edge off any day's hike. They top flatbread with chicken-apple sausage, steam mussels in a tomato-garlic broth, and mix ranch elk with mushrooms for a ragout served with mustard spätzle. Later in the day, the menu gets even more interesting with elk under a cassis glaze, pork tenderloin with a morel and cognac sauce, and caribou in a blueberry-port reduction. But watch out for those mountain-high prices—$33 for both the elk and the caribou.

We like breakfast at Deer Lodge best. When the mountains are quiet, it is still a bit of an alpine wilderness. A very civilized wilderness, but a wilderness nonetheless. So it seems justifiable to indulge in a mixed grill of elk-cranberry sausage and two kinds of bacon with eggs, potatoes, toast, and preserves. Or a game hash with onions, tomatoes, potatoes, corn, and two poached eggs. There are lighter offerings too, like toasted bagels, cottage cheese, and house-made granola, but the thin mountain air pushes us to the more hearty fare.

The food at Deer Lodge is Rocky Mountain substantial and great for pre- and post-hike consumption. It is rich and deep in flavours and always well executed. Considering the locale of the lodge, they also manage to maintain a professional service staff. And the setting just makes everything taste all the better.

www.deerlodgelakelouise.com

Des Alpes
Swiss-French

702 – 10 Street, Canmore
Phone: 678 • 6878
Tuesday – Sunday 5 pm – 10 pm
Reservations recommended — Fully licensed — Non-smoking
V, MC, AE — $$$

Run by a Swiss couple who came to Canada in the early '80s, Des Alpes is in a large log building, with the restaurant on the lower level and roomy living quarters on the upper one. The dining area is appropriately alpine, a hybrid of contemporary Canmore and traditional Switzerland. Tables are well spaced for views of the mountains and private dining, and there is a separate room for groups.

Des Alpes only does dinner. This is partly because the weekday lunch trade goes for quicker, lighter, cheaper fare, but it is also partly a lifestyle issue. Family and quality of life are more important to the owners than being open all the time.

The food at Des Alpes is terrific. The menu consists of Swiss-French preparations like cheese fondue, veal émincé, and lamb filet baked with herbs and garlic, and it is globalised with chicken curry and tiger prawns Jakarta. They use the best ingredients, prepared with exacting skill. No skimping on anything. It's rich, rich food, full of cream and flavour. The veal émincé of thinly sliced meat in a mushroom and onion sauce is a classic rendition—delicate, creamy, and complex to the taste. Even the salads are robust. The Caesar is bathed in a unique dressing and laced with garlic and Parmesan. No less intense is a tomato salad with blue cheese, onions, and a balsamic vinaigrette.

The breads and desserts are made in-house and they are wonderful. One of the owners is a member of a major baking family in Switzerland, and it shows. Thick, crusty sourdoughs, delicately layered chocolate-banana-rum cakes, all filled with luscious calories. Quality is the word from end to end.

Service is also skillful, in a quiet, unobtrusive Euro style. Dinner is an experience here so take your time and relax into the evening. And the prices don't seem as extreme anymore. Des Alpes was one of the first independent restaurants in the area to break the $20 entree mark. But with everyone else joining in, the $24 steaks and the $22 prawns don't seem so high. And $15 for the chicken émincé or the chicken curry seems like a bargain, as does $5 for the Caesar and $4 for the soup of the day.

With its high standards, Des Alpes remains one of our favourite places in the Bow Valley. It may leave us groaning from the richness, but then, calorie counts are lower in the mountain air.

Divino

Contemporary

817 – 1 Street SW
Phone: 263 • 5869
Monday – Saturday 11:30 am – 10:30 pm
Reservations recommended — Fully licensed — Patio — Non-smoking section
V, MC, AE, DC, Debit — $$ – $$$

Dᴵⱽᴵⁿᴼ started out in the early '80s in a space that had once been a tailor shop in the historic Grain Exchange Building. The angular display windows were converted into highly visible and sought-after seating areas, with other tables lining a corridor and clustering under a skylight in the back. A number of years later, Divino took advantage of the demise of their neighbour, The Love Shop, knocking down the wall that separated the two businesses, installing a wine bar, and creating a character-filled room with more than double the seating.

Divino has two distinct personalities. During the day, big east-facing windows draw in light bouncing off the PanCanadian tower across the street. Corporate power-lunchers suck back ginger rotini salads with grilled chicken, snow peas, and red grapes or lamb-pistachio burgers with caramelized onions and Ermite cheese. Seated at small bistro tables, they juggle notepads and briefcases as they try to find room for the wild mushroom pizzas. It's uptown and hyper, with brisk service and expense accounts.

But after dark, the look softens with table candles and warmly lit, stained glass chandeliers. The menu stays the same, but the pace slows as couples from the Beltline and visitors from the Palliser enjoy their wine and dinner. The tone is more romantic as the tiny tables now allow for intimate conversations. Sound still bounces around the walls, but it's not deafening—it's at a level that provides privacy without pain.

The menu changes slightly from time to time, but maintains its Contemporary California-Italian tone. One recent cool summer day, I had the daily soup, a beet and Gorgonzola blend that had a discouragingly pink tone but an excellent flavour balance. The purée of beets was offset by the piquancy of the blue cheese, creating a rich and refreshing soup. Then I had the smoked salmon and shrimp clubhouse sandwich, a tall construction that included applewood cheddar and a slather of chipotle mayo between thick layers of bread. It was almost impossibly thick, with far too much bread for the rest of the ingredients. I found that removing one of the bread slices improved its overall balance. Which ultimately made for a wonderful sandwich.

Divino exudes a class and casualness that is amplified by the staff. It's been around a long time, so no one is trying to prove anything. Divino is just about good food served well in an interesting room.

Dutchie's

Caribbean

3745 Memorial Drive SE (Glencrest Centre)
Phone: 204·8197
Monday – Wednesday 11 am – 8 pm
Thursday – Saturday 11 am – 11 pm
Reservations accepted — Fully licensed — Non-smoking section
V, MC — $ – $$

D UTCHIE'S is located in the space that started off as Lloyd's Caribbean Bakery & Bellyful and eventually became Sam's Caribbean One Stop. Unlike its predecessors, Dutchie's is not named after the proprietor, but rather after a kind of stewing pot often used in Caribbean cooking. The menu is pretty much the same as those of the previous owners: jerk chicken, brown chicken, curried goat, stewed fish. Nothing elaborate, but guaranteed to satisfy any urges you may have for spice.

The space is pretty much the same too. It's a narrow, nondescript strip-mall bay that seats a couple of dozen. There's not much for Island identity, but the tables are cleanly topped with tablecloths and cloth napkins. Chances are the owner himself will take your order if he isn't serving drop-in customers looking for a pattie to go. Or one of the kitchen staff may pop out to help.

The owner is from Antigua and his style of food is much like that of Jamaica, with a few spice variations. I tried one of his house-made patties (Dutchie's is one of the few places not to use Lloyd's wholesale patties) and it was very good—flaky pastry filled with well-seasoned, mildly spicy beef.

It set me up perfectly for a plate of stewed brown chicken with rice and peas. Again, nicely spiced with big chunks of chicken, some fresh vegetables, and more rice and peas than I could eat. A good deal for $9. But the preparation was typically Caribbean, which means that it was cooked to death. Though the flavouring was excellent, the chicken was dry and the rice and pea pilaf was far past its prime. On the one hand, it is unfair of me to criticize the food for being true to its heritage, but on the other, I wish they wouldn't cook it to such dryness. What I particularly did enjoy about the brown chicken was the complexity of the spicing. It was rich and robust with cinnamon and cloves and intense—but not over the top—with Scotch bonnet peppers.

Dutchie's is pretty casual, but I found the service as fast and pleasant as I have ever found in a Caribbean restaurant. It's laid-back, but appropriately so.

If you liked Lloyd's and Sam's, I think you'll like Dutchie's. Just don't expect anything terribly elegant.

El Sombrero

Mexican

520 – 17 Avenue SW
Phone: 228·0332
Tuesday – Friday 11:30 am – 2 pm, Monday – Thursday 5 pm – 10 pm
Friday & Saturday 5 pm – 11 pm, Sunday 5 pm – 9 pm
Reservations recommended — Fully licensed — Patio — Non-smoking section
V, MC, AE, DC, Debit — $ – $$

WITH its perch above 17th Avenue, El Sombrero has an excellent view of the world passing by outside. (That view includes the terrace at The Living Room next door.) Normally, second floor eateries do not have an easy go of it, but The Sombrero is doing just fine.

It is in a space that feels like an old apartment, or at least an old office suite, with its group of small rooms cobbled into a cafe. It has a crowded, homey feel that goes quite nicely with the down-home Mexican menu. On any given night, the room is filled with families, young couples, and members of the Latino community, all enjoying the tastes of Mexico. And they have added a sunny deck that oversees 17th Avenue even more closely. If you like to sit above the crowd, this is a great spot.

The menu covers the typical range of burritos, enchiladas, rellenos, and quesadillas. They also have the less common carne asada a la Tampiquena (marinated, thinly sliced steak), chuletas de cerdo con achiote (pork chops marinated in achiote), and mejillones al estilo Popeye (mussels, Popeye-style). It is a good menu in terms of variety, especially considering the lack of creativity in so many Mexican restaurants.

I like the quality of the mole at El Sombrero. It is rich and dark with chocolate, without being bitter, and its silky smoothness is spiked with chilies and deepened with nuts. Poured over soft corn tortillas filled with shredded chicken to create enchiladas de pollo con mole, it makes for a dense, sultry dish. With sides of rice and refried black beans for $11, it is also a bargain. Great quality, great value. Their tostadas are likewise good, topped with beans, lettuce, avocado, and chicken.

El Sombrero has the odd distinction of being one of the few Mexican restaurants in the city that does not automatically offer a bowl of chips and salsa with a meal. They tried charging for them for a while, but soon moved to the "available on request for free" mode. I realize there is a cost involved, but they might as well bury that in the price of the entrees. Customers expect chips and salsa quick and free at Mexican restaurants.

Regardless, El Sombrero offers good food at reasonable prices. The atmosphere is conducive to margaritas and nachos, and the view is great. Relax and enjoy.

Escoba

Influenced Cuisine & Wine

513 – 8 Avenue SW (Penny Lane)
Phone: 543·8911
Monday – Friday 11 am – 11 pm, Saturday 4 pm – 11 pm
Reservations recommended — Fully licensed — Non-smoking section
V, MC, AE, DC, Debit — $$

FEW underground restaurants thrive, but one that excels in spite of its obscurity is Escoba, located in the basement of Penny Lane. Escoba—meaning "broom" in Spanish—is a windowless space with a wine-cellar look. There are heavy wooden pillars, a rugged concrete floor, and fenced-in wine racks along a couple of walls. It's a weighty stone decor that seats about seventy in borderline claustrophobia. With low ceilings, crowded tables, and a pervasive dimness, Escoba will feel comfy for some but overly close for others.

In this era of hard-to-define cuisines, Escoba has labelled theirs "Influenced." Influenced by who or what is not clear, but it sounds good. The menu sets up as being strongly Contemporary with slight overtones from Latin America and Asia. With the availability of fresh ingredients from around the world and the creativity of a new wave of young chefs, the sky is the limit on what can be created. Escoba offers spring rolls with feta, toasted pine nuts, and spinach with a sweet chili aïoli; tiger shrimp and asparagus in a Dijon and tomato cream sauce over linguine; smoked salmon, provolone, and capers on pizza; and roasted eggplant, sun-dried tomato, and feta on mixed greens. Whatever the style, it sounds good.

And it tastes pretty decent too. Dropping in for lunch, a friend and I tried a couple of sandwiches. Mine had roasted portabello mushrooms with eggplant, zucchini, red pepper, artichoke relish, and Asiago. His had chicken with honey mustard, Asiago, banana peppers, and greens. They were thick constructions, made with quality ingredients and packed with flavour. Excellent, difficult-to-eat sandwiches that each came with a side of roasted vegetables and a choice of soup for $12. The soup of the day was carrot, and aside from being too thick, it was a tasty purée. The mushroom soup was rich with a hint of Dijon.

Escoba prides itself on a good wine list (with many decent wines by the glass) and a cellar-like setting that creates a wine-bar tone. It is not for those who have trouble with tight, enclosed places or for those wanting a private meal. (It amazes me how deftly the staff can maneuver among the tightly spaced tables.) But if you are looking for a quick escape from the hurly-burly of downtown business, just a few steps down the stairs carries you a long distance.

Fleur de Sel

French Brasserie

2015 – 4 Street SW
Phone: 228 • 9764
Tuesday – Friday 11 am – 2 pm, Tuesday – Sunday 5 pm – last guest
Reservations recommended — Fully licensed — Smoking at bar only
V, MC, AE, DC, Debit — $$ – $$$

B RASSERIES are rooted in the working-class background of French breweries. In the early 1800s brewmasters, realizing that their beer attracted crowds, developed menus to keep patrons eating—and drinking—longer. They went for simple stuff: sausage with sauerkraut, pots of beans with preserved duck, fresh oysters, and other tasty food that went well with beer. Over time, brasseries became more elegant, more decorated and linened, but they still tended to keep the approach simple.

Fleur de Sel isn't quite so old. It opened in 1998 in the Tivoli building and has used the space well: high ceilings, exposed brick walls, and a long curved bar sweeping into an open kitchen all give hints of the brasserie heritage.

Brasserie cuisine lives on at Fleur de Sel. (*Fleur de sel*—literally "flower of salt"— refers to a type of salt that is panned in France and resembles small flowers.) Under the skilled hand of owner-chef Patrice Durandeau, it encompasses a broader range than the original brasseries, with some dishes moving towards Contemporary tones. Durandeau, an excellent *saucier*, applies his skills to dishes ranging from beef tenderloin with pickled ginger and glace de viande (intensely beefy, with light ginger undertones) to traditional mussels in mustard and crème fraîche (rich, velvety smooth, each mussel bursting with flavour).

A homey cassoulet is a treat with flageolet beans that are slow cooked with chunks of sausage, a smoky pork chop, and a grilled lamb chop. The combination is outstanding, making as elegant a cassoulet as I have had. Yet this is still a rustic dish. Served in a heavy crock, a meal in its own cooking pot, it is the essence of brasserie food.

The grilled tuna in a wasabi beurre blanc—again leaning towards the Contemporary—is a brilliant dish. The vegetables are excellent too—large green beans sautéed in butter and garlic, sautéed potatoes, whatever suits the season.

Desserts run to the more traditional chocolate mousse, profiterolles, and fruit tarts. A seasonal plum tart was particularly outstanding.

There are few faults with Fleur de Sel. The food is unfailingly rich in an era of light and fatless. The tables are very close, and although the main room is non-smoking, when folks light up at the bar, it can't help but filter throughout the room. Seating about forty, it is a small place.

Fleur de Sel is unrepentantly French and uncompromisingly excellent. You may want to go to an extra workout afterwards, but it meets the need for those special occasions when only the best will do.

Florentine

Contemporary Comfort Food

1014 – 8 Street SW
Phone: 232 • 6028
Monday – Friday 11:30 am – 2 pm, Monday – Wednesday 5:30 pm – 9 pm
Thursday – Saturday 5:30 pm – 10 pm
Reservations recommended — Fully licensed — Non-smoking
V, MC, AE, Debit — $$ – $$$

FLORENTINE has seen a number of owners and chefs since its arrival in 1994. And each new person has brought a slightly different spin to the place. But through it all, the restaurant has retained an elegance and a commitment to quality. Recently, Florentine joined the Wildwood Restaurant Group, creating a great pairing with its robust neighbour Bonterra.

Chef Michelle Ducie and pastry chef Wendy Olson are responsible for maintaining much of Florentine's creative style. The menu ranges from lobster and avocado salad with basil-lemon brown butter to grilled salmon with a quinoa and caramelized onion pancake. Ingredients are global, but the approach is flavour and satisfaction first. In addition to ordering à la carte, Florentine offers prix fixe options at $48 for three courses and $54 for four courses. Caution though—it can be difficult to consume more than two courses because this is hearty food. We always manage, however, to leave room for their tasty desserts.

A black-bean soup brings a tartness and heat to the bowl that is soothed by an ancho chili crème fraîche. The beans are the backdrop to the soup rather than the focus as is typically seen in Latin American bean soups. It's a spin that works for me, although traditionalists may not find the variety of flavours to their liking.

A pork schnitzel takes me back to my youth, except for its tenderness. My memories are of much tougher meat. And the spätzle with grainy mustard and port jus are a decadent contrast to the mild pork. Mom never cooked like this.

The coconut shrimp curry with lemon grass-scented jasmine rice is an Occidental approach to a Thai dish that works well. The flavours are rich and deep. Now in a Thai restaurant you'd get more shrimp and it would likely cost less than the $25 price tag, but it is nonetheless a good dish.

Florentine offers a rustically Mediterranean atmosphere that features the rough concrete floors of the original owner (this was part of the press rooms for the old *Albertan* newspaper). Seating about forty, it's cozy and stylish—each table is topped with a decanter of filtered water and a bottle of wine with a food-pairing suggestion attached.

Florentine has gone through a lot of changes in the last few years, and I hope that it has now entered a period of tranquility. It remains a lovely spot for dinner, with equally lovely food and service.

www.florentine@wildwoodgroup.net

Galaxie Diner

Diner

1413 – 11 Street SW
Phone: 228•0001
Monday – Friday 7 am – 3 pm, Saturday, Sunday & Holidays 8 am – 4 pm
Reservations not accepted — No alcoholic beverages — Non-smoking
Cash only — $

A trip to the Galaxie Diner is like a visit to Mayberry via the *Twilight Zone*, with a bit of *Friends* thrown in. It's definitely part of another universe, but thankfully, a friendly one.

The Galaxie is a tiny red-vinyl, twirly-stooled diner seating a couple of dozen. But it's not a nouveau diner—this stuff is genuine. The napkin dispensers, the stools, even the Kellogg's breakfast cereal display, are all the real thing. An abbreviated lunch counter seats six on those stools, while four vinyl-coated booths pack in another sixteen. In the window nook, two small tables hold another four. It's cozy, with the kitchen consuming the centre of the room. Everything has the slightly dented look of a real diner, including the jukebox selectors in each booth. But the Galaxie is non-smoking, which is a huge bonus. And the food is way better than in the greasy diners of my youth.

They don't make a lot of things at the Galaxie, but what they do, they do with quality. There is the all-day breakfast with the usual eggs and bacon and a darned good breakfast burrito—two large flour tortillas filled with scrambled eggs, sautéed peppers and onions, a pile of home fries, and a side of salsa and sour cream. If this were New Mexico, I would expect a hotter bite to the burrito, but regardless, it's tasty and fresh. The Galaxie burger is another favourite: it's a huge house-made beef pattie with cheese, bacon, mushrooms, peppers, and onions served between two slabs of toasted bread and with a pile of home fries. Very filling. And good value at $5.50. The home fries can be a touch salty, but are otherwise excellent.

They don't really do dessert here. But they do have ice cream, and they make killer milkshakes, served in those huge metal tumblers. They also don't do dinner—it's only open during the day.

All this seems to suit the neighbourhood. And much of the time, anyone who comes into the Galaxie knows not only the owner but a lot of other people too. The Galaxie has strong community support, which is obvious from the weekend lineups.

It helps that the place is casual—things are fairly relaxed here. And time seems to melt to the point where the '50s take over from the '90s. The jukebox wails, the customers laugh, a Studebaker pulls up. For a few moments, you're in another universe and a pretty interesting one at that.

Golden Inn
Chinese (Cantonese)

107 – 2 Avenue SE
Phone: 269·2211
Sunday – Thursday 4 pm – 3 am, Friday & Saturday 4 pm – 4 am
Reservations accepted — Fully licensed — Non-smoking section
V, MC, AE, Debit — $ – $$

THE GOLDEN INN is one of those Chinatown joints where culinary time appears to have stood still. The room is large and characterless, the service impersonal, and the style a form of Cantonese that harkens back decades. Yet it remains a classic in its genre.

The Golden Inn takes an unprepossessing position on a quiet section of 2nd Avenue SE. The room is long and wide and high, with a few decorations making a vain attempt to break up the wall expanse of off-white. The non-smoking section is indeterminate, especially since staff are wont to smoke in the room. But this is in keeping with what passes for service. Waiters shuffle across the floor, barely stopping to drop dishes at the tables. At one end of the room, a staff member assembles plates, bowls, and spoons with what seems like the most noise possible. That must be why so many of the dishes are chipped. The Golden Inn is neither friendly nor unfriendly—service is just neutral, the bare minimum needed to do business.

But the food remains good. The Law Ding black-bean chicken is salty, thick with sauce and chunks of chicken, and laced with beans and onions. The braised 8 Joe duck incorporates seven other meats with incredibly tender duck breast. And the simple mixed vegetables is a delightful mix of baby corn, broccoli, bok choy, and huge mushrooms. Not overly thickened, just lightly sauced.

Be forewarned that this food requires attention and is far from delicate to eat. The chicken is chopped whole, skin-on, bone-in. So you get everything. The duck comes on the bone too, so there is a lot of detailed chewing and expulsion of bony and fatty bits. Do not take anyone that you are trying to impress.

The Golden Inn also has some of the oddest hours in town. They do no lunch business, preferring to open at 4 in the afternoon and to stay open until 3 or 4 in the morning. Needless to say, the crowd becomes quite interesting after about 2 a.m. This is a night owl's hangout and, as such, has the bleary-eyed tone that seems appropriate in the wee hours.

Time has passed the Golden Inn by in food style and service, but the great thing is, they don't care. Customers of all stripes keep coming back to enjoy the fare and the experience of another time and place.

Harbour City

Chinese (Cantonese)

302 Centre Street S
Phone: 269 • 8888
Sunday – Thursday 9 am – 2 am, Friday & Saturday 9 am – 4 am
Reservations recommended — Fully licensed — Non-smoking section
V, MC, AE, Debit — $ – $$

D IM SUM is from the Eastern school of Chinese cooking—it is seen in Canton and Shanghai, two areas that do not use a lot of spice in their cooking. Instead, they use the natural qualities of the foods, enhanced by comparatively simple bean and soy sauces.

A lively Chinatown restaurant that really understands dim sum is Harbour City (obviously a reference to a much different city than Calgary). A broad path that circles their dining room has tables on either side so that the dim sum carts can always pass by closely for customers' easy inspection. And these carts flow abundantly in both directions, carrying a selection of the over 100 different dim sum treats they can produce.

The first dim sum to roll by us were balls of sticky rice wrapped in lily leaves. Flavoured with chunks of pork and chicken in a savoury bean sauce, this sticky rice was the best I have ever had. Sticky rice is frequently spongy and sour, but this dish retained a firm texture and a wonderful flavour. It was a portent of good things to come.

We really enjoyed the shrimp dumplings, big lumps of ground shrimp wrapped in translucent rice dough. But the steamed scallop dumplings were even better— fresh, light, simply done. We liked the steamed squid in black-bean sauce and the dense, almost rubbery texture of the steamed beef balls. Even the taro root dumplings and the barbecue pork buns were exceptional. But top honours of the day go to the charming Catherine who (after I had powered out) tried the steamed chicken feet, tripe, lung, and spleen. She declared the spleen the tastiest, very similar to liver.

That is the great thing about dim sum. You can try all sorts of things, and the more people you have, the more things you can try. It is also noisy, messy, and a lot of fun for the whole family, as long as they are a little adventurous.

The staff here are good at explaining the dishes and somehow keeping track of the bill. Dim sum items are mostly $2 to $3 with some going up to $5, making it a pretty reasonable meal. It is hard to eat more than $10 to $15 worth of dim sum per person.

Harbour City also carries a full menu of other Cantonese dishes and has extremely long hours. It is definitely one of the better places in Chinatown.

Heartland Cafe
Bakery & Cafe

940 – 2 Avenue NW
Phone: 270·4541
Monday – Friday 7 am – 8 pm
Saturday & Sunday 7 am – 6 pm
Reservations not accepted — No alcoholic beverages — Benches outside — Non-smoking
V, MC, AE — $

THERE is a popular local hangout hidden in Sunnyside. Just far enough away from the bustle of 10th Street, the Heartland Cafe is a rustic, friendly place that harkens back to turn-of-the-last-century Calgary.

From the outside, Heartland is an old brick building with a few benches. There is always someone in Birkenstocks sitting on one of these benches, sipping a latte and reading the paper. Frequently they are smoking a rollie because inside it is delightfully smoke-free. It is also of fluctuating temperature due to the presence of hot baking ovens and questionable insulation and ventilation. So expect to be a little cool in the winter and a little hot in the summer.

Also expect to find some tasty food—thick cheddar-dill scones, moist raspberry-yogurt muffins, drippy cinnamon buns, and sweetly iced carrot cake. The place may look like a holdover from the '60s, but the fare is way better. No carob here. It is food done professionally in an artisanal style. Full of flavour, but rustic and somehow socially conscious—sweet, but in a brown sugar sort of way. Heartland fills the air for a few blocks around with the fragrance of fresh baking.

I particularly enjoy the scones here ($1.65). I like these treats to be made with density, with the strong taste of dill and cheddar. Scones that are great on the day of baking with a dark-roasted coffee but that turn into hockey pucks after twenty-four hours. Heartland does them like that. They also do a variety of soups ($4.25) and sandwiches such as tuna or chicken-cheddar melts ($5), plus a vegetarian chili for a reasonable $4.50. And they make some of the better coffees in the over-caffeinated Kensington area.

Lunch at Heartland is a comfortable, casual event. When the high-ceilinged room fills with people, sound bounces around to create a quilt of privacy. So even if the seating is a bit tight, it remains quite discreet. Only seating about thirty, it can be difficult to get a table—not because of the number of people, but rather because the customers seem to stay forever. This is the kind of place where people go to talk and talk and talk.

Heartland is cute and very much a part of its community. And it is worth a visit, even if you are from the burbs.

The Highwood
Culinary School

1301 – 16 Avenue NW (John Ware Building, SAIT)
Phone: 284·8615
Monday – Friday for lunch, Monday – Thursday for dinner
Reservations essential — Fully licensed — Non-smoking
V, MC, Debit — $$

SQUEEZE in another dozen tables and The Highwood would look like a high-tone restaurant in New York or Los Angeles. The colours are muted yellows and greens, the granite and burled wood bar sweeps across one end of the room, and black and white clad staff maneuver trays and trolleys around veneered pillars. Pan-smoked salmon and seared scallops with a herb beurre blanc and cheese mousseline with spinach on barley risotto are presented on pristine china. Diners lounge on plush velveteen banquettes as soft light spills into the room, creating a sumptuous atmosphere.

The Highwood used to feel like an upscale school cafeteria, which makes sense since it is a training centre for students studying for hospitality careers. It underwent nearly a million dollars worth of renovations a few years ago and is now one of the nicest dining rooms in the city.

The Highwood offers students the best of the best to hone their skills. In the kitchen are rows of industrial stoves, huge coolers, massive dough mixers, and immense ovens—the kind of equipment students can only hope to work with when they graduate. Under the tutelage of expert teaching chefs, they create dishes from sushi and wood-fired pizzas to noisettes of lamb and bananas Foster.

Of course, someone has to eat all these creations and that's where we, the public, do our part for higher education. And for a modest price.

At dinner, a five-course meal is $25 plus GST and gratuity, just enough to cover food costs and a little more. For that, you get a choice of appetizers, followed by a soup and a salad. Then a choice of entrees—fare like tandoori-style prawns with yogurt-cilantro raita or Oka-stuffed rack of lamb. If you're still ambulatory at this stage, they roll out the dessert trolley or present a selection of cheeses.

Lunch is à la carte (except for a Thursday buffet) and a little pricier but still a bargain, with bison casserole at $8.95 and glazed duck salad with candied ginger and orange emulsion at $3.95.

Sure, not everything is perfect—these are students after all. But that is to be expected in a learning environment. You will find an unceasing earnestness and a keen desire to learn. On our many visits, we have never encountered any "attitude" in the service.

Then there's all that room between the tables. It is ostensibly to allow plenty of room for novice servers, but we find it helpful for giving sated diners more room to waddle their way out.

Il Girasole

Italian

636 – 10 Avenue SW
Phone: 263•6661
Monday – Friday 11:30 am – 2 pm, Tuesday – Saturday 5:30 pm – last guest
Reservations recommended — Fully licensed — Patio — Non-smoking
V, MC, AE, DC, Debit — $$ – $$$

AMID all the look-alike Italian restaurants, one of the best can be missed. Although it is very close to downtown, Il Girasole is just across the railroad tracks, making it easy to overlook.

If you are a train buff, it is the best place in town. They deliberately built the restaurant with huge windows looking onto the tracks a few metres away. Not that you need a distraction inside Il Girasole. It is a bright, pretty room, elegantly appointed with well-spaced tables topped with cream-coloured linens. There's a private room at one end for up to twenty-five and another banquet room that will fit sixty. The dining room itself is sided by an open kitchen so that waves of rich Italian cooking wash over you as you wait for dinner.

And the food is worth any wait. We devoured an appetizer platter of mussels, prawns, and calamari, each in its own delicious sauce. All the seafood was perfectly prepared. Then we had a light salad in a simple oil and balsamic vinaigrette, just right to freshen our palates after the seafood (we were dining in the slow, multi-course Italian style).

Next, we moved on to some veal parmigiana and a linguine carbonara. The veal was lightly breaded and savoury with just the right amount of cheese. It was nicely served with a simple spaghetti coated in olive oil, roasted garlic, and just a hint of hot chilies. The carbonara was equally tasty, but could have used a little more pancetta. Not that it wasn't rich enough. Speaking of rich, for dessert we had fresh strawberries covered with a hand-whipped zabaglione—egg yolks and sugar frothed with Marsala into a sweet cream.

The hand whipping was done by owner Tony Gloria who, with his wife Pina, run Il Girasole as a very hands-on operation. Wearing red aprons, they greet the customers, cook the food, and serve the tables. They also have skilled staff to help keep the quality high. There's always a lot of personal care and attention at Il Girasole.

Considering the quality, the prices aren't that bad. At dinner, salads and appetizers run mostly at $6 to $10, with the top pasta appetizer at $14—that's for the vermicelli with caviar though. For pasta entrees, add $5 to the price. Meat or seafood dinners range in the $20s, so it is not your bargain-basement Italian place.

Don't overlook Il Girasole. It is as colourful and intense and warm as the sunflower it is named after.

Il Sogno
Italian (Neapolitan)

24 – 4 Street NE
Phone: 232 • 8901
Tuesday – Friday 11:30 am – 2 pm, Sunday 10:30 am – 2 pm
Tuesday – Sunday 5 pm – 9 pm
Reservations recommended — Fully licensed — Smoking at bar only
V, MC, AE, DC — $$ – $$$

I l Sogno lives up to its name—it is Italian for "the dream." The owners have taken over three bays of the De Waal Block, a large brick building that faces onto 4th Street NE, and have developed a two-room, sixty-seat restaurant. The high tin ceiling has been exposed and painted a bronze tone. Creaky wooden floors, lightly sponged walls, and white linened tables complete the look. It is spare yet elegant. There is nothing extra in the room—what is there serves a purpose. In the daytime, sunlight floods the space, creating sharp edges and clean lines; in the evening, candlelight bathes the rooms in a golden glow. Il Sogno is one of those places where the food tastes better just because the room is so nice.

But the food definitely backs up the look. The menu reflects the taste of the Neapolitan chef, so there is a lot of seafood, items like mussels poached in black pepper and lemon or sea bass steamed with cherry tomatoes, clams, and white wine. There are also plates like veal chops with sautéed spinach, rabbit with rosemary and roasted tomatoes, and beef tenderloin with truffled oyster mushrooms and provolone.

We started our dinners with two dynamite appetizers—fresh pears and air-dried beef, prosciutto, sun-dried tomatoes, and Parmesan. And that was just the first one. The second was seared scallops on sautéed wild mushrooms. At $9 and $13 respectively, worth every penny. The pear was exactly ripe and blended perfectly with the beef and prosciutto, the cheese and tomatoes adding to the balance. And the scallop dish was huge—three large scallops with a big pile of mushrooms. This could be a lunch in itself.

For our main courses we ordered linguine with mussels, clams, and prawns at $16 and sautéed prawns with a roasted red-pepper pesto on risotto at $21. Both were good, but the nod goes to the risotto, an excellent balance of prawns, smoky pepper flavour, and creamy risotto. Every mouthful was a delight. The linguine was good too—skillfully prepared—but I thought its cherry tomato sauce was too light for the strength of the mussels.

Probably the highlight of the night was the white-chocolate cremino—a kind of Italian crème brûlée. Outstanding. Add to that some fine service and an excellent wine-by-the-glass list, and you have a very good restaurant.

Indochine

French-Vietnamese Fusion

315 Stephen Avenue Walk SW (+15 Level, Bankers Hall)
Phone: 263•6929
Monday – Wednesday 11 am – 7 pm, Thursday – Saturday 11 am – 9 pm
Reservations recommended — Fully licensed — Non-smoking
V, MC, AE, DC, Debit — $$

IN a world of Fusion cuisines, perhaps the oldest and still most successful is French-Vietnamese. It has had a long time to develop—since the mid-1800s when the French first occupied Vietnam (or Indochina). The fragrant flavours of lemon grass, lime leaves, and nuoc mam fish sauce are combined with French cooking styles to create intense and elegant dishes. One of the best places to find this melding is at Indochine.

The menu does have familiar dishes for fans of Vietnamese noodle houses. There are the soups and salad rolls and lemon grass chicken, all skillfully prepared. But then there are the ginger mussels. Steamed in a ginger, garlic, and black-bean broth, it is one of the best mussel dishes in the city. The black beans and ginger perfectly complement the large mussels. With fresh baguette to mop up the sauce, it is an excellent appetizer.

We've tried the Crepe d'Indochine—a fluffy yellow crepe made with rice flour and turmeric, stuffed with pork, marinated shrimp, and bean sprouts. Light and tasty. And the grilled salmon sandwich is superb—pieces of fish are lightly sautéed with onions and capers. The baguette is the doughy variety, which works well on this kind of sandwich. It comes with either a green salad or some Provençale-style frites dusted with sea salt and rosemary. Very nice.

There is a great sense of presentation with the contrasting of colours and textures. The salmon sandwich is served on a banana leaf, the fries are tucked into a second curled leaf. The mussels are similarly well displayed with bowls of fish sauce for dipping and marinated carrots to add colour and taste. Fresh flowers from the owner's second business—the Garden Follies florist—adorn the plates.

Sometimes when cuisines go upscale, so do the prices. Indochine's have understandably risen in the last few years, but they still aren't bad, especially considering that the address is Bankers Hall. The crepe is $10, the ginger mussels $9.75, the sandwich $12. Most things are under $15.

Indochine has a casual environment with an unusual indoor patio. If possible it is best to avoid the lunch rush—though service is fairly quick, it is so popular that it can feel a little harried and crowded. It is much more relaxing in the evening or on the weekend.

All in all, Indochine serves good food. When Kipling said, "East is East, and West is West, and never the twain shall meet," he had obviously never tried the French-Vietnamese food of Indochine.

Indulge

Casual Gourmet

620 – 8 Avenue SW
Phone: 229·9029
Monday – Friday 7 am – 6 pm, Saturday & Sunday 10 am – 2:30 pm
Reservations accepted, recommended for weekend brunch — No alcoholic beverages
Non-smoking
V, AE, Debit — $

INDULGE is one of the many recent arrivals in the downtown core that keys on the area's breakfast and lunch crowds. But instead of having a flashy decor, Indulge is surprisingly understated. It looks like a casual '70s granola bar, with a counter cutting off the kitchen from the dining area and with its large room, square wooden tables, and bits of art on the walls. You step up to the counter to order from overhead chalkboards, which is difficult because, once you are close enough to order, you can't actually see the chalkboards anymore. So you have to do that shuffle of stepping back and forth to see the boards and place your order. As I said, it's like a '70s granola bar. This is not complex, just a bit awkward.

But worth every moment of awkwardness. The staff are very service oriented, and when I couldn't decide on which soup to have, I was offered little samples of each. The lunch menu follows a fairly simple soup-and-sandwich format, but the two chefs really know their stuff. A red-lentil soup was one of the best I've ever had. A carrot-apple soup was just as good. And sandwiches of grilled vegetables and ham with Asiago were great. There's nothing fancy about these preparations—they're just intelligent, simple, and not overworked.

Breakfast and weekend brunch are just as flavourful. (And at brunch there is table service!) My omelette of house-roasted peppers and brie was lovely. And their French toast with candied almonds and maple syrup, sided with cranberry-turkey sausage, was exceptional.

Sweets are much the same way: simple and intense. Their brownies are dense, rich, chocolatey squares, and the sun-dried cranberry scones are a buttery, flaky effort.

Indulge makes great food. And what they put out in the restaurant is a fairly narrow example of their capacity. On their catering side, they do things like langoustine- and Gorgonzola-stuffed mushrooms, citrus-braised osso bucco, and maple-pecan baked brie. There is a lot of creativity here.

And value. One lunch of a soup, a sandwich, and three desserts (two to take home) was $10. I liked it so much that, after my first lunch, I went back with Catherine for a second one—two soups, a sandwich, and three more desserts for $16.

Indulge is a comfortable non-smoking environment, the kind of place where it feels OK to sit for a while and read the paper. The kind of place where it feels OK to indulge.

Istanbul
Turkish

2005 – 4 Street SW
Phone: 229·0542
Daily 11 am – 10 pm
Reservations recommended — Fully licensed — Patio — Non-smoking
V, MC, AE, Debit — $$

THIS restaurant space has seen a long list of either unlucky or downright bad ideas. I can think of at least four places that have come and gone, from a Dutch pancake eatery to a pie shop to a couple of mediocre Mexican attempts. So I was a bit wary when I saw the return of the Istanbul to this location. I say return because the owners ran a smaller and more casual cafe on 14th Street SW for a while.

The new Istanbul is very well conceived. They have kept the ceramic tile floor (I think that appeared in the Mexican phase), painted the walls in Mediterranean tones of off-white and deep blue, and topped the tables with linens. The menu spans the more familiar Eastern Med dishes of kebabs, stuffed grape leaves, calamari, and baklava. But it also presents the less commonly seen Turkish specialties like piyaz (white bean salad), mücver (zucchini patties with yogurt garlic sauce), karniyarik (beef-stuffed eggplant), and kuzu pirzola (Turkish rack of lamb). So customers can go as comfortable or as exotic as they want.

I tried the piyaz and enjoyed the blend of white beans, tomatoes, onions, parsley, and sumak. It was a gentle salad—the balance was good, but it lacked intensity. Still, nicely fresh. Then on to the lamb kebabs, two skewers of marinated lamb interspersed with onions and green peppers. So many places use cheap and gristly meats on their kebabs, but not the Istanbul. This was good lamb and that makes all the difference. It was tender and tasty and not overcooked. Served with a pile of well-prepared rice and various grilled vegetables, it was a great plate of food for a reasonable $14. I had to finish dinner with my favourite Turkish dish, sutlac (rice pudding). Just as good as my years-old memory of Turkey, creamy rice was topped with crushed pistachios and cinnamon. Lovely.

The Istanbul also features pleasant service and a short but intelligent wine list. This is the kind of place where you can have a quick and light meal or a serious feast.

It's about time someone turned this ill-fated room into a winner. It is a much better location than its history reveals. I think Calgary's only Turkish restaurant will be a strong player on the busy 4th Street restaurant scene.

James Joyce & The Joyce on 4th
Irish Pubs

114 Stephen Avenue Walk SW	*506 – 24 Avenue SW*
Phone: 262•0708	*Phone: 541•9168*
Sunday – Thursday 11 am – midnight	*Monday – Friday 11:30 am – midnight*
Friday & Saturday 11 am – 1 am	*Saturday & Sunday 9 am – midnight*
No non-smoking section	*Non-smoking section*

Reservations recommended — Fully licensed — Patios
V, MC, AE, Debit — $ – $$

STROLL down Stephen Avenue and faint strains of Celtic music reach the ears. A black banner protrudes from the old Toronto Bank Building, marking the entrance to the James Joyce Irish Pub. Pass through the double wooden doors and you are hit with a wall of warmth, the lilt of laughter, the waft of beer and tobacco, and the soft glow of chandeliers. Welcome to the downtown Joyce.

This is a pub, but not just any pub. It is a lively Irish pub with cozy corners, good food, Guinness at three temperatures, and a gigantic air handling system to suck away the excess smoke. It is a pub we like. And Guinness is a big draw here. Served at Irish (46 to 48°F), European (44 to 46°F), or North American (40 to 42°F) temperatures to satisfy all customers, it forms the molasses-black backdrop of the Joyce. The ale also appears in some of the food, such as the beef and Guinness pie where the meat is marinated in it and baked under a thick, flaky pastry. It's a rich and pleasing meat pie, perfect with Guinness in the glass.

Other Irish classics include a savoury lamb stew, a stellar corned beef and cabbage, and a very decent fish and chips. The chips themselves are grand—thick, fresh, lightly crunchy on the outside, soft on the inside. And then there are the potato nachos, an invention of the Joyce. Responding to patron requests for nachos but wanting to maintain an Irish spin, the cooks crosscut potatoes, fry them, and layer on onions, peppers, tomatoes, cheese, and sour cream.

Not everything on the list is heavy, meaty, and fried. There are a few salads, and it's rumoured that someone even ordered one once. (When in Rome, or Dublin...)

The Joyce has recently enlivened 4th Street SW with a new location in the old Bizou space. Serving a similar menu, The Joyce on 4th has the Victorian look of overstuffed couches, fireplaces, and pounded tin ceilings. It's a roomy place with a distinct non-smoking area and a south-facing patio. The Guinness here is served only at the cool North American temperature, but the welcome is just as warm as downtown.

What sets the Joyces apart from most of the growing number of Irish pubs is the sincerity and quality of the effort. They are comfortable places with friendly staff and good food, just what we'd expect in Ireland. And the Guinness is always creamy.

JoJo Bistro
Parisian Bistro

917 – 17 Avenue SW
Phone: 245•2382
Monday – Friday 11:30 am – 2 pm, Monday – Saturday 5:30 pm – 10:30 pm
Reservations recommended — Fully licensed — Smoking at bar only
V, MC, AE, DC, Debit — $$ – $$$

IT seems every time I go to JoJo, they have changed the look: they are always repainting and shifting the seating around. Right now, the colours are sponged gold and dark purple, and there's a bench with tables running along one wall and a row of tables along the other. JoJo is a long, narrow room that typifies the French bistro style, with one exception. The crisply set tables are devoid of ashtrays because JoJo has limited smoking to the bar area only.

JoJo offers a menu of classic dishes such as duck confit with white beans, mussel soup with saffron, and sweetbreads in a mustard sauce. At both lunch and dinner, you can order off the full menu or opt for the table d'hôte—three courses for dinner and two for lunch. At dinner, for instance, you can order the mussel soup followed by a venison osso bucco and a Grand Marnier crème caramel, all for $33.50. For $15.50 at lunch, they offer a choice of appetizers and then such main courses as a Caesar salad with duck confit or a seafood brochette, followed by coffee or tea. Not bad at all, especially for the quality.

I opted for a lunchtime potato soup and a bavette. A bavette is a cut of beef from the back of the sirloin, a piece that is a little chewy but flavourful, especially when well aged and cooked medium rare. And that's one thing you can be sure of at JoJo—they are going to grill a medium-rare steak medium rare. With some good pommes frites on the side, it was a tasty main course. The potato soup too was nicely prepared—nothing fancy, but thick and creamy.

Much of French cuisine is just simple, high-flavour food. It looks appetizing on the plate, there is nothing fussy about it, and it tastes good. We seem to be in an era where a lot of chefs are trying to impress us with the complexity of their preparations and the immensity of their ingredients. In doing so, they sometimes lose the flavour focus of the dishes themselves. The fundamental question is this: does it taste good? Seems awfully simple, but some chefs are going for pretty before tasty.

Anyway, JoJo goes for flavour first. It's good food, fairly simple and straightforward. Frankly, it's a relief not to have to think about the food once in a while. Sometimes it's nice just to enjoy the company and the simple pleasure of a well-cooked meal.

Jonas'

Hungarian

937 – 6 Avenue SW
Phone: 262•3302
Monday – Friday 11:30 am – 2 pm, Monday – Saturday 5 pm – 10 pm
Reservations recommended — Fully licensed — Non-smoking section
V, MC, AE, Debit — $

WE used to enjoy the Tokay and the Silver Tray, but in our culture's move away from the heavier Eastern European cuisines, we lost the elegant food of Hungary. So I am glad to see the arrival of Jonas' Restaurant.

Named after its Hungarian owner, Jonas' has an Eastern European cafe feel. The room is long and narrow, and it's windowless except for right at the front. The cinder-block walls are hung with Hungarian weavings, and diners huddle over candles at tables where many chairs are pointed toward the walls. There is an air of privacy, almost a darkened conspiracy to the room.

And then there is the staff, friendly ladies who explain the food in loving terms. And they have good reason to be proud. Although the menu is only marginally more expansive than the decor, it is a collection of Hungary's favourite foods. There's chicken paprikash, cabbage rolls, schnitzel, and even goulash. All the hearty, robust dishes with all the calories that have made Hungarian an outcast cuisine. But for those who want to be careful, most of the dishes are offered in half portions as well as full sizes.

The liver dumpling soup ($1.45 for the small, $2.45 for the large) features delicately light dumplings swimming in an excellent chicken stock. Nothing heavy about this. For that, you can try the Hungarian goulash, thick with beans and sausage, a large serving of which would be a meal in itself ($2.75 for the small, $4.95 for the large).

A small entree of paprikash or cabbage rolls or schnitzel will cost a stunning $4.65, and these are servings many places would call full sized. Large entrees start at $6.25 for the beef stew and top out at $9.95 for the breaded catfish. The paprikash has a velvety sweet pepper sauce over tender drop noodles and chunks of chicken. And the schnitzel with pan-fried potatoes is everything I would expect in a schnitzel.

For dessert there are palacsintas—crepes with various fillings such as chocolate sauce and ground walnuts. And the food goes well with their selection of Hungarian wines by the glass. I hadn't had Szeksardi in years. It hasn't changed.

So Jonas' is very good. Don't expect the elegance of a grand Hungarian restaurant. Instead, expect a cozy Hungarian cafe. As a Hungarian friend told us the night we saw her at Jonas', it's cheap and cheerful and easier than cooking it at home.

Juan's

Mexican

807 – 1 Street SW
Phone: 266•0051
Monday – Saturday 11:30 am – 2 pm, 5 pm – 10 pm
Reservations recommended — Fully licensed — No non-smoking section
V, MC, AE, Debit — $$

A quiet place next to the Grain Exchange Building, Juan's has been around since 1989. It leans more to the traditional than to the trendy with walls covered in Corona posters, Mexican road maps, and tortilla presses. The room seats about thirty at tables squeezed closely together, and on a hot summer day, it's downright warm. The rest of the time, it's quite pleasant, though even one smoker can cast a pall over the room.

And yes, there is a Juan. Smiling, pleasantly professional, late of Oaxaca via Mexico City and the Four Seasons, Juan Cruz brings a wealth of experience to his job. He's as fine a host as you will find in the city, and his food isn't bad either.

Every table is waiting with a basket of tortilla chips and a bowl of salsa. His salsa is fresh and has a bite—not too big, but if you are averse to spice, order up some guacamole and enjoy the creamy smooth flavours of this avocado dip. It's unusual to get good guacamole in Calgary, partly because decent avocados are hard to find here, but Juan goes the extra mile to make sure his is *muy delicioso*.

If you like soup, two of Juan's are a must. The tortilla soup of chicken broth with tortilla strips, avocado, and cheese is a light alternative to the Tabasco-style cream of pinto beans, a serious, stomach-filling soup of puréed beans.

Juan offers other Mexican classics like Caesar salad and avocado salad as well as chicken enchiladas with mole sauce and huevos rancheros. His cuisine is pan-Mexican—it's not dedicated to any particular region, but is rather a sampling of the whole country. There's a red snapper dish from Veracruz, a chicken breast smothered in a pungent arbolito pepper sauce from Oaxaca, and some ceviche from Acapulco.

Juan's sauces have depth and character. Chocolate darkens the mole while chilies add an underlying bite. You may find more strength and complexity down south, but these will not leave you wanting.

What you should leave is room for dessert, definitely a highlight at Juan's. He continues to make one of the best flans (crème caramel) in town and a fine, fine rice pudding. But for the full Mexican package, try the crepas con cajeta, a couple of crepes folded over heated cajeta—condensed, super-sweet, caramelized goat milk. With a dollop of whipped cream and the obligatory maraschino cherry, you're guaranteed a major sugar buzz.

Kane's Harley Diner

Diner

1209 – 9 Avenue SE
Phone: 269•7311
Sunday – Thursday 7 am – 8 pm, Friday & Saturday 7 am – 9 pm
Reservations accepted — Fully licensed — Non-smoking section
V, MC, AE, DC, Debit — $ – $$

Back in 1957, Kane's Harley-Davidson shop opened in Inglewood as a purveyor of big bad bikes for big bad boys. Kane's was successful, and in 1997, moved into new digs in the old liquor store across the alley. The former bike shop was then available, and the owners decided to capitalize on the Harley image by turning it into a diner.

Kane's Harley Diner is legit—it is not a sanitized, theme-park diner. It is Harley first and undeniably foremost with its omnipresent orange and black trim. And it is biker-friendly with its exclusive bike parking out front and a rear exit that leads directly to Kane's sparkling new shop, rebuilt after a fire in 2000.

Kane's seats about 100 at booths and tables, with a soda bar along the back for twenty more. The bar uses Harley mufflers as kick-rails, and there's a Harley logo in the flooring, framed Harley ads on the walls, and even a Harley jukebox wailing great bike and diner tunes. The room is brightened by the high ceilings and windows onto 9th Avenue and by the smiles of a friendly staff. It is a surprisingly comfortable atmosphere.

The cuisine is diner classic with humongous breakfasts, one-pound burgers, good clubhouses, serious steaks, and grilled bologna sandwiches. There is meat loaf, pork chops with mashed potatoes, ribs, hot dogs, and chili—high-carbo, bike-riding vittles that may explain the general girth of many bikers and the size of Harley seats. There is also a list of "weeds," salads of spinach or coleslaw or iceberg lettuce, if you feel so inclined.

We opted for the big breakfast buzz, Catherine choosing the Flathead pancakes and me, the Ultra—three eggs, two slices of bacon, two sausages, two slices of ham, and two pancakes. Catherine loved her Flathead, served with real maple syrup and soft, unsalted butter. She always likes pancakes, but cold butter can send her into an early-morning funk; to her, this is a major culinary misdemeanour because spreading it on hot pancakes tears them. My Ultra was everything I would expect of a high-carbohydrate, high-cholesterol breakfast. Quality ingredients all round. Good sausage, crisp bacon, eggs perfectly over easy.

We like Kane's. Whether for breakfast or a good diner lunch, it fits the bill. Kane's is a terrific place for bikers, car-folk, strollers, and bladers. I would not necessarily park a Yamaha bike outside, but otherwise, you will be made welcome and served some good food.

Kashmir
Indian (Mughlai & Kashmiri)

507 – 17 Avenue SW
Phone: 244·2294
Tuesday – Friday 11:30 am – 1:30 pm, Tuesday – Sunday 5:30 pm – 10 pm
Reservations recommended — Fully licensed — Non-smoking section
V, MC, AE, DC, Debit — $$

WHEN the Moti Mahal moved to 14th Street a few years ago, the original Moti owners, the Singh family, returned to that 17th Avenue location. They spiffed up the two rooms and opened the Kashmir.

The restaurant looks very nice. They retained the basic bi-level space, enhancing it with some new window treatments and lights. The tables shine with white china, and the rooms have an elegant yet comfortable feel.

The Kashmir's menu includes many of the familiar dishes found in most local Punjabi restaurants: there is chicken mukhani, lamb jalfrazie, and various tandoori dishes. But there is also chicken Kashmiri, prawns Kashmiri, and paneer pujiah. These dishes demonstrate the difference between the Kashmiri and Punjabi cuisines.

Kashmiri food is rich but not as complex as that of the Punjab where many dishes depend on layers of spices worked subtly into the food. The Kashmiri style relies more on cream so there is not the necessity to use as many spices. There is still lots of flavour, just not necessarily the depth of spicing. The Mughlai influence, which comes from the reign of the Mogul emperors hundreds of years ago, introduces pricier ingredients like saffron, fruits, and nuts to elevate Kashmiri cuisine to Taj Mahal status.

The chicken and prawn Kashmiri dishes, for example, incorporate apple and cream into mild, rich sauces. The paneer pujiah mashes paneer, the Indian version of cheese, together with onions and mushrooms to create a coarse, curd-like dish. And on request, the Kashmir will make their margis kofta, a Scotch egg type of concoction where a hard-boiled egg is wrapped in ground lamb and served in another rich, creamy sauce. The lamb, egg, and spicy sauce make an intriguing combination.

Other menu items include spiced spinach, prawns in a vindaloo sauce, and beef Goa finished with coconut milk. Of course, there are dhal and other vegetarian entrees as well as soft, tender naan.

The Kashmir offers mango-flavoured ice cream and gulab jamun as well as a list of cocktails and wines. My beverage preference for this type of food is always a Raj or a Big Rock beer, and they carry both.

Service is a perfect fit with the food and decor: it's elegant in a quiet Northern Indian way, with gracious and helpful staff. There is much to enjoy in this type of food, and the Singhs have made the Kashmir one of the most pleasing Indian restaurants in the city.

Kensington Berliner
German

1414 Kensington Road NW
Phone: 283·0771
Tuesday – Sunday 11:30 am – 2:30 pm, 5 pm – 10 pm
Reservations recommended — Fully licensed — Patio — Non-smoking section
V, MC, AE, Debit — $$

JUST west of the hub of Kensington sits a tiny mall with a big log facade. It looks more like Banff than Hillhurst, but it creates an atmosphere that is at once urban and woodsy. It works perfectly for the Hostel Shop and its next door neighbour, the Kensington Berliner. The Berliner had a rustic look and hearty menu long before the logs arrived, and they mesh together nicely.

I wanted to sit on the new and improved patio, but on a warm summer day, I was chased to the cool interior by overly friendly wasps. Inside there are forty-four seats at various tables and booths. The tone is softly Germanic with more wood and small lamps and a Bach soundtrack. The deep tones of German music put me in the mood for some serious eating, so I indulged in a robust lunch of sauerkraut soup and sausages. That's the kind of food you'll find at the Berliner. And its menu covers the whole country, from the herring with sliced apples to the schnitzel with fried eggs and anchovies to the sauerbraten with raisins.

German cuisine is not the most popular in a culture that often concentrates on lighter fare, so if just the sound of this food makes your stomach expand, you are not alone. But every once in a while, it's great to have a big plate of spätzle and sauerkraut topped with grilled sausages. And the Berliner does this well. My sausages were nicely grilled and served with both sweet and hot mustards. The sauerkraut was tart but not too sour, and the spätzle was lightly chewy without being tough. Greens? Well, there was a slice of tomato on there somewhere, and I'm sure sauerkraut still qualifies as a vegetable. To double up on my greens, I added the sauerkraut soup, a hot and mouth-puckering broth filled with cabbage and shards of smoked ham. Very nice.

Now there are some salads on the menu, but this is not the place to look for a light meal. Even the seafood dishes are covered in creamy sauces. Desserts are either an apple strudel—a very good one at that—or a German cheesecake. And they feature eisbein, the marinated pork hock dish that John F. Kennedy ate before declaring "Ich bin ein Berliner."

So if you're up for a little taste of Germany, look no farther than the Kensington Berliner.

The King & I
Thai

822 – 11 Avenue SW
Phone: 264·7241
Monday – Thursday 11:30 am – 10:30 pm, Friday 11:30 am – 11:30 pm
Saturday 4:30 pm – 11:30 pm, Sunday 4:30 pm – 10:30 pm
Reservations recommended — Fully licensed — Non-smoking section
V, MC, AE, DC, Debit — $$ – $$$

I've always had a fondness for good musical theatre and back—way back—in my drama days, I performed in a production of *The King and I* (that was well reviewed, I might add). Great songs, great story, lots of concubines. Whenever I visit The King & I restaurant, I have to restrain myself from breaking into "Getting to Know You." Now that's not totally my fault. The framed Broadway posters and pictures of Yul Brynner and Deborah Kerr just make me want to sing and dance. And so does the food.

The King & I presents the full Thai menu, from beef satay and tom yam kung soup to Matsaman curries and coconut rice. It is fresh and light and cleanly spiced. No muddy flavours here.

The som tum salad combines shredded green papaya with tomatoes, carrots, and slices of shrimp in a tart vinaigrette, creating a crisp, tangy dish. Lovely. And the chu chi vegetables are a light and cool collection of fresh produce laced with chili, basil, and coconut, perfect on a hot summer's day. We always enjoy the pad kra pao kai, stir-fried chicken with fresh basil and chilies, but found the chicken itself to be skimpy on our last visit. For the $14 price tag, they could have been more generous. And it could have used a little more oomph in the flavour too.

Prices generally are not low at the King & I. The chu chi vegetable dish is also $14, and individual bowls of coconut rice are $2 each. Most entrees are in the $13 to $15 range, and some of the seafoods are pushing into the $20s. Not necessarily bad value, but higher prices than we're used to seeing in Thai restaurants.

But The King & I has always tried to be a little different. The tone is upscale, with renovations a few years ago creating a stylishly light bamboo interior. It's a classy look with tawny shades of paint, mildly Asian room dividers, subtle lighting, and lots of natural wood.

And service is crisp. Uniformed staff are quick with the menus and the dishes, not rushing but providing a smooth flow to the meal.

Eating with a fork and spoon, I am reminded again of how King Mongkut incorporated the ideas of the West while maintaining the traditions of Siam. This King & I has done the same thing quite successfully.

Shall we dance?

Kootenay Park Lodge
Mountain Home-Style

Vermilion Crossing, 42 kilometres south of Trans-Canada on Highway 93
Phone: 762·9196
Victoria Day weekend – last weekend in September:
Daily 8 am – 10 am, noon – 2 pm, 6 pm – 8 pm
Reservations recommended — Beer & wine only — Veranda — Non-smoking
V, MC — $$

O PENED as a Canadian Pacific Railroad wilderness lodge in 1923, the main building of Kootenay Park Lodge has changed little since the early days. A wood veranda sweeps around two sides of it, providing shelter under the huge spruces. Inside, the room focuses around a stone fireplace, with mounted animal heads peering down on diners. Everything is wood, from the floorboards to the heavy log walls. It is so rustic and relaxing that after the two-hour drive from Calgary, any stresses just melt away.

Outside the main lodge sits a collection of small log cabins available for overnight stays. Closer to the road, the owners have opened a new service station and Visitors' Centre for those looking at only a brief pit stop. The revival of Kootenay Park Lodge is the work of Francis and Paul Holscher, a mother and son team who have preserved the best parts and upgraded the rest. The Visitors' Centre fits perfectly in the park, and the old lodge looks better than ever.

And then there is the food. Everything tastes better in mountain air of course, but the cooking here is exceptional, in a mountain-lodge, home-style way. The breakfast menu offers the usual fare of eggs and bacon, hot oatmeal, French toast, and pancakes, as well as a house special of fruit- and yogurt-filled crepes and a sundae of layered granola, fruit, and yogurt. The dinner menu is a collection of burgers, crepes, and pastas with a few mountainy dishes thrown in—things like rainbow trout with hollandaise sauce and sirloin strips with fresh mushrooms in a red wine sauce. The Caesar salad is a classic version, made with real bacon and a forceful dressing. The chicken breast with satay-style peanut sauce shows the Holschers' Dutch heritage. For dessert, there are ice cream offerings but also fruit clafoutis with raspberry sauce and whipped cream. It is a surprising menu in its diversity and a comforting list in its simplicity. Perfect for Kootenay Park.

In 2001, Kootenay Park Lodge reinstated lunch, which I am happy to see. I missed their club sandwich. Thick slices of chicken, bacon, and tomato on homemade bread, it defines what a club should be. And it's great with their mountain fries.

So for those traversing Kootenay Park, the lodge is a great place to relax, if even for just a moment. It is both rustic and contemporary, a historic spot on the edge of the wilderness that is accessible by pavement.

www.kootenayparklodge.com

La Brezza

Italian

990 – 1 Avenue NE
Phone: 262·6230
Monday – Friday 11:30 am – 2:30 pm, Daily 5 pm – 11 pm
Reservations recommended — Fully licensed — Non-smoking section
V, MC, AE, Debit — $$

THE restaurants of Bridgeland are awaiting the redevelopment of the General Hospital site since its demolition removed their lunch trade. One of the places hanging in there is La Brezza, a small Italian restaurant seating about forty in what was once a 1940s residential bungalow.

It has always had a homey look—they knocked out a couple of walls, leaving the basic layout. There is a cozy funkiness to it, but you have to enjoy a crowded, noisy environment to really have a good time here. But sitting in the sun-washed former living room, the food rolls out fragrantly, an upside to the closeness. Another major plus is that the main room has gone totally non-smoking; a separate area downstairs is available for those who wish to dine with tobacco.

The black-vested staff are professional in that Euro-waiter way. They never forget about you, but they are not intrusive either. The owner, the ebullient Marco Abdi, is usually on hand to add his personality to your visit. He is a gracious host, one who knows the restaurant industry well.

Food-wise, La Brezza has really matured over the years. The menu contains reasonably standard Italian fare—the pastas and veals and minestrones—but it is done well. The fettuccine alla Brezza is superb, the pasta done al dente in a rich, creamy mushroom and bacon sauce. Some wild mushrooms are included to give the dish more depth. Likewise, the penne amatriciana is an excellent bowl of pasta with bacon, tomatoes, and peppers. La Brezza also does excellent seafood. The mussels in white wine, the shrimp with lemon, and the calamari in tomato sauce are all very traditional preparations made with gusto and quality. The sauces will have you reaching for more bread to capture the last drop.

And La Brezza is generous with their bruschetta. It is a signature dish here, an excellent blend of tomatoes, onions, peppers, herbs, and a lot of garlic. It has a real bite. Served with fresh-from-the-oven focaccia, it is a treat to start your meal with this, and they are happy to bring more if you want. And there is no cost.

So La Brezza is still impressive. It is casual and oddly funky with its bungalow decor. It can get a bit claustrophobic, but the food and the service are both top notch.

La Cantina
Golf Clubhouse

11618 Valley Ridge Park NW
Phone: 221·9682
Monday – Thursday 10 am – 11 pm, Friday – Sunday 6:30 am – 11 pm
Reservations accepted — Fully licensed — Patio — Non-smoking
V, MC, AE, Debit — $ – $$

CATHERINE remembers learning to ski around here in the late '60s when this area was a little ski hill called Happy Valley. Things have sure changed. The site is now a well-maintained, difficult, and picturesque public golf course. It's easy to dismiss or just plain forget about the restaurants at public links. Most are surprisingly dark and filled with an overabundance of smokers chowing down on mediocre post-golf meals. But La Cantina at Valley Ridge is one of those few good public course eateries with nice food and verdant views. After a self-flagellating round, it makes an excellent refuelling station. But just as importantly, it's a good community resource for the folks of Valley Ridge. This is not an area filled with great restaurants, and I'd be quite pleased to have a cafe like this in my neighbourhood.

Breaking from the typical golf course mold, La Cantina's menu has a mild Tex-Mex/Southwestern tone to it. No fears though—you can still find a good clubhouse sandwich and a list of burgers along with the early morning breakfast necessities. There are also quesadillas, fajitas, and queso fundido as well as steak sandwiches and Caesar salads.

The food is hearty and delivered fairly fast—two golf requirements. A chicken and rib combo was a tasty blend of smoky ribs drenched with barbecue sauce and a quarter chicken that had been cooked on the rotisserie. Each meat was tender, well flavoured, and distinct from the other. It was subtle in a world where golf fare tends to be heavy-handed with flavour. And it was as messy as any chicken-rib combo should be.

One of my golf buddies arrived early for our afternoon tee time and scarfed back the Dallas Dunk sandwich of pulled chicken, crisp bacon, and cheese in a toasted baguette. Served with a homemade dipping gravy, this sandwich impressed him enough that he ordered another one for our after-golf meal. He liked it just as much as the first.

The side dishes hold up to the main items well too. The fries, the rice, the refried beans are all decent versions, and a bowl of clam chowder was as good as any in the city.

Price-wise, both the course and the clubhouse offer good value. The chicken-rib combo was $13, and only a few other dishes are over $10. A big meal for a hungry foursome came in at $65, including a healthy and well-deserved tip.

La Cantina is a hidden gem in the northwest, one that's too good for just us golfers.

La Chaumière
Continental

139 – 17 Avenue SW
Phone: 228 · 5690
Monday – Friday 11:30 am – 2 pm, Monday – Saturday 6 pm – midnight
Reservations recommended — Fully licensed — Patio — Non-smoking
V, MC, AE, DC — $$$

FROM what I remember of my French classes, a *chaumière* is a thatched cottage, a rustic country place. Not at all like the suave château on 17th Avenue that houses one of Calgary's finest restaurants. La Chaumière has been around for twenty-three years and has built a well-deserved reputation for elegant dining and posh service.

The building resembles a high-tone conference centre more than a thatch-roofed cottage, but the main dining room is stylish and personal. Seating about sixty, it is set with large, comfy chairs around a fountain of flowers. A patio sprawls west to Rouleauville Park while south windows brighten the space. La Chaumière offers quiet, understated elegance; it's a breath of fresh air among some of the over-designed and over-loud rooms that abound.

Over the years, the food has always moved to keep pace with the market. It is still fundamentally Continental, with duck confit, foie gras, bouillabaisse, and chateaubriand with Béarnaise sauce. But there is a commitment to local ingredients, with Bassano carrots, Yukon Gold potatoes, Hotchkiss greens, and of course, Alberta AAA beef. And preparations have moved beyond the classics to include items like grilled swordfish on eggplant and spigarello and hoisin-glazed salmon. Yet they balance the menu with port demi-glace, escargots, and soufflés to please the traditionalists.

We indulged in La Chaumière's lobster bisque and the wild mushroom soup of the day. Both were skillfully prepared with silky undertones. Since it was a cool and rainy day, I opted for the beef and veal stroganoff in a rich morel sauce, a delightfully light and herb-fresh rendition of the oft-heavy stew. Catherine's seafood niçoise was equally warming with softly poached bits of salmon and tuna on a bed of olives, beans, and greens. We finished with one of the city's better crème brûlées, gilded with a cardamom and citrus-zest Chantilly cream (unnecessary, but who were we kidding—we ate it anyway).

Service at La Chaumière remains a high point. The staff are as well trained and professional as any for miles around. That is largely due to the efforts of co-owners Joseph D'Angelus and Joe Mathes, skilled practitioners of the fine art of service. There are few better.

In all, La Chaumière deserves its reputation as one of the best. They have stayed with the top end of the market and have not let it drift away like so many of their now-absent compatriots. They remain a landmark of local cuisine and service.

La P'tite Table
French

52 *North Railway Street, Okotoks*
Phone: 938·2224
Tuesday – Friday 11 am – 1:30 pm, Tuesday – Saturday 5:30 pm – 10 pm
Reservations recommended — Fully licensed — Patio at lunch — Non-smoking
V, MC, Debit — $$ – $$$

L
A P'TITE TABLE is a lovely French cafe settled into a pretty little town. Like many cafes in France, it is pressed up against the main thoroughfare. Its old tin siding lends an air of maturity to the outside. Inside, there is high-quality food and skilled staff toiling in the kitchen. But this is not Vence or Chagny or Saumur. It's Okotoks.

Thierry and Cidallia Meret took over the French restaurant in the old Post Office building in 1996 and crafted a lovely little dining room. They have since expanded to include fourteen more seats and air conditioning.

La P'tite Table specializes in a Contemporary version of traditional French cooking. The lobster bisque is thinner than that of decades past, with clear, intense flavours and a serious depth. Sitting in the bowl, this soup is unimpressive, but rolling over your taste buds, it demands attention. There's no breast of duck shellacked with an impenetrably sweet orange glaze; here, an essence of cranberry tarts up the orange sauce. They smoke Atlantic salmon over Quebec maple for a real Canadian flavour, then serve it with an herb baguette and a grainy mustard cream cheese. Amazing. On one of our visits, a daily special of steamed sea bass layered over a leek and citrus sauce was intense and subtle all at the same time. Lightly dusted with crushed pink peppercorns, it made for a beautiful plate.

But the best part may be the vegetables. There are nearly a dozen different items on your plate: a yam tart, a half-moon of turnip, carrot flowers, a string bean, spears of asparagus, a braised radish, a dollop of delicious lentils. These lentils are so good, they halt conversations and nearly bring a tear to the eye (to Catherine's anyway).

Then there are the desserts like lavender crème brûlée or chocolate profiteroles. Their tarte Tatin is sweet and hot, with its caramelized apples complemented by vanilla ice cream. The île flottante continues to be the winner for me with its fluffy wedge of baked egg white drizzled with caramel, floating in a vanilla cream and topped with toasted almonds.

A confidence exudes from the kitchen at La P'tite Table. It's not showy or pretentious, and there's nothing over the top. Presentation is good, but not outlandish; flavours are intense without being obnoxious. This is food with presence and substance. Service is pleasantly professional and all thirty-six seats are non-smoking.

Need I say more? Who needs Vence or Chagny or Saumur when we have Okotoks. La P'tite Table *est merveilleuse.*

www.la-ptite-table.com

La Tasca
Spanish

2138 Crowchild Trail NW
Phone: 210·5566
Tuesday – Friday 11:30 am – 2:30 pm, Tuesday – Sunday 4:30 pm – 10 pm
Reservations recommended — Fully licensed — Non-smoking section
V, MC, AE — $$

I wasn't overly excited to see that a restaurant called La Tasca had opened across from McMahon Stadium. The area, known as Motel Village, has never been an exciting restaurant destination, so I wasn't expecting much. But this was one of those occasions when I was happy to be proven wrong.

La Tasca, which means "tapas bar" or "place to enjoy food and drink," offers a tapas menu as well as a full Spanish one. Tapas are $6 to $8, and the full menu includes a roasted half chicken with a sherry velouté for $14 and salt cod in a tomato-wine sauce for $16.

A white bean salad features perfectly cooked beans, beautifully roasted and peeled red peppers, and a bundle of crisp romaine in a balanced garlic and olive oil vinaigrette. For $6, it is $3 or $4 less than what you might pay in one of our trendier cafes. A Caesar salad—admittedly not Spanish—is equally well prepared.

We had a paella Valencia-style, the kind I have been looking for since one memorable night in Madrid in 1978. This was a beautiful pan of golden saffron rice with big chunks of sausage and veal and chicken, a pile of shrimp, and a couple of small lobsters. Marvelous. At $36 for the two of us, way more than enough for one meal and no complaints as to the quality.

La Tasca itself is a large, 100-seat restaurant with a scenic view of McMahon Stadium and the Crowchild Trail pedestrian overpass. It is in an unprepossessing strip mall and takes a very sharp turn off of Crowchild to reach. So be careful.

The place used to be the restaurant Why Not Italian?, and they have kept the Mediterranean look inside with the wrought iron, the tile floor and the red ceramic rooftops. Various areas are available for both large groups and quiet couples and adequate separation exists for smokers and non-smokers. There's a Gipsy Kings soundtrack, and on the evening we visited, a young man was playing a classical guitar.

Also on the upside, there is a decent wine list with some good Chilean choices by the glass. Plus friendly and professional service. Unfortunately, they lost their very talented chef from the early days and went through some inconsistencies as a result, but have emerged as one of the better restaurants in the northwest.

Laggan's
Bakery & Deli

Samson Mall, Lake Louise
Phone: 522·2017
Daily 6 am – 7 pm (varies seasonally)
Reservations not accepted — No alcoholic beverages — Non-smoking
Cash or Canadian/US traveller's cheques only — $

L AGGAN'S is not so much a place to eat as it is a place to refuel. Plus, if you want to get a snapshot of the human side of Lake Louise, this is the place to go. At any time of day, there seem to be lineups and almost constant confusion as the stressed staff serve an endless stream of visitors. Japanese tourists line up for a quick snack along with Brits hunting for a good cup of tea, while Scandinavian hikers and Australian skiers fill their packs with carbo-goodies for the day's efforts. Outside there is often a scruffy looking batch of over-pierced wanderers smoking rollies and playing with a dog. Ah, Lake Louise.

Inside it is bakery-hot and noisy with customers moving slowly along the counter toward the ordering area. There is no menu, just display counters filled with the likes of granola cookies, meat pies, and sandwiches. There is an overhead chalkboard, but most of the ordering is done with the pointing method. The long and narrow room seats about twenty-eight and is in never-ending motion.

If you can survive the heightened level of activity, the food is pretty good. The cranberry-chocolate chip cookies are sweet and gooey, perfect for a hike to the Plain of Six Glaciers. A few of those treats—always fresh because they go so quickly— pack as many calories as a person needs. They also carry cold cuts, sausage rolls, and such if you want to stock up on more proteins and fats for your day, and there are the requisite juices and fruits as well.

Laggan's has become the necessary pit stop for visitors who shy away from the prices around the lake and who want to spend their time outside at Louise rather than inside in a dining room. A few short, noisy moments in Laggan's and you are set for the day.

Laggan's also makes for a good rest stop for those passing through. Two hours out of Calgary, it is just off the Trans-Canada and is flanked by a grocery store, gas stations, and a great mountain bookstore.

Lake Louise Station

Contemporary Canadian

200 Sentinel Road, Lake Louise
Phone: 522·2600
Dining room: Daily 5 pm – 11 pm; Lounge: Daily 11:30 am – 11 pm
Dining cars: Daily 6 pm – 9 pm
Reservations recommended — Fully licensed — Patio
Non-smoking dining room & dining cars, smoking in lounge
V, MC — $$ – $$$

IN 1910, Canadian Pacific built a train station at Lake Louise to welcome Eastern tourists to the Rockies. Constructed from huge logs and decorated in the lodge theme of the day, it was meant to impress the visitors. But when train travel fell out of favour, the station was mothballed and largely forgotten. Fortunately, it was too nice a building to forget forever. Lake Louise Station reopened in 1994 as a restaurant, and it is lovely.

In the former main lobby, now a lounge that serves lunch and dinner, huge oak and leather chairs are surrounded by vintage benches, clocks, and stained glass windows. Next to it, the dining room features a display case of early twentieth century CPR silver and china and a great view of passing trains. And down the siding sit two dining cars, the Delamere and the Killarney. The Delamere dates back to 1925, and the Killarney was built in 1906 for Lord Shaughnessy, President of the CPR.

Dining choices at Lake Louise Station range from casual family eats to game-oriented gourmet experiences. The dining room and lounge menu is a comfortable cross-cultural collection of bruschetta, shrimp with a ginger-plum sauce, smoked salmon, and French onion soup. It also features rack of lamb, venison, and big cuts of Alberta beef that international tourists devour, even at premium prices.

We started our lunch with a seafood chowder featuring salmon, scallops, shrimp, and a touch of cognac. Each piece of seafood had retained its individual flavour, creating a tasty but not overpowering soup. And the Caesar salad was a fresh, crunchy version with lots of tangy flavour and no brown edges. The BLT and the Station burger were likewise excellent. The BLT was made on fresh, thick slices of whole wheat bread, and the bacon was nicely crisp. The burger, a six-ouncer with back bacon, cheddar, and a good bun, was a down-home Canadian classic.

The two dining cars go upscale with seared scallops, marinated salmon, pheasant in a Zinfandel sauce, and grilled caribou in a blackberry reduction. It's more elegant and more dollars, with entrees heading into the low $30s. But it's a dining experience in a railway setting that is unequalled in the Rockies.

Lake Louise Station is a great place for train buffs, history fans, and food lovers. Whether you just want to watch the train while sipping a drink, have a tasty and reasonably priced lunch, or dine in historic surroundings, it is a wonderful place.

Las Palmeras

Mexican

3630 – 50 Avenue, Red Deer
Phone: 346·8877
Monday – Thursday 11:30 am – 10 pm, Friday & Saturday 11:30 am – 11 pm
Sunday noon – 9 pm
Reservations recommended — Fully licensed — Non-smoking section
V, MC, AE, DC, Debit — $ – $$

Las PALMERAS used to be in a strip mall up Ross Street on the east side of Red Deer. It was bright and lively in a Central American style. But in 1996 they moved to a free-standing space at the top of the South Hill.

This new location maintains the simplicity of the old one. The room itself is nothing special—its best asset is the abundance of windows. Most of the furniture is of the backyard variety, and the decor has a bit of the old tiki room, fake-palm-tree feel which creates a casual atmosphere that goes with the food.

Las Palmeras offers one of the most interesting and authentic Mexican menus in the province. There are prawns in red chili sauce, chicken enchiladas, chile rellenos, and shrimp quesadillas. And a personal favourite—carnitas. That is a marinated pork loin dish almost never seen this side of the border. The pork is lean and tasty, rolled in cloves, oregano, and ancho chilies, and they serve it with two warm and fresh corn tortillas. The tortillas alone are enough to make me go back. Las Palmeras make their own—something few restaurants do—and they are perfect with the carnitas. Add in some tasty refried beans and rice, plus guacamole and salsa, and the carnitas make for a tasty meal. At $12.50 it is not cheap, but worth every penny for the skill involved.

My friends enjoyed the Acapulco chicken crusted with herbs and spices and charbroiled to juicy perfection, as well as a non-Mexican dish of shrimp fajitas (fajitas are actually from Texas) that was generously spiced and portioned. The margaritas were a hit too.

All the meals are sizable at Las Palmeras, and there is no reluctance to lay the flavours on. So often we see timidity in spicing Central American food, but Las Palmeras is proof that, if you are true to the traditions, it can work. On a Tuesday evening in Red Deer, Las Palmeras was very busy.

Good service helps too. The couple who run the place are originally from El Salvador, as are many of their staff, and they bring a quiet, gracious style to the room.

They also bring a few Salvadoran dishes to the menu, like pupusas (corn tortillas filled with pork, cheese, and vegetables) and an appetizer of cassava fried with pork.

We Calgarians don't usually head north for Mexican food, but Las Palmeras is definitely worth the ninety-minute drive. Folks in Red Deer are lucky.

Latin Corner

Latin American

109 Stephen Avenue Walk SW
Phone: 262·7248
Monday–Friday 11:30 am–10 pm, Saturday 5 pm–10 pm
Reservations recommended — Fully licensed — Patio — Non-smoking section
V, MC, AE, DC, Debit — $$

I T's great to see a restaurant that is fun and energetic and zesty—like a Ricky Martin video. The new Latin Corner is that and much more.

I say new, but it is actually the return of the Latin Corner in a bigger, more elaborate form. The original Latin Corner was wedged into an old Dairy Queen on 4th Street SW. It was a fine place to escape the winter cold with its basic Latin American food and rich black-bean soup. The owners—a former Venezuelan bullfighter named Gustavo Yelamo and his Czech wife Nadia—were, and are, one of the big attractions of the Latin Corner. They are a lively, elegant couple with immense restaurant skills and huge personalities.

The new Latin Corner is a long, narrow space where sandstone walls and old skylights have been uncovered, creating a warm cantina look and a comfortably cavernous feel. It's stylishly Latin with terrazzo tile floors and a frightfully small kitchen along one side.

This is full-tilt Latin American fare: many of the dishes do not include a lot of vegetables. When you order the lamb shanks, for example, you get two lamb shanks in an anise sauce with a small pile of quinoa, a light grain. That's it. And many other dishes are heavy on the meats too. But that is the culture. So be aware of that when you order. There are vegetable dishes on the menu, like the black-bean soup or the black-bean salad or a vegetable casserole, but if you order a meat dish, that is predominantly what you get.

I tried the black-bean soup, which was as good as ever, and the tamarind-glazed beef ribs. This last dish came with yucca and plantain, as well as some great potatoes and a fabulous slaw. A good deal at $14.

Most entrees are in the $12 to $14 range, with the platters to share going from $35 for a paella to $55 for the Brazilian Gaucho, a feast of skewered beef, chicken, chorizo, and salads. Tapas run from $6 to $9.

The Latin Corner is an impressive restaurant, and late in the evening, it becomes a lively Latin party place. Don't expect a quiet evening here. But do expect to have some fun. The great setting, interesting menu, and terrific owners have brought "La Vida Loca" to Stephen Avenue.

Lazy Loaf & Kettle
Bakery & Cafe

8 Parkdale Crescent NW   130 – 9 Avenue SE (Glenbow Museum)
Phone: 270·7810   Phone: 266·1002
Monday – Friday 7 am – 11 pm   Monday – Friday 7:30 am – 5 pm
Saturday & Sunday 8 am – 10 pm   Saturday & Sunday 9 am – 5 pm
Patio

Reservations not accepted — Beer & wine only — Non-smoking
V, MC, AE, Debit — $

THE LAZY LOAF & KETTLE is still the only cafe I have ever reviewed that's run by someone I went to school with. Wetaskiwin Composite to be exact, in the late '60s and early '70s. A lovely young lady that I sat beside in Chem 30 happens to own, with her husband, the Lazy Loaf. I like what they are doing and it has nothing to do with the fact that we grew up together.

The original Loaf is a small but constantly expanding place in Parkdale Crescent. Their specialty is a serious two-pound loaf of bread that contains no dairy, eggs, or fat. It does, however, feature nine grains, plus unbleached flour, carrots, wheat germ, and barley malt—lots of good stuff. It makes excellent sandwiches and incredible toast. Two pieces of this for breakfast and you will never have McGavin's again.

Both locations feature this bread, and others, wrapped around cold cuts and vegetarian combinations. Very good and reasonably priced. There is not a lot of selection at either spot—soups, salads, and the sandwiches, plus some cookies and cakes and the best Nanaimo bars in the city. They are the kind of Nanaimo bars that I ate growing up—which may explain my extra pounds. They also do a full grill breakfast at the Parkdale cafe—bacon, eggs, hash browns, that sort of thing.

The best time to visit either Loaf is when their cinnamon buns are still warm from the oven. They roll their nine-grain dough into sticky, cinnamon-dripping, raisin-oozing spirals. These are not those over-frosted ones that you find in chain outlets, but big, steamy, gooey things that warm and fill your stomach for hours. They are the best cinnamon buns, for my taste, that are available within driving distance. Excellent with a good cup of coffee or, in the summer, with one of their frozen cappuccinos.

The Loaf on Parkdale Crescent has the look and feel of a leftover coffee house or granola bar from the '60s with its wooden tables, chalkboard menu, crowded walk-up ordering area, and pre-'70s music. And the Glenbow cafe makes a perfect rest stop for museum visitors and conventioneers. Both Loaves offer excellent value and high quality. Just what I would expect of a gal from my hometown.

Le Beaujolais
French

Corner of Banff Avenue & Buffalo Street, Banff
Phone: 762·2712
Daily 6 pm – midnight
Reservations recommended — Fully licensed — Non-smoking
V, MC — $$$

L E BEAUJOLAIS is the classic French restaurant of Banff. It has perched above the corner of Banff Avenue and Buffalo Street for over twenty years, serving classic Continental cuisine now infused with some New World ingredients. It continues to wow global visitors and locals alike, and for serious food enthusiasts, it has become a necessary part of the Banff experience.

Le Beaujolais has been successful by flowing with the times. It used to be that a jacket and tie were *de rigueur*, but nowadays, a decent polo shirt is formal enough. Mountain chic, so to speak. And service has grown more subdued and comfortable over the years. Some of the waiters are downright chatty. Chef de Cuisine Philipp Weingartner is given great breadth in the kitchen, so fresh techniques have brightened up the classic cuisine. This shows the benefit of consistent ownership since day one, with Albert Moser at the helm.

The quality of the food has not changed. It is still excellent. The salmon is marinated in-house and smoked for Le Beaujolais by Valbella Meats in Canmore. The tomato cream soup with seared scallops is a gentle balance of earth and sea. And the chateaubriand remains a beefy standard.

Looking closer at the menu, we see Contemporary culinary ideas such as jasmine-smoked quail with kumquat chutney, ostrich carpaccio with tête de moine cheese, and lightly seared tuna sashimi with ginger-infused red pepper coulis. This tuna is superb, one of the best pieces of fish to ever pass my lips. Farther along the list, we see a civet of Merlot-marinated caribou, mushrooms, and blueberries, an outstandingly rich stew glistening over sage-butter polenta. Lovely flavours, silky textures.

Le Beaujolais offers dishes à la carte and in table d'hôtes. Prices for three-course table d'hôte combos were $52 and $58 in the summer of 2001, but the menus change a couple of times a year. Ordering à la carte is a bit more expensive.

My dinner of tuna, tomato soup, caribou, and crème brûlée was perfectly timed and served under the silver dome of classic French cuisine. Catherine's prawns, soup, and salmon (we shared the brûlée) was a pleasant parallel. I could quibble with the intensity of the gin in the tomato soup (not enough) or the texture of the brûlée (inconsistent), but overall presentation, quality, and service were delightful.

My wallet may not be able to handle Le Beaujolais on a daily basis, but when only the best will do, it's great to know that they are up to the challenge.

info-pages.com/beaujolais

Leo Fu's
Chinese (Szechwan & Mandarin)

511–70 Avenue SW
Phone: 255•2528
Monday–Friday 11:30 am–2 pm, Sunday–Thursday 4:30 pm–10 pm
Friday & Saturday 4:30 pm–11:30 pm
Reservations recommended — Fully licensed — Non-smoking section
V, MC, AE, DC — $$

EVER since I first reviewed Leo Fu's in 1987, it has been my first choice for Szechwan food. The Koo family who own Leo Fu's are constantly on the lookout for new ideas and recipes to enhance their menu, and their selection remains one of the most interesting and adventurous in the city.

The orange-flavoured beef and orange-flavoured chicken are outstanding—crispy chunks of sautéed meats are coated in a spicy, savoury orange sauce. The General Tso's chicken is intense in a hot red-bean sauce. If you like it mild, try the lemon chicken, the roast pork with snow peas, or the sweet and sour shrimp. For more intensity, there is chicken in garlic sauce or salt and pepper squid. They do ginger beef, as well as ginger chicken and ginger squid, and they are excellent. They even make some fabulous Szechwan-style chicken wings if you are looking for something really different.

Leo Fu's food is always good, not only because of the excellent sauces but because of the high-quality ingredients they use. Following the Mandarin tradition, most of the trimming and cleaning is done in the kitchen, so you see a minimum of bones and fat left on the meats. When the plates go back to the kitchen, they are empty and not covered in a slick of grease.

Looking for flaws, there are few. First, it is not cheap. It is not outrageous either, but that high quality comes with a price tag. Most dishes are a bit more than other Chinese restaurants, but worth it. Second, there are occasionally problems with smoker/non-smoker separation. It would be great if they went totally non-smoking like so many of our other better restaurants.

Leo Fu's occupies an obscure location that is usually full and bustling with activity. It's been painted in blues and golds and has a warmth and friendliness that come from years of being the best.

They have opened four new restaurants over the last few years in the Salt Lake City-Provo area of Utah. Now that is a long way to go, especially for takeout. To accommodate this expansion, part of the family has moved south, but Leo Fu's continues to prepare fabulous food right here in Calgary.

Note: In early 2000, John Koo passed away, leaving daughter Maria in charge of the restaurant. John was a great chef, restaurateur, husband, and father. He was also one of the kindest and most stylish men we have ever known.

Lina's Italian Market
Italian Market & Cafe

2202 Centre Street N
Phone: 277·9166
Market: Monday – Friday 9 am – 8 pm, Saturday & Sunday 9 am – 5 pm
Cafe: Monday – Saturday 11 am – 2 pm for lunch, Daily 2 pm – closing for coffee/desserts
Reservations not accepted — Fully licensed — Non-smoking
V, MC, Debit — $

SINCE it opened in 1995, Lina's has become one of the most popular shopping destinations for Italian foods and housewares in Calgary. It's mostly a grocery store, filled with more balsamic vinegars and extra-virgin olive oils than you can shake a package of linguine at. The sparkling clean meat and cheese counter is filled with cold cuts and homemade sausages, as well as specialty meats like rabbit or goat. There's a good selection of cheese, plus big pots of olives, pickled calamari, and a tasty house-made bruschetta topping. I really like their tiramisu, and if you do too, there are containers of it waiting in the coolers for you to take home.

There's also a forty-seat cafe that fills every day with dozens of hungry folks looking for a good Italian lunch. They serve fresh panini made from cold cuts and cheese, a little eggplant spread, and a crusty roll. But even better are the dishes from the hot table. On any given day, Lina's cooks prepare a meat special or two, a pasta special or two, and a couple of vegetable dishes. They do not make a lot of food. It is almost like visiting someone's house: when they run out, they run out. But if you time your visit right, you might get a tomatoey veal stew or a spicy Italian sausage with sautéed onions, mushrooms, and zucchini, roasted potatoes, and a deadly plate of pasta. And the lasagna here is rich and creamy smooth, with nicely balanced flavours.

I have paid a lot more for lesser-quality cannelloni at fancier places. All the ingredients are at their fingertips, and they use them effectively. The staff whip up food in traditional ways: I once had a roasted chicken leg rubbed with rosemary and garlic that took me back to Northern Italy. This is as authentic as it gets, even to the point where the staff get concerned if you do not clean your plate.

In the summer of 2001, Lina and her gang moved across Centre Street to a space that is more than twice the size of the original one. That means more of everything, from produce to fresh meats to take-away meals. There's more staff, better parking, and more elbow room in the cafe. The ceilings are high, the new espresso machine pumps out a good brew, and now Lina has even more fans than before. *Bella!*

Lion's Den

Diner

234 – 17 Avenue SE
Phone: 265 • 8482
Daily 9 am – 10 pm
Reservations accepted — Fully licensed — No non-smoking section
V, MC, AE — $

THERE is a little place near the west edge of the Stampede grounds that many of us just drive by day after day—which is a pity because it's filled with character and characters. There are too few places like the Lion's Den, the fiercely independent diner that serves up jokes and debates along with a great plate of fries.

The Lion's Den is a small cafe that seats about forty in a room full of tables, vinyl-cushioned booths, and swivelling counter stools. The space is decorated with memories of the Olympics, the Stampede, the owners' kids, and other community activities. It's a hodgepodge with a curiosity shop appeal that is amplified by a television and a jukebox. Often the TV and the music are both playing, providing a cacophonous backdrop to any discussions.

Got a pet peeve? Would you like a new one? Owner Rico Festa will be happy to oblige, and he'll throw in a handful of really bad jokes. The restaurant is his personal soapbox, and it is worth the price of admission just to hear his daily comments.

Meanwhile in the kitchen, Rico's wife Rose cooks up some very good diner food. The menu covers huge territory from sauerbraten and corned beef on rye to veal cutlets and pizza.

I almost always have the clubhouse on brown with a side of fries. The clubhouse is a diner classic, and this is not one of those gussied-up versions found in yuppie places for $12.95. This is a nicely layered combo of crisp bacon and fresh turkey with tomatoes, lettuce, and mayo for $6. It's hard to beat, especially with some hand-cut and freshly fried chips that are crisp and blazing hot.

A bowl of macaroni soup in a light broth with hints of tomato is ladled into a large, flat bowl. This would be a $6 soup at many fancier places around town, but at the Lion's Den, it is scooped into an old diner-ware bowl for $2. And it is better than most of the swanky joints, with the delicate flavours of the broth and the macaroni blending perfectly. Rose is one heck of a cook.

The Lion's Den is a kind of community centre that attracts all kinds. They serve a regular clientele that ranges from paramedics and police officers to Stampede workers, lawyers, and downtown CEOs. It's an eclectic bunch that comes for the unmatched combination of rhetoric, cheap prices, tasty food, and good will.

Little Chef
Family Dining

555 Strathcona Boulevard SW (Strathcona Shopping Centre)
Phone: 242·7219
Monday – Saturday 9 am – 9 pm, Sunday 9 am – 8 pm
Reservations recommended — Fully licensed — Patio — Non-smoking
V, MC, Debit — $ – $$

Lots of places call themselves "family" restaurants, which usually means mediocre, microwaved food, lousy coffee, poor service, a smoky atmosphere, and indestructible furniture. But the Little Chef typifies what a family restaurant really should be.

The walls are pink, the light is soft, and the floor is carpeted. There is a big Pepsi cooler and an ice machine behind a large service counter, and the tables are well spaced to create a comfortable, open feel. It has an atmosphere that is agreeable for seniors, young couples, families with kids, and teenagers—a real multi-aged crowd.

Adding to this pleasant environment is a staff whose smiles are genuine and who respond quickly and efficiently. Catherine—well-known for complaining about being cold—once asked for a warm cup of water and was instantly given a steaming mugful with a thick wedge of lemon. No questions and no charge.

The menu at the Little Chef is basic but far from mundane. There are turkey sandwiches, beef dips, and Caesar salads. But there is also orange-ginger beef, salmon stir-fried with a hot pepper sauce, and steak and kidney pie. Catherine—who also complains about the lack of good steak and kidney pies around town—thought it was marvelous. It had a strong beef taste, tender chunks of kidney and steak, and a superb pastry crust. I am told that when they do a liver and onion special, it is the first thing to disappear off the list. So for all you organ-meat fans, this is the place.

The spinach salad that preceded the pie was also excellent. It was a good serving of clean, crisp spinach loaded with mushrooms, bacon, hard-boiled eggs, and an excellent vinaigrette. At $9 for both the salad and the meat pie, this was outstanding value.

I tried the pork back ribs, which were a smoky, tangy, messy rack of meaty ribs served with a pile of rice and a stack of julienned vegetables. The vegetables show the thoughtful skill of the Little Chef. Instead of using a giant sack of frozen peas and carrots, they slice fresh carrots, zucchini, celery, and peppers into long, thin strips. These are then cooked quickly with each order.

For dessert there are homemade fruit tarts along with cheesecakey things. Again, excellent pastry on the tarts. My coconut cream pie was great.

The Little Chef serves good food professionally in a pleasant, non-smoking atmosphere at reasonable prices. Even the wine list is intelligent. What more could a person ask?

The Living Room
Contemporary Interactive

514 – 17 Avenue SW
Phone: 228•9830
Monday – Friday 11:30 am – midnight
Saturday & Sunday 10 am – 3 pm, 5 pm – midnight
Reservations recommended — Fully licensed — Patio — Non-smoking
V, MC, AE, Debit — $$

ONE of the hot new restaurants of 2001 is The Living Room. Interesting name, suggesting a casualness that is reflected on the menu. They call their food Contemporary Interactive cuisine, indicating a certain amount of customer interaction in some of the dishes. Like the fondues and the bouillabaisse that are done at the table.

The Living Room has adopted a current look—the colours are this moment's taupey earth tones, there's contemporary art on the walls, and the lighting is delicate. But underlying this stylish appearance is also a great depth. The food has been well thought out—it's somewhat ambitious without overreaching, it's tasty, and it's not badly priced.

Catherine had a sandwich of sliced lamb with a three-onion jam and oven-dried tomatoes on brioche, with a side soup of an asparagus velouté. An excellent lunch and for $10, great value. The soup was velvety and rich, the lamb tender and piqued with the onion jam. For our palates, the tomatoes were an unnecessary addition: we thought the acidity of the jam and the tomatoes fought against each other.

My roasted chicken breast sandwich with red peppers and mozzarella on focaccia was equally good, but my soup—the oyster chowder—was the real highlight. I like food that surprises me a little. And this chowder did just that. The creamy, rich chowder base was highlighted by lemon grass, lime leaves, and lime juice, giving it a real citrus bite. Not everyone is going to like it, but we sure did.

The Living Room uses a lot of citrus. They do appetizers of arugula and duck confit with a tangerine dressing and fresh oysters with lemon and horseradish. Their lemon tart with gooey Italian meringue is mouth puckering, and the crème brûlée is rich and subtle with its backdrop of lemon and ginger. Very delicate and complex at the same time.

Other lunch dishes range from a brie and roasted-garlic strudel at $9 and a venison carpaccio at $12 to a dynamite bouillabaisse for two at $22 and gnocchi with pancetta and caramelized onions at $15. The dinner menu is much the same, but with the addition of items like osso bucco and a chef's five-course menu for $65. (The chef, Andrew Keen, was formerly at Umberto's in Vancouver and the Bear Foot Bistro in Whistler.)

So The Living Room is a fine restaurant with a chic look and some interactive cuisine. At last, it's "in" to play with your food.

Lok Tao

Chinese (Cantonese, Beijing/Peking & Swatow)

414 – 16 Avenue NW
Phone: 277·0113
Monday, Wednesday & Thursday 11 am – midnight
Friday 11 am – 12:30 am, Saturday 3 pm – 12:30 am, Sunday 3 pm – 11 pm
Reservations recommended — Fully licensed — Non-smoking
V, MC, AE, Debit — $$

O N a particularly homely stretch of 16th Avenue, there is an appropriately unnoticeable joint serving the food of Peking, Canton, and Swatow. Swatow is a coastal area north of Hong Kong with a cuisine that features mild spicing, seafood, and fresh local produce. It's a fairly unknown style around here. The owner of Lok Tao is one of the few chefs in town from Swatow, and even she does not have too many of the region's dishes on her menu.

We ended up ordering four non-Swatow dishes—pan-fried roast chicken with ginger and onions; prawns and chicken with baby corn and mushrooms in a honey-pepper sauce; beef and asparagus in black pepper; and mango chicken. The sauces were strong and well balanced, light on oil and with almost no MSG. It was fresh and flavourful food, the vegetables crunchy, the meats tender.

The mango chicken was a delightful blend of fresh, tart mango and slices of lean, tender chicken. The beef and asparagus had a lovely balance of beefy flavours, and the prawns and chicken arrived sizzling on a cast-iron pan. The only breading in the meal was a light dusting on the pan-fried chicken. It was our favourite dish with its spicy, crunchy exterior and its tender interior.

Desserts are the typical deep-fried banana and the not-so-typical deep-fried mango and taro root. With a little ice cream and a light syrup, they were not bad, though more than a little sweet.

I like the quality of ingredients and the great sense of balance. I can't complain about the size of the portions or the prices either. Those dishes for four adults, plus rice and a fifth plate of beef and broccoli for a youngster dining with us, came to $56. Most items are $7 to $10, with seafood a bit higher.

The food is only part of the experience at Lok Tao. The rest is the friendly service and a pair of the homeliest bathrooms in the city. Well beyond description, you just have to see them. Suffice it to say that the miniature pea-green, metal-flaked tiles and the baby-blue commode are a visual experience.

The owner is a real presence both in the dining room and in the kitchen, providing advice and service to all. It seems that she knows everyone.

Lok Tao is casual, the decor is nothing special, and it is squeezed right up against 16th Avenue. But it is everything we have come to expect from a good Chinese restaurant—interesting dishes, great service, and reasonable prices.

Louisiana
Cajun & Creole

227 – 10 Street NW
Phone: 270 • 0634
Monday – Saturday 11 am – 11 pm, Sunday 9 am – 9 pm
Reservations not accepted — No alcoholic beverages — Patio — No non-smoking section
V, MC, AE, DC, Debit — $

THE LOUISIANA RESTAURANT used to be a popular little Cajun and Creole place in Motel Village before it got demolished a few years ago. But it has returned as Louisiana Fried Chicken, a hole in the wall that seats all of twenty-two. It looks like a fast-food outlet, which it is, with newspapers and magazines strewn about, muddy tracks on the floor, and full ashtrays on the counter. It is not the least bit stylish.

But I have a feeling that old fans of the Louisiana won't really mind. It never was a place to go for style. It was always a little grotty and way too smoky. Folks went there for the enormous servings of good Louisiana food at surprisingly low prices.

And you can find that same big food at the new place. It's heavy-duty stuff with loads of salt and fat—nothing at all delicate about it. There is also nothing green about it. There might be a little lettuce and tomato on your po' boy sandwich and that's about it.

But it's good. The chicken po' boy drips out of a huge bun with a creamy sauce. It's tender and rich and overloaded with chicken. The ribs are slathered with a sticky Cajun barbecue sauce, and a bowl of Cajun peel-and-eat shrimp is a spicy meal in itself. These shrimp are also the most expensive dish on the list at $12.95. The sandwiches are $7 or $8, with almost everything else under $10.

The biggest menu change from the old place is the introduction of fish and chips and the Louisiana chicken, a spicy, battered version which again is sold in bulk— they actually have what they call a 5-Piece Chicken Snack. (A snack?) They also serve an all-day breakfast.

I do want to stress how unprepossessing this place is. It's a fast-food joint with absolutely no sense of style. You order at the counter if you can see over the pile of boxes, you will likely have to clean your own table if you plan to eat in, the washrooms are out the door and down a hall, and the only thing that cuts the odour of stale cigarette smoke is the smell of heavy Cajun food. The Louisiana is a one-man operation, and given the number of customers going through the place, he doesn't have a lot of time for the front end of the business.

So don't say I didn't warn you.

Mamma's

Italian

320 – 16 Avenue NW
Phone: 276·9744
Monday – Friday 11:30 am – 2 pm, Monday – Saturday 5 pm – 11 pm
Reservations recommended — Fully licensed — Non-smoking section
V, MC, AE, DC, Debit — $$

BACK in 1978, Mamma's opened with great enthusiasm. It was one of the first big Italian restaurants—it had a fountain, some skylights, and a white plaster and light wood interior to go along with the pastas and veals and espressos. It was difficult to get into for quite a while; even with over eighty seats in the main dining room, they were constantly full.

Now, twenty-three years later, the restaurant holds up surprisingly well. The main room is divided into four areas, creating private dining options while still retaining an openness. There's hardly a bad table in the room, and many have the option of being pulled together to seat large groups. The plaster and wood are still there, having gained a patina of age. Mamma's seems as timeless as the Mediterranean.

But there have been changes. In 2000, the original owner retired and a stylish gentleman named Sal Daklala took over. He is in the process of refreshing the place, though he has wisely kept most of the old staff as well as the menu.

Mamma's food is the solid, traditional Italian fare of fettuccine Alfredo, veal parmigiana, and tortellini soup. But this is not the bargain basement stuff of discount cafes. This is the real thing, with fresh cream, top-quality seafood, and tender veal.

The carpaccio is a well-constructed dish of thinly sliced beef tenderloin drizzled with a mustard cream and topped with caperberries and shards of Parmesan. Lovely. The prawns sautéed with tomatoes, onion, and garlic are a delight, sparkling with fresh flavours and piqued by the licorice taste of a finishing splash of Pernod. The pastas are equally well prepared. The fettuccine alla Mama is a creamy blend of shrimps, scallops, and asparagus that is gentle on the palate. For a more robust assault, the spaghetti amatriciana pushes bacon, onions, and garlic into a rich tomato sauce.

This is satisfying food, enough to keep us away from the dessert menu. But there you will find the usual Italian suspects of tiramisu, zabaglione, crème caramel, and gelato.

Mamma's has stood the test of time because they have always taken their work seriously, served good food, and treated their customers well. There is every sign that this will continue. Twenty-three years is a great accomplishment in the restaurant industry, and we expect them to be going just as strong in another twenty-three.

Maple Leaf
Canadian

137 Banff Avenue, Banff
Phone: 760·7680
Daily 11 am – 11 pm
Reservations recommended — Fully licensed — Non-smoking section
V, MC, AE — $$ – $$$

THE MAPLE LEAF commands a big corner of Banff Avenue where the King Edward Hotel used to be. The old hotel was reconceived into a Hard Rock Cafe for a while, but in the late fall of 2000, the Maple Leaf sprouted in this spot. And it is the full embodiment of the Molson beer commercials that proudly proclaim our national pride.

The Maple Leaf is a lovely two-storey restaurant that seats 225 amid Rundle rock and moose heads and bulrushes and cedar. I almost expect to be waited on by Red Green and Celine Dion look-alikes. The space has private rooms, large group tables, and big windows looking onto downtown Banff. But it does have its challenges. There is a huge staircase opening to the second floor that crunches the seating up there: a number of tables for two are placed in what is really an upstairs walkway. Avoid these if you can. And the downstairs dining area is quite close to staff territory: cash registers and service areas are too unshielded from diners, causing unnecessary distractions.

Apart from the uptown, backwoods decor, there is the food—a serious attempt at Canadian cuisine. There is wild boar with juniper berries, Arctic char with sage butter, buffalo curry with peach chutney, and salmon done three ways. There are Malpeque oysters, Alberta beef, and PEI mussels done with peameal bacon and Big Rock ale. The Leaf should be on the list of anyone looking for our national cuisine.

Execution is best on the proteins. A maple-smoked pork chop had a delicately smoky bite that was enhanced by a not-too-sweet barbecue sauce. The sauce created a tangy, almost tart glaze on the lightly cured chop. But although the string beans had a pleasant, grilled saltiness, the mashed potatoes and steamed broccoli were too ordinary for the rest of the plate. And pre-fab carrot bullets in mid-summer? Please. I also found a zucchini-basil soup to be a good start, but it needed a swirl of crème fraîche or some crumbled goat cheese to elevate it to superlative.

Still, the ideas are strong and the service is friendly. The Maple Leaf is showing both locals and visitors alike just what eating Canadian is all about. They aren't perfect yet, but then neither is the culture they represent. I'm sure that given more time, the Maple Leaf will become one of the better places in Banff. I'll definitely be back.

www.banffmapleleaf.com

Marathon
Ethiopian

130 – 10 Street NW
Phone: 283 • 6796
Non-smoking (except 1 table)

924 – 17 Avenue SW
Phone: 802 • 1588
Non-smoking
Patio

Monday – Friday 11 am – 2:30 pm, 5 pm – 10 pm, Saturday 11 am – 11 pm
Sunday 5 pm – 10 pm
Reservations recommended — Fully licensed
V, MC, AE, DC, Debit — $$

THE food of Ethiopia is rich, elegant, and complex, layered with the intense flavours of berbere (a blend of chilies) and niter kibeh (butter with herbs). It is presented without utensils, to be scooped up with injera, the traditional bread made with the millet flour called teff. Every dish seems exotic, from the incular firfir (eggs with onions, tomatoes, and chilies) to the yaterkik alicha (split peas with curry, ginger, and garlic). Partly it's the names, partly it's the wide range of vegetarian dishes and the combinations of ingredients, and partly it's the presentation.

We don't know a lot about the food of Ethiopia in this part of the world, but many of us are familiar with the runner Abibi Bekela. It is he that the Marathon Restaurants honour with their name, a national hero who brought Olympic gold to Ethiopia in the 1960s.

When visiting one of the Marathon locations, order a combination house special—great value at $24 for two people. We did, and a huge platter came covered with injera and topped with two lamb dishes, one beef dish, and four vegetable ones. Injera looks like a very large, thick, spongy crepe, and you rip pieces off to scoop up the stews from the platter in front of you. Everything is chopped quite finely so knives aren't required.

Our lamb and beef were excellent, but we really enjoyed the vegetarian dishes. The yatkilt alicha (cabbage and carrots with chili, garlic, and ginger) and the azifa (lentils in a mustard sauce) were both flavourful and fairly healthy. For meat eaters, there was the kitfo, lean raw beef bathed in spiced butter and spiked with chilies—as much intensity and cholesterol as you'd ever want.

There is no Ethiopian tradition for dessert, but there certainly is for coffee. Historical tradition tells us that an Ethiopian goatherd found that his flock became extra frisky whenever they ate the berries off a certain kind of bush. He tried a few himself, enjoyed the buzz, and named the beans after his hometown of Kaffe. The Marathon, on advance request, will perform a rustic coffee-roasting ceremony, after which they will serve the freshly roasted coffee in traditional cups.

The decor at both locations is low key, but perhaps that's appropriate for one of the last cuisines to be "discovered" by the Western world. Service is pleasant, though slow and steady. So don't be in a rush. Remember, marathons take a long time. (The lunchtime buffet, however, can have you in and out like a sprinter.)

Maurya
Indian

1204 Kensington Road NW
Phone: 270·3133
Sunday – Friday 11:30 am – 2 pm, Sunday – Thursday 5 pm – 10 pm
Friday & Saturday 5 pm – 11 pm
Reservations recommended — Fully licensed — Patio — Non-smoking
V, MC, AE, DC, Debit — $$

THE MAURYA goes against the old tendency of Indian restaurants to drape themselves in red and gold. Instead, they have created a cool white room on Kensington Road, a space that could be perceived either as stark and minimalist or as simply stylish and understated. Regardless, the Maurya looks a lot different than some of the older places around town that serve Indian cuisine.

The food here is as skillfully prepared as anyone's. The Maurya offers a traditional list of tandoori meats such as the murgh malai tikka (creamy chicken), seafood specialties like prawn malai in coconut milk and mustard, and a nice selection of vegetarian dishes. The last time we went, the pappadams were so fresh, they were still a bit warm from the oven.

On that visit, we chose the palak paneer and the Peshwari chole, the first featuring chunks of house-made paneer in a thick spinach purée, the second, a mix of chickpeas, cashews, and raisins. Both dishes showed richness and intensity of flavour, but the chole could have used more cashews and raisins. And if you are not into puréed spinach, forget the palak paneer. The highlight of our meal was the murgh bharta, a dish of finely chopped tandoori chicken sautéed with onions, tomatoes, cream, and spices. So rich, so tasty. Scooped up with a fluffy naan, it was a full-bodied, complex dish that tasted just as good reheated as leftovers.

Indian food always surprises us, and our experience at the Maurya was no different. We frequently order three dishes, two of which are typically vegetarian. When they arrive, they never look like all that much food, but we usually have enough to take home for lunch the next day. Sure, a couple of naan, a plate of rice, and a few pappadams all contribute to our fullness, but it's mostly those creams and spices that fill us up.

In addition to its simple decor, the Maurya has a glassed-in tandoor oven, so the chef is in full view. Which is more than can be said for the Maurya itself. Although it is a decent size at sixty-five seats, it is partly obscured and hidden from street view by a brick electrical box.

Regardless, residents of the Sunnyside and Hillhurst communities look at the Maurya as one of their favourite eateries. Call ahead—it can get quite busy at times.

The Mecca

Diner & Southern Barbecue

10231 West Valley Road SW
Phone: 288·2500
Tuesday – Friday 7 am – 2 pm, Saturday & Sunday 7 am – 3 pm
Friday – Sunday 5 pm – last guest
Reservations not accepted — Fully licensed — Patio — Non-smoking section
V, MC, AE, Debit — $

THE MECCA is the closest thing we have in Calgary to a real roadhouse diner. A couple of decades ago a trailer was plunked onto a gravel lot on the west end of town. Sometime later, an extra room or two were added, and it became a quick pit stop for skiers on their way to the mountains.

It's still there, the parking lot is still gravel, and it sits almost unnoticed among the Prairie grasses. More development has crept up around it lately, but it still stands alone near the intersection of the Trans-Canada and Stoney Trail, just west of Canada Olympic Park. It has changed hands a few times, most recently in late 2000. Though it's been perked up with some fresh paint and had the menu upgraded, The Mecca is still a classic. They have kept the hook-and-eye latches on the washrooms and, unfortunately, the smoking section. With low trailer ceilings and limited air circulation, it can get a bit close.

But the food is fresh and hot off the grill. The pancakes are thick, the bacon is crisp—though not as crisp as Catherine would like—and the hash browns are made from real potatoes. The Griz is as hearty a breakfast as most can handle: three eggs, bacon, ham, sausage, hash browns, toast, and a couple of pancakes. Excellent value for $8.45.

The biggest innovation of the new owner is the addition of some Southern barbecue dishes. On Friday, Saturday, and Sunday evenings, they serve beef brisket and ribs, pork butt and ribs, and chicken that have all been slow-smoked in the Southern US barbecue tradition. The recipes are from the award-winning Ron Shewchuk of Rockin' Ronnie's Butt Shredders, and good recipes they are. For $11.95, you get a choice of meats, plus baked beans, coleslaw, corn bread, and a bun. The atmosphere is perfect for this kind of full-tilt, messy food.

The entertainment is good too. On any given weekend you may find Tom Phillips and the Men of Constant Sorrow, the Ronnie Haywood Trio, or Billy Cowsill (yes, that Billy Cowsill) & the Co-dependents performing at The Mecca. It's that kind of place.

As well, The Mecca's service is friendly, quick, and reasonably professional. The atmosphere may be smoky, but The Mecca is definitely a stop worth making.

www.meccacafe.ca

Mescalero

Contemporary Southwestern

1315 – 1 Street SW
Phone: 266 • 3339
Monday – Saturday 11:30 am – last guest, Sunday 11 am – 2 pm, 5 pm – last guest
Reservations recommended — Fully licensed — Patios — Non-smoking section
V, MC, AE, DC, Debit — $$ – $$$

WHEN the warm weather arrives, one of the nicest places to be is on the patio at Mescalero. With its terra-cotta flower pots, plastered walls, and fountain, it is almost more Santa Fe than any restaurant in Santa Fe.

The original Mescalero patio is a walled enclosure shaded by huge poplars. The fountain trickles on one side while umbrellas and heaters fill the space. It's quite lovely. A newer patio is similar, if lacking the patina of age. Both hold warmth well into the evening and do not seem overly popular with bugs. They are very private and removed from the street.

Focusing on Southwestern cuisine that was inspired by the fire-damaged interior of the building, Mescalero offers dishes like chorizo, artichoke, and poblano pizza or steamed mussels in a sun-dried tomato and chipotle cream. The menu incorporates a wide range of intense flavours, and the skill comes in balancing them all.

Mescalero makes the finest plate of nachos for miles around, with cheese and chilies layered on multicoloured corn chips. I've also had a pheasant and fresh vegetable burrito that was terrific. Breaking from their Southwestern theme, their Tower of Terror tenderloin is one of the best beef dishes in the city, especially served with a wild mushroom-sherry gravy. Meaty! And a dish of raw, chunky tuna in a wasabi cream was outstanding.

Desserts are creative with fresh fruits incorporated into crumbles, tortes, and ices. I had a fresh cherry pie once that was everything it should be—sticky-sweet with baked fruit, a flaky crust snapping under my fork.

Ordering at Mescalero can be tricky. You get two food menus: the regular sheet that lists about twenty tapas, plus the daily sheet that features more tapas as well as entrees. If you are hungry, you can order a tapa and an entree, but that is a lot of food. The entrees are huge and the tapas are somewhere between large appetizers and small meals. A couple of tapas is usually more than enough. Whatever your inclination, the menu is quite flexible, and the expert staff are helpful in guiding decisions.

So whether it's a soft summer night on the patio or a sun-washed winter lunch in the dining room, Mescalero is stylish, sophisticated, and unique and comes without the heavy New Mexican price tag.

Mimo

Portuguese

4909 – 17 Avenue SE (Little Saigon Centre)
Phone: 235·3377
Monday – Thursday 11 am – 10 pm
Friday & Saturday 11 am – 11 pm
Reservations recommended — Fully licensed — Non-smoking section
V, MC, AE, DC, Debit — $$

D ESPITE Mimo's simple-sounding address, finding it is a feat of great navigational skill. Surrounded by a motley collection of businesses just off 17th Avenue, Mimo is in the back row of the Little Saigon Centre.

Major renovations in 2000 created a lovely new dining room totally out of context with the area. They moved the restaurant out front where there are windows— albeit without much of a view—and created a new Portuguese sports bar in the back where the restaurant used to be. With crisp linens on the tables and staff in white shirts and black slacks or skirts, it's a formal yet comfortably casual room.

Once there, your nose will be assaulted by the zesty aroma of Isabel and John Da Costa's Portuguese cooking. Much of that comes from the rich olive oil called azeite, the only hot-pressed olive oil made in a world of cold-pressed ones. The Portuguese extract every drop of flavour from their olives, and its earthy, peppery flavour is transferred into the food.

Mimo's paella soaks up the azeite, as well as the essence of the mussels, squid, scampi, clams, and crab that fill it. This is as flavourful a paella as you are likely to find. For a slightly more delicate meal, there's the frango no chorrasco, a barbecued half chicken with fried potatoes. Juicy and slightly spicy, it's hard to believe you're not in Lisbon. (If you're going to order it, Isabel ideally likes to have at least a day's notice for proper preparation—the chicken is just a little bit more tender than if you order it when you arrive at the restaurant.) If you like more spice, try the camarao ao alho, or garlic shrimp—they are coated with far more chilies than garlic. And make sure to order a bottle of Vinho Verde beforehand. It goes down quickly with this shrimp.

There is a lot of salt and oil in most of this food. It's a part of the culture. Some dishes, like the bacalhau, push it too far for my palate. But I really enjoy the bitoque, a tasty steak topped with a fried egg and served with french fries. For something completely different, try the carne de porco a alentejana, a casserole of pork and clams. It's a combination that works surprisingly well.

Mimo is an opportunity for a virtual visit to the beaches of the Algarve or the wineries of Oporto. And it is very much worth the navigational effort it takes to find.

Misai

Japanese

1915 – 32 Avenue NE
Phone: 250·1688
Daily 11 am – 2:30 pm, Sunday – Thursday 5 pm – 10 pm
Friday & Saturday 5:30 pm – 11:30 pm
Reservations recommended — Fully licensed — Non-smoking section
V, MC, AE, DC, Debit — $$

WE are seeing a broadening of Japanese food styles these days—it's not just sushi, tempura, and noodles any more. We now have an Isakaya-style Japanese restaurant, which is one set up for sharing dishes along the lines of Chinese food.

It's the new Misai Restaurant, which probably has the most extensive selection of dishes we have yet seen in Calgary. Their menu is numbered up to item 2,425—I think they have left gaps in the numbers, perhaps to allow for future growth.

The Misai is in a space that has been many restaurants over the years, but it is not even remotely recognizable as any of its predecessors. They have created a long, narrow room with a sushi bar running its length. Booths line one wall, and in the back, there are the private tatami rooms complete with sliding doors, chair backs, and shoe racks. It is a pleasantly Oriental room with slate tile, wood trim, and a nifty hideaway shelf under the sushi bar to stash your belongings.

The menu seems aimed at both locals and tourists, especially the Japanese tourist. The Misai offers free evening shuttles from northeast hotels where many tour groups stay. Smart.

There is an abundance of fried appetizers, from squid legs to beef and cheese to salmon with pumpkin. I tried the ebi harumaki—prawn spring rolls at three for $5. They were light and crunchy and not particularly tasty. Nothing I'd go back for. They also have grilled appetizers like gyoza dumplings, capelin, and beef tongue. And there are salads, ramen noodles, and various entrees like grilled fish with rice, miso, pickles, and salad for $10. Reasonable prices.

I ordered a good sushi combo that came with soup and salad. Clean cuts of tuna and salmon nigiri with tasty rice. Nice tekka rolls with chopped tuna. Not a bad lunch for $12. The only negative was the salmon-skin cone that I also ordered. They lost that order twice—first they gave me a lovely plate of tuna sashimi that wasn't mine and then they lost the reorder. When the cone finally arrived, I still wasn't impressed. It came off as slimy, not the crisp and crunchy version that it should have been.

Other than the cone mix-up, service at the Misai was pleasant in the traditional Japanese style. And generally, I was impressed. It is nice to see a good independent place in the northeast doing well.

Moroccan Castle

Moroccan

217 – 19 Street NW
Phone: 283•5452
Tuesday – Thursday & Sunday 5:30 pm – 10 pm, Friday & Saturday 5:30 pm – 11 pm
Reservations recommended — Fully licensed — Non-smoking
V, MC — $$

THE MOROCCAN CASTLE presides over the small kingdom of West Hillhurst in a building that has recently had a full caravan makeover. Customers sink into cushioned benches to dine at low tables in private areas divided by curtains. Deep red walls are subtly lit, and tent-like carpets drape overhead, creating a sumptuous desert atmosphere.

The experience is quite unique. Meals at the Moroccan Castle are often full evening events that start with a ritual handwashing with rose water, a tradition inherited hundreds of years ago from Middle Eastern traders, followed by a procession of dishes.

The b'stilla pie appetizer is a wonderful combination of shredded chicken, eggs, onions, and almonds wrapped and baked in layers of phyllo pastry. About the size and shape of a Camembert round, the hot b'stilla is dusted with cinnamon and icing sugar before serving. This brings an aromatic sweetness to a savoury dish that is already overflowing with flavours of chicken and nuts and flaky with phyllo.

Couscous is another tasty Moroccan dish. Made from semolina flour (from the Latin *simila*, meaning "flower of flour"), couscous is a tiny pasta-like pellet that is steamed and served with various meats and vegetables. At the Moroccan Castle, the Couscous Royale comes with lamb, shrimp, chicken, and merguez—a Moroccan sausage—as well as nuts and dried fruits. The dish is rich with the natural flavours of the fruits and meats, and the couscous itself is the perfect neutral backdrop for soaking up all the tasty juices.

Other menu items include more couscous dishes, a spicy harira soup, a carrot and orange salad, and some tajine stews with such combinations as lamb, prunes, and almonds or chicken, lemon, and olives.

The food can be eaten by hand—specifically the right hand, and then, only the thumb and the first two fingers. But if you feel like using cutlery, go ahead; hands are traditional, but these days in Morocco, the knife and fork are much more common.

Service at the Moroccan Castle is discreet and professional, in fitting with the setting. There are French overtones to both the food and the service. (France had a serious interest in Morocco for many years, and the language of business for many Moroccans continues to be French.) But the underlying style here is very Moroccan, a desert friendliness that balances the French formality.

So the Moroccan Castle takes us to the casbah without leaving West Hillhurst. It is a short trip for such an interesting cuisine and pleasant cultural experience.

Murrieta's
West Coast

808 – 1 Street SW
Phone: 269·7707
Monday – Wednesday 11 am – midnight, Thursday – Saturday 11 am – 2 am
Sunday noon – 10 pm
Reservations recommended — Fully licensed
Non-smoking dining room, smoking in bar/bistro
V, MC, AE, DC, Debit — $$ – $$$

MURRIETA'S is quite an accomplishment—a combination of respect for history with the buzz and energy of a hot new restaurant. They took over the second floor of the Alberta Hotel building and enclosed the old atrium to create a ninety-seat dining room, wrapping it with a large bar and bistro. The main room features sandstone and brick under a huge skylight and an open kitchen along the south wall. It is quite striking.

The menu keeps pace nicely with the look. Barbara Lippuner came over from The Ranche and has created a tasty West Coast menu. There's a large variety of seafood, from pan-roasted prawns and smoked salmon flatbread to seafood linguine and Arctic char prepared four ways. And it is done very well.

The pan-roasted prawns are cooked to just-done and are served in a creamy and skillfully salted sauce. Delightful. As are some mussels, steamed and paired with chorizo in a roasted red pepper and tomato sauce. The seafood linguine is filled with scallops, prawns, salmon, halibut, and more mussels as well as asparagus and chervil, all in a vodka cream sauce. Very rich. But for really rich you can't beat the butternut squash and goat cheese ravioli topped with toasted pine nuts and bathed in butter and fresh sage. It's almost too rich to serve as a main course. Personally, I would prefer just a few as an appetizer.

At dinner, those pasta dishes run about $15 to $17, and the appetizers are around $9 or $10. Other dishes include a bouillabaisse or some black cod or a fourteen-ounce New York steak all at $25, salads from $6 to $10, and flatbreads from $9 to $14. Lunch prices are a bit lighter.

It is good food served in abundance by a professional staff. For such a new restaurant, they display a great sense of maturity. I think Murrieta's (which is named after a California winery that was named after the Mexican folk hero-bandito) is a great addition to the dining scene. And I applaud a restaurant that is totally committed to matching New World wines with New World cuisine.

My only concern with Murrieta's is that they maintain the division between the dining room and the bar-bistro section, keeping the bar activity on the other side of the wall. We like the current tone of the dining room and hope to return frequently.

Nellie's
Breakfast Cafe

2308 – 4 Street SW
Phone: 209·2708

738 – 17 Avenue SW
Phone: 244·4616
Patio

Monday – Friday 7:30 am – 4 pm, Saturday & Sunday 8:30 am – 4 pm
Reservations not accepted — No alcoholic beverages — Non-smoking
V, MC, Debit — $

Most mornings I'm happy with a big cup of French roast coffee and a bagel or a bowl of Cheerios. But some days I want a big old gut-busting plate of sausage and eggs with thick toast and pots of jam. But where can I get that? I have railed long and loud about the lack of decent breakfast places in town. Fortunately, when I'm in my grumpy-hungry morning mood, I can rely on the two Nellie's to stuff my face.

Named after Nellie McClung and her nearby historic residence, the two Nellie's are small, rustic joints. The original strikes an agrarian tone on 17th Avenue. The 4th Street one is a little bigger, seating about thirty in crowded but non-smoking confines at colourfully topped tables. It is a pretty enough place, with barnyard shades of green and rusty red offset with cow murals and blackboard menus.

Nellie's is not known for delicate, low-calorie breakfasts. This is "big food"—an order of French toast comes with two large pieces of sourdough, the omelettes use three eggs, and the pancakes cover a huge platter. Then there is the Belly Buster, my point of reference for Nellie's. With the Buster you get three eggs, a choice of bacon, ham, or sausage, a choice of French toast or pancakes, a choice of bread for your toast, and finally, hash browns. For $8.75, this is a lot of food.

But you do not have to eat big at Nellie's. You can get a fruit plate or, on Sundays, there is the Lite Brunch Combo of grilled banana bread with fruit and yogurt. Sorry, that's as light as Nellie's gets.

Lunches of the soup-and-sandwich sort are available, but Nellie's is made for breakfast. That's what everyone seems to order. And the breakfast concept matches the service. Staff buzz about with coffee pots in one hand, platters in the other, and pencils tucked behind their ears. They are pleasant people and a New Age version of the old diner waitresses—these ones have tattoos and nose rings. They come by this lineage honestly. One of the owners is the daughter of Edna, the woman who has run the Blackfoot Truck Stop for over forty years.

Nellie's is a good concept. They have a handle on what they want to do and they know how to do it. And given Calgarians desire for a good breakfast—just check out the weekend lineups—they are bound to continue their success.

Nellie's Breaks the Fast
Breakfast & Lunch

516 – 9 Avenue SW
Phone: 265•5071
Monday – Friday 6 am – 2 pm, Saturday & Sunday 8:30 am – 3:30 pm
Reservations recommended — Fully licensed — Rooftop patio — Non-smoking section
V, MC, AE, Debit — $

THEY say breakfast is the most important meal of the day. I'm not exactly sure who "they" are, but regardless, the message often falls on deaf ears in a city where starting work after 8 a.m. is considered a minor sin. We line up at drive-through coffee bars, grab day-old muffins from bakers who haven't got today's out of the oven yet, and think of lunch as the first meal of the day. No wonder out-of-towners don't understand our lust for the twelve o'clock lunch.

But come the weekend, things lighten up a bit. Sure there's soccer practice, ballet lessons, strategic planning meetings, restaurants to review... but I digress. Sometimes there's an opportunity for a leisurely breakfast, and Break the Fast, as it is known, is a terrific destination.

It sits perched above 9th Avenue atop a steep set of stairs. One wall is papered with vintage album covers—*Led Zeppelin III*, *Patsy Cline's Greatest Hits*, The Stones' *Some Girls*, and the like—allowing your mind to wander back a few decades while you wait briefly for caffeine. The staff, an interesting lot, buzz around with coffee pots in hand and arms loaded with steaming trays of good food. Break the Fast is active and laid-back at the same time.

We tried two of their omelettes, one filled with apples seasoned with cinnamon, apple mint, and apple liqueur and topped with melted white cheddar, the other stuffed with chorizo, salsa, and more white cheddar. Both came with fried red-skinned potatoes and a choice of Winnipeg rye, multi-grain, sourdough, or raisin toast.

They have a great breakfast menu complete with more omelette choices, whole wheat pancakes, eggs Benedict, fruit crepes, the basic combos of eggs any style with bacon, ham, or sausage, and more. Most items run $6 to $9. And they don't lie about their bacon. At Break the Fast, if you want it really, really crisp, you get it really, really crisp.

Break the Fast also offers a basic lunch menu of salads, sandwiches, and burgers, with a few perogies and cabbage rolls thrown in. I understand that these are quite popular and well executed, but I wouldn't know. With a name like Break the Fast, I feel obliged to concentrate on the most important meal of the day.

Oh! Canada
Canadian

815 – 7 Avenue SW
Phone: 266 • 1551
Monday – Thursday 11 am – 8 pm, Friday 11 am – 9 pm
Reservations recommended for lunch — Fully licensed — Patio — Non-smoking section
V, MC, AE, Debit — $$

FIRST, a few words on Canadian cuisine and whether or not there is such a thing: Of course there is. Any time there are farmers and fishers doing their jobs and cooks using what is produced, there is a food culture. Canada is one of the best food-producing nations in the world—our salmon, maple syrup, wheat, and beef are beyond compare. And increasingly, we have more people who know how to handle these ingredients well. But our geography dictates that Canadian cuisine be regional—what is prepared in the Maritimes is quite different from that in Quebec or Alberta or British Columbia.

In reality, we eat Canadian cuisine a lot without really thinking about it. So it's interesting to see a restaurant like Oh! Canada boldly proclaim our nationality. This is a fairly new place, and its menu, created by the talented Dickson Yip, spans our country.

We shared appetizers of portabello mushrooms topped with lobster and Leoni Grana Parmesan cheese (that's from Camrose) and a quesadilla stuffed with smoked salmon and goat cheese. Both were very nice. And the cheeseburger of Alberta beef with smoked applewood cheddar and more portabellos was great. My ribeye steak with roasted peppers and corn bread was pretty good too, although the vegetables were better than the steak, which wasn't all that tender. But the corn bread—made with corn flour so that it didn't crumble apart like the ones made with cornmeal—was excellent.

Other items on this all-Canadian menu include a smoked meat sandwich, a seafood salad with a blueberry-orange dressing, whiskey-fennel sausages, buffalo linguine, buckwheat honey crème brûlée, warm bumbleberry crisp, and apple pie with maple-cinnamon ice cream. Aside from a slightly soggy crust, the apple pie was good.

Oh! Canada's biggest problem is the room. It was built in the early '80s and, with its pink and grey tones, it looks it. It's a great space with a huge glass wall and high ceilings, but it is awkward, wedged onto the courtyard side of the Nova building. And the space will never be an evening destination—it is too deep in the downtown office core. Its main draw is during lunch and after work, so the food will stay fairly simple.

Simple, but very tasty and very Canadian.

Oriental Phoenix
Vietnamese

104 – 58 Avenue SE
Phone: 253·8383
Monday – Thursday 11 am – 9 pm
Friday & Saturday 11 am – 10 pm
Patio

503 – 4 Avenue SW
Phone: 262·3633
Monday – Thursday 10:30 am – 9 pm
Friday 10:30 am – 10 pm
Saturday 5 pm – 10 pm

Reservations recommended — Fully licensed — Non-smoking sections
V, MC, AE, DC, Debit — $ – $$

WHILE many local Vietnamese restaurants are simple, tiny, hole in the wall, family-run efforts, the Oriental Phoenix is a large, slick operation that seems to get larger and slicker all the time. In 1999 they took over a former Hurley's on 58th Avenue, spruced it up and opened a fresh, multi-roomed eatery and a super patio. (You can't beat the excitement of watching cars run the flashing red lights of the LRT tracks from your seat on the patio.) The downtown location is a slightly darker conversion of an old steak house. With crisply uniformed, smiling staff and a popular menu, they are becoming the Earl's of the Vietnamese food scene.

Fundamentally, the Phoenix serves good food. Not the best—that honour goes to the Saigon—but it's good food at good prices. There are over 100 items on the menu, from the crisp cha gio rolls and green papaya salad to the deep-fried quails, curry chicken, mussels in black-bean sauce, and satay beef. Most are quite nicely prepared.

Following Calgary's obsession with bún (the bowls of rice vermicelli topped with various meats and vegetables), that is what we often order. Bún is an excellent meal and an excellent deal. Their shrimp, beef, and chicken version, for $8.95, is my favourite. The meats are grilled to a salty, crispy perfection. Brochettes with boneless beef, skinless chicken, and four lovely prawns are lain over a bowl of noodles with vegetables, and they bring a bowl of nuoc mam for splashing over the combination. The dish is a light blend of meaty flavours, crunchy vegetables, and slippery noodles. It is the noodles themselves, however, that let the dish down. The Phoenix overcooks them to the point where they fall apart. This is not just an occasional problem—it seems to happen every time I have ordered bún at a Phoenix.

I also think that their salad rolls have certain shortcomings. Although all the ingredients are there, they could use more greens, and the rice wraps can get pretty chewy.

The Oriental Phoenix has a real strength in their sauces—strong, pungent hoisin and fresh, sharp nuoc mam. And their service is invariably brisk, friendly, and professional. I have to credit the Phoenix for helping to make Vietnamese food increasingly more popular. They may well be the Earl's of the Vietnamese market, and for their mix of food, service, and decor, they deserve their continued popularity.

Owl's Nest

Contemporary Continental

320 – 4 Avenue SW (The Westin)
Phone: 508 • 5164
Monday – Friday 11:30 am – 2 pm, Monday – Saturday 5:30 pm – 10:30 pm
Reservations recommended — Fully licensed — Non-smoking section
V, MC, AE, DC — $$$

FOR many years the Owl's Nest was "the" place for special occasion dinners—birthdays, anniversaries, promotions, and the like. It had that sumptuous hotel dining room feel, the service was impeccable, and the food was the rich and traditional Continental cuisine served in the best hotel restaurants. The Owl's Nest featured the food of one of Canada's most respected chefs, Fred Zimmerman. Dining here was a fabulous experience. But following Zimmerman's retirement, the restaurant became a little stale.

And the market has generally gone away from hotel dining, preferring instead to indulge in the more exotic and innovative foods of independent restaurants. Places where the rooms are more lively and the prices are lighter. Hotels have been struck with a dilemma—fight the trend or go with it. The Marriott closed the once-swanky Traders. The new Sheraton in Eau Claire farmed-out their food service to Fionn MacCool's and the Red Devil. The Hyatt created the one-size-fits-all Thomsons. So there remain only three top-end hotel dining rooms—the Delta's Conservatory, the Palliser's Rimrock, and the Westin's Owl's Nest.

The Westin decided to buck the trend and return the Nest to its former full-service, big-occasion status, and that's nice to see. We need a few places like this, where the staff pull out the table to allow the customer to slide into a booth. Where roses and matches with your name embossed in gold are brought to your table. Where the lobster bisque—so silky and rich—is finished at the table with brandy and cream. Where a chateaubriand for two is baked in a thick, thick crust of sea salt and presented under a silver dome. Where lobster thermidor and Dover sole and escargots are not museum pieces, but reinvented and respected classics.

The Owl's Nest food is now fresh and elegantly prepared by chef Martin Heuser. The classics are done the way they should be and the Contemporary items like the Salmon Dome are a creative swirl of smoked salmon and gravlax wrapped around salmon tartar and topped with caviar. The sauces are rich and decadent, and the desserts are beautifully sinful.

And always the service. Gracious, graceful, and attentive but not oppressive or intimidating. Under the direction of the skilled Reg Lewis, the staff exude the confidence that comes with the knowledge that the food is very good.

The Owl's Nest is back, and in force.

Pau Hana Grille

Euro-Asian

1851 Sirocco Drive SW (West Market Square)
Phone: 217 • 3000
Tuesday – Friday 11 am – 2 pm, Tuesday – Thursday & Sunday 5 pm – 9 pm
Friday & Saturday 5 pm – 11 pm
Reservations recommended — Fully licensed — Non-smoking
V, MC, AE, DC, Debit — $$

THE term *pau hana* is Hawaiian for kicking back after work and enjoying life. A good name for a restaurant. And a good name for this one.

The Pau Hana is a nice looking place—it has fifty-eight seats and a tiki room atmosphere with big bamboo chairs and a couple of fountains. There's no mistaking that you are in a strip mall, but it is quite comfortable nonetheless. And it has become popular with the folks in the Westhills area.

Pau Hana serves an upscale menu with beef short ribs braised in brandy and Sapporo beer and sea bass in ponzu sauce, both in the low $20s. So this is not a little strip-mall diner. They are serious about the food. It is an interesting concept to create a Euro-Asian Fusion cuisine. Hoisin-marinated chicken with a cranberry-quince syrup or beef tenderloin with shiitake and black-bean cream sauce—these are ideas that are well worth a look.

We started with a nice plate of salt and pepper squid. It felt clean and light on oil, with a crisp batter. It was a basic deep-fried squid though, light on the salt and pepper. With a sweetish orange-chili plum sauce for dipping, it was a pleasant enough appetizer, however, and big enough for the two of us. Since it cost $10, that is a good thing. For our main courses, we had the roasted half duck with wild rice risotto and a maple-balsamic reduction and the seared scallops with couscous in a blackberry-vodka sauce. Both dishes were nicely presented, with the duck draped over the risotto and the scallops skewered and placed over top of the couscous. They were good too but a bit understated.

I've been most impressed with some of the less ambitious dishes. A simple wrap of chicken and fruit chutney was outstanding, and the cream of shiitake-mushroom soup makes my short list of all-time great soups. Full-bodied without being unnecessarily thickened, this soup is rich and creamy and almost a meal in itself. Served with puff pastry sticks, it has been a huge hit with anyone I've suggested it to.

I wouldn't say that everything works all the time at Pau Hana. But when the envelope is pushed this much, there will always be greater and lesser successes. I'm just happy to see such creativity and to see someone running an interesting place west of Sarcee Trail. Pau Hana is rounding into an excellent eatery.

www.pauhanagrille.com

Pelican Pier

Family Seafood Restaurant

4404 – 14 Street NW
Phone: 289·6100
Monday – Saturday 11 am – 10 pm, Sunday noon – 9 pm
Reservations not accepted — Fully licensed
Non-smoking 5 pm – 8 pm, non-smoking section otherwise
V, MC, Debit — $ – $$

WHILE judging an oyster shucking competition, I pumped the other judge, a seafood supplier, for various fishy information. Like where he goes for fish and chips. His preference, he told me, was Pelican Pier, which I remembered from its Eau Claire days. But I had not eaten there since its move to 14th Street, so I decided it was time to trawl the seas of Nose Hill.

Pelican Pier is much more than just a quick fish and chip shop. It's a full-blown restaurant with about thirty different seafood dishes, from shrimp bisque and breaded oysters to grilled salmon and Creole snapper. And of course, fish and chips.

Before I even got to the fish and chips, I tried a cup of their chowder. I couldn't decide between the seafood chowder and the Manhattan clam chowder, so my server suggested a blend of the two, a concoction known as a bowl of red and white. It was a good bowl of soup, thick with clams and chunks of fish, plus potatoes and other vegetables. Good quality seafood and vegetables that were not overcooked.

Then on to the fish and chips—a couple of lightly breaded pollock filets served steaming hot over a pile of fries, with a bowl of house-made tartar sauce on the side. For $7.25, it was a good plate of food. The fish was nicely prepared—lightly battered, not one of those three-inch thick, doughy jobs that just traps all the grease. Pelican Pier's seems halfway between a breading and a battering, a great alternative for those who love fish and chips but really don't want all that heaviness. And with the tartar sauce, it was one of the best fish and chips I have had. The pollock itself was fine too. (You can always upgrade to cod, haddock, halibut, or salmon for an extra $3 to $7, a great option.) They don't slack off on the fries either. Long, freshly cut, crispy chips—a perfect complement to the fish. They also offer more of these if you would like, at no extra charge. A nice touch.

Pelican Pier is not a bad looking place. Split into two halves, it is appropriately coastal, with lobster traps and fishnets dangling from the ceiling and posters of fish lining the walls. Condiment trays load the tables, and if you listen real hard, the traffic on 14th can sound like waves lapping the shores. I almost expect to see Captain Highliner waiting tables.

Pfanntastic Pannenkoek Haus
Dutch Pancakes

2439 – 54 Avenue SW
Phone: 243·7757
Tuesday – Friday 11 am – 8 pm, Saturday & Sunday 8 am – 8 pm
Reservations recommended Tuesday – Saturday, not accepted Sunday
Fully licensed — Non-smoking section
V, MC, AE, Debit — $

WE had our first Dutch pannenkoeks at a seaside cafe in The Hague. They weren't much to look at—big, thin pancakes, more like crepes really, dotted with chunks of mushroom and smoked bacon. We thought we would need a half-dozen to fill up. But a few bites into them, we realized that the beauty of Dutch pancakes is more than skin deep and that we were enjoying a complex, dense, subtle, filling meal.

We have further appreciated pannenkoeks at the Pfanntastic Pannenkoek Haus in a nondescript strip mall just north of where Crowchild meets Glenmore Trail. It's the brainchild of an exuberant former oil-patch employee and a quiet gentleman chef from Holland. Together they have created a menu of over sixty kinds of pancakes.

The Pfanntastic itself is crisp and clean, but could just as easily be serving Canadian pancakes. The style is casual, and the menu rarely breaks the $10 mark. When it does, it's for such treats as the major dessert pannenkoek with warm cherries, ice cream, whipped cream, kirsch in a little chocolate cup, and chocolate sauce—all for $10.95. This is economical dining, and the food is top notch.

Unlike pizza joints, you can't hide a lack of toppings under a thick tomato sauce. These pancakes are about a quarter-inch thick, so everything is visible. The pancake itself has a pleasant, mild flavour, somewhere between a crepe and a Phil's buttermilk. Prepared in twelve-inch rounds, the toppings are typically cooked into the batter. And the toppings range from spek (Dutch bacon) with eggs cracked into the pancake to saskatoons to cheese and leek. The possibilities are limitless, as long as the ingredient isn't too wet. Nobody likes a soggy pancake.

We sometimes sweeten our savoury pancakes with the warmed, molasses-like stroop syrup—similar to maple syrup with bacon. One sweet pancake that intrigues us is the brown sugar with lemon juice, sweet and tart at the same time. But if you like sweet and savoury, there are combos like bacon and apple or ham and pineapple. Yes, a Hawaiian Dutch pancake.

They also have excellent soups like the chicken and vegetable with dumplings, a beautiful stock with feather-light drop noodles. Plus, they do omelettes and some uitsmijters—open-faced sandwiches.

Like Canadian pancakes, we don't get a hankering for pannenkoeks every day, but when we do, nothing else fits the bill. The Pfanntastic holds to their tradition well, bringing a little taste of Holland to Calgary.

Pies Plus
Pies & Light Meals

12445 Lake Fraser Drive SE (Avenida Place)
Phone: 271·6616
Tuesday – Friday 8 am – 9 pm
Saturday & Sunday 8 am – 6 pm
Cash or cheque only
Patio

Bragg Creek Shopping Centre
Phone: 949·3450
Monday – Friday 10 am – 6 pm
Saturday & Sunday 10 am – 7 pm
V

Reservations not accepted — No alcoholic beverages — Non-smoking
$

SOMETIMES simple is best. These days we see desserts with complex preparations, a number of international ingredients, and lengthy three-line descriptions. Many of these are fabulous. But sometimes we just want a slice of apple pie with a flaky crust, a light dusting of cinnamon, and maybe a scoop of vanilla ice cream. Or a fresh peach pie in season or a banana cream or a lemon meringue. Aside from making them at home, there are few places to find these simple pleasures. Not that there is any shortage of syrupy fillings oozing out of precast pie crusts. Lots of neighborhood bakeries and grocery stores have one of these goopy renditions.

So what should a pie be about? A fruit pie should be about the fruit, a cream pie, about the key flavour—be it coconut or chocolate or banana—in a custard base. What they should not be about is cloying sweetness or a treacle of fake ingredients. (Have I had too many bad pieces of pie or what?)

If you feel like me, go to Pies Plus. Get real fruit with real flavour, pastry made on the spot, and service from people who understand pie. The folks at the two Pies Plus locations have been around about seventeen years and have worked their repertoire up to over 100 varieties.

We are single-fruit pie purists in our house, but we may occasionally indulge in one of their strawberry-rhubarbs or a blueberry-raspberry. What we enjoy is the presence of the fruit, unadulterated by excess sugar, and the abundance of the fillings. These are not those thin little community-bazaar pies where the filling is stretched too far. These are heavy with fruit. Much of the time, the pies are made from high-quality frozen fruit due to seasonal availability, but when they use the fresh stuff, the results are even better.

Pies Plus also does a range of light meals and snacks, like soups, sandwiches, muffins, quiches, and meat pies, and they offer seasonal specialties such as tourtière and plum pudding. Always fresh, always high quality. They have good coffee too.

The Pies Plus locations can get quite busy—especially in Bragg Creek—so be patient. They are friendly, lively places where having a piece of pie can be fun. You'll pay a little more, but for a piece of the real stuff, it is worth it.

The Pines

Contemporary Canadian

537 Banff Avenue (Rundlestone Lodge), Banff
Phone: 760·6690
Monday – Friday 7 am – 10:30 am, Saturday & Sunday 7 am – 11:30 am
Daily 5:30 pm – 10 pm
Reservations recommended — Fully licensed — Non-smoking
V, MC — $$ – $$$

BANFF used to be a place for pancakes and bad coffee. But some sparkling new Contemporary places have emerged in the last few years, places that are creating impressive food with excellent service to go along with it.

Situated discreetly in the Rundlestone Lodge, The Pines is one of the best. But it's easy to miss. The Rundlestone is too far north on Banff Avenue to attract the bulk of tourists who trawl for dinner on the strip, and the restaurant has no street frontage. Once you're inside the dining room though, it speaks of Banff without hitting you over the head. The neutral tones and highlights of natural wood are elegantly understated, and the room looks onto a small wooded park.

The menu is wonderfully Contemporary Canadian, a compilation of Canadian ingredients combined in the low-fat, high-flavour style of the day. Carpaccio is made from cured buffalo, honey-glazed salmon is served with a wild rice quiche, and caribou is sided with an apple polenta. The chefs draw on their European backgrounds to bring out the best in the dishes, and they offer fabulous blends of flavours and textures.

An ostrich steak crusted in black pepper was moist and intensely flavoured—the best piece of ostrich I have yet to eat. It was as rich and dense as a good beef ribeye. But the plate was made by the gratin of potatoes and apples, a kind of scalloped potato dish with apples tossed into the mix. A terrific idea. With a medley of julienned vegetables rolled in phyllo pastry, this was an outstanding meal.

Catherine's dish was perhaps even better—a maple- and orange-glazed duck breast with pecan-crusted bacon on barley risotto. They could not have designed the dish any better to meet her taste. The duck was unbelievably tender, and the maple-scented bacon was as crisp as she likes it. Though not done in a really creamy risotto style, the barley was nutty and a perfect complement to the poultry. With some oregano-flavoured vegetables, it was an impeccable plate.

I should also mention our appetizers, served tapas style: shrimp and crab with asparagus aïoli and shredded pumpkin; smoked Valbella goose and air-dried duck with pickled vegetables; and basil-marinated brie with pepperonata crostini. They were excellent selections, beautifully prepared. The brie was too young, but otherwise, no complaints.

So Banff has come a long way from pancakes, thanks to places like The Pines. And even the coffee isn't half bad.

Piq Niq

Eclectic European

811 – 1 Street SW
Phone: 263·1650
Monday – Friday 11 am – 2 pm
Wednesday – Saturday 5 pm – 10 pm
Reservations recommended — Fully licensed — Non-smoking
V, MC, AE, DC — $ – $$

THE quietest and most unassuming place on 1st Street is Piq Niq, a tiny cafe on the ground floor of the Grain Exchange Building. Overshadowed by its larger neighbour Divino, Piq Niq seats a couple of dozen in a rustically renovated room.

The floors are the original hardwood, and the doors and windows harken back a few decades. Water pipes have been exposed overhead, and floor tiles have been uncovered to create a softly historic atmosphere. The room is topped by a huge chandelier that was rescued from a renovation of the Westin Hotel. It consumes almost the entire ceiling.

At lunch, Piq Niq serves a simple, tasty list of panini on focaccia or ciabatta or baguette. With a couple of soups, a few salads, and a handful of pastas, it is a short but well-executed menu that puts a creative spin on the typical soup-and-sandwich lunch.

One cold and rainy day, the soup du jour was a hearty beef barley, an excellent start to the meal. So was the tomato-basil soup. With a noticeable presence of basil, it was a tomatoey, rich version that did not need to rely on cream. The soups were great fronts for a chicken breast on focaccia and an Italian sausage on ciabatta. Both sandwiches were packed with meats and cheeses, smothered in pesto and tomatoes, and layered between fresh breads. They had everything that I want in a sandwich, including roasted peppers that had been peeled. Other sandwich offerings include pear, leek, and Gorgonzola; beef sirloin with provolone and mushrooms; and pastrami with Gouda. Nice ideas. And reasonably priced with soup or salad for $10 to $12.

At night, Piq Niq gets more serious with a menu of duck confit, beef tenderloin in a mustard and Marsala jus, caramelized salmon, another handful of pastas, plus a live jazz club downstairs called Beat Niq. They have managed to hold most entrees under $20, providing excellent value.

Service fits with the soft, subtle atmosphere. The staff remain in the background until they are needed and then perform their jobs professionally. This includes crusting the crème brûlée at your table with a small blowtorch. And an excellent brûlée it is, with its crisp, warm top and extremely creamy contents. This is one of the top two or three brûlées in the city.

Piq Niq has matured nicely since it opened in 1994, becoming an assured establishment that appears to be very comfortable with itself.

www.beatniq.com

Pita's Plus Donair

Lebanese

3132 – 26 Street NE (Interpacific Business Park)
Phone: 735·1116
Monday – Friday 9 am – 9 pm, Saturday 9 am – 7 pm
Reservations accepted — No alcoholic beverages — Non-smoking
Cash only — $

AMONG the many value- and quality-laden cafes of the northeast, Pita's Plus stands out as one of the best. They serve a short, simple, and mostly homemade menu of tabouleh, hommous, pita pies, and donairs that are both good and cheap.

The most expensive item on the menu is the chicken donair plus—that's a big pita wrapped around lettuce, tomatoes, onions, chicken, and either tahini or what they call sweet sauce. This thing is huge and it's all for $6.

What is most exceptional about it is the chicken. Most chicken donairs are similar to beef donairs, whereby chunks of fresh meat are layered onto an upright skewer that roasts the meat while it rotates. Cooked bits are cut off and made into sandwiches. At Pita's Plus, they oven-roast whole chickens, blend the meat with various spices, and then wrap it in pita. Those spices, combined with the sweet sauce that I chose, add a great depth of flavour and make these sandwiches quite unique.

They top a thin house-made crust with delicately spiced ground beef for their pita pie. Not the prettiest thing I've ever eaten. It has the look of a hamburger pizza, but is very savoury and comparatively light. These are all of $2 each, or $2.50 if you want cheese added.

We really enjoy their tabouleh, the salad made with chopped parsley and bulgar wheat. Very nicely balanced, not too much lemon, just tart enough. And the falafel passes muster too.

Pita's Plus also has the best rice pudding in the city. It's done Middle Eastern style with fragrant rose water heightening the creaminess of the pudding. There are no raisins in this version, but the pudding is topped with cinnamon to bring out the flavours. It's so nice and is also all of $2.

Pita's Plus is a sparse place where you order at the counter to either take out or carry your food to a table on a red cafeteria tray. The floors are lino, the forks are plastic, and the menu has been hand constructed. It's a multi-generational family operation with friendly service and grandkids running about.

So if you head out to Pita's Plus, don't expect anything fancy in the space or the service. Just expect very fresh food prepared with care.

Plunkett's
Casual Fine Dining

12445 Lake Fraser Drive SE (Avenida Place)
Phone: 271·7120
Monday – Friday 11:30 am – 2 pm, Monday – Thursday 5 pm – 8:30 pm
Friday & Saturday 5 pm – 9:30 pm
Reservations recommended — Fully licensed — Non-smoking section
V, MC, AE, Debit — $$ – $$$

I N a word, or perhaps a year, I would describe Plunkett's as "1980." It's about twenty years behind the cutting edge in cuisine. Before you think me an unkind boor, I should tell you that those were words given to me by the skilled chef-owner Brian Plunkett as I was thinking the very same thing.

At Plunkett's you will see a reiteration of past culinary traditions. There are escargots, coquilles St. Jacques, and baked tomatoes. Plunkett's is aimed at the large group of people who don't really care about the latest food trend, those who want something traditional and reliable. And it delivers.

The room itself is set up like a traditional dining room with crisp linens and nicely spaced tables. They have taken over a spot in Avenida Place that was most recently a steak house and have neutralized the space, highlighting the windows and providing a minimum of decoration. Everything is spotless, including the cutlery and glasses. They pay serious attention to the look and feel of the place.

They do the same with the service. It is professional and discreet, there when it needs to be, absent when it doesn't. And it fits in with the casual tone of a fine neighbourhood restaurant.

As does the food. The Stilton and leek soup is a gentle balance of blue cheese and onion flavours, a skillful concoction. And the mixed green salad with goat cheese is a pleasant plate with a sun-dried tomato vinaigrette. (The goat cheese and vinaigrette are about as trendy as Plunkett's gets.)

I was a bit disappointed in the broiled seafood brochettes over a saffron risotto. Chunks of salmon and the scallops and prawns were all perfectly prepared, but the risotto was actually just long grain rice tinged with saffron. Nice, but not actually a risotto.

No culinary envelope is being pushed at Plunkett's. It's good food no doubt, skillfully prepared, but if you are looking for innovation, look elsewhere. This is the kind of place I would take my parents, with their tame palates and need to identify everything on the plate. That doesn't make it bad or invalid. Plunkett's is actually a brave concept. It can be difficult to do food that is familiar—everyone knows how it should taste, which can make it less forgiving. But Plunkett's does it well and for a large and appreciative market.

It's up to you to decide whether Plunkett's is dated or classic. As for me, I think it's classic.

Post Hotel

Continental

200 Pipestone Road, Lake Louise
Phone: 522 • 3989 or 1(800) 661 • 1586
Daily 7 am — 11 am, 11:30 am — 2 pm, 5 pm — 9:30 pm
Closed in November
Reservations recommended for dinner — Fully licensed — Non-smoking
V, MC, AE — $$$

M ANY claim that the best food in the Rockies is at the somewhat understated Post Hotel. Understated because the 120-seat room is so frequently full that the owners feel little need to advertise. So there are no glossy ads proclaiming the Post's prowess. Even looking at the room, it would be easy to surmise that it's just another mountain hotel cafe. Though certainly pretty enough, it has been cobbled together from the old lodge and a newer building, so the ceilings are low and the setting is lodge-like. And the lunch menu presents what at first appears to be an unremarkable list of burgers, sandwiches, and salads.

But be assured, this is one of the best places to eat for miles around. Looking closer at the menu, those salads are topped with goat cheese croutons and the burgers come with caramelized onions and Gruyère or a cranberry-onion marmalade. And a soup of the day was cream of herbs.

Cream of herbs? What the heck is that? I ordered some and, wow, was it good! Rich and light at the same time, the flavour of fresh herbs blending with the cream into a beautiful soup. They didn't tell me exactly which herbs they used, but I tasted oregano and basil and tarragon.

I also had to have some of the Post's fries. It may seem odd to come to a place that serves Brome Lake duck and Alaskan crab cakes to eat french fries, but the Post makes the best. They are the only place we know that consistently does the double-dip style of fry cooking. And in peanut oil no less. Try them. They are the perfect match for the clubhouse with its grilled chicken, bacon, avocado, and black-bean mayonnaise on house-baked bread. A great sandwich.

Lest you think that's all they do, at night the menu slides up to $38.50 for the caribou strip loin on a pear-Armagnac sauce or fallow deer medallions on a rosehip sauce with Arctic cranberries. And the house-baked pastries are always a treat—Valrohna chocolate cake, cherry phyllo strudel, fresh fruit crumble, and more, starting at $9.

The Post is consistent in their food and in their service. They seem to glean the best available staff, who are always crisp and attentive. It helps that the hotel owner is a constant presence on the premises.

It doesn't get much better than the Post. And that's OK by me.

www.posthotel.com

Priddis Greens
Casual Clubhouse & Continental

Priddis Greens Drive, Priddis
Phone: 931·3171
Golf season: Daily 7 am – 10 pm
Off season: Friday 5:30 pm – 10 pm, Saturday 10:30 am – 10 pm
Sunday 10:30 am – 2 pm
Reservations recommended — Fully licensed — Sundeck — Non-smoking section
V, MC, AE, DC — $ – $$$

THE PRIDDIS GREENS GOLF & COUNTRY CLUB restaurant overlooks the course and the Foothills, providing a sweeping view out to the Rockies. Unhindered by development, it is a gorgeous, verdant panorama. Sunlight pours through the tall second-floor windows into a comfortable room that works for both casual and formal occasions.

The food here is very good, something of a rarity at golf courses. It is common to find decent clubhouse sandwiches in places like this—it is their natural environment after all. And the Priddis version is a winner with its juicy turkey and crisp maple bacon on thick slabs of bread. But they offer more than the golf fare of chicken fingers, nachos, and burgers. There are gravlax sandwiches, pesto pizzas, fajitas, and rotini coq au vin. If you are looking for upscale and Continental, there is a list of classics like escargots Bourguignonne, crown of lamb, and veal Nicolas.

But we prefer to relax at Priddis with an $8 sandwich rather than a $22 duck breast. It seems to match the setting better for us. If, however, you get a hankering for a bowl of lobster bisque with your burger, they make an exceptional one.

We also like the buffet Sunday brunch, probably the best in our area. Tables groan under the weight of smoked fish, eggs Benedict, waffles, hips of beef, bacon, cheeses, salads, and layered cream cakes. It's not cheap at $22 ($20.75 for seniors and $12 for kids ten and under), but as buffet brunches go, it is pretty good value.

Priddis is partly successful because of one of the best and most experienced food and beverage managers in the area—Bernard Duvette. M. Duvette is a gracious and skilled host, charming to his customers while totally in control of a well-trained staff. It is always a pleasure to dine in a room under his supervision.

Priddis is a private course but the restaurant is public, so you do not have to be a member or even a golfer to enjoy the beauty and the quality of Priddis Greens. It is one of the best quick getaways we have and is only a few minutes away from the city on paved roads.

From Macleod Trail, drive west on Highway 22X (the Marquis of Lorne Trail) for approximately 25 kilometres. Turn left on Priddis Greens Drive (watch for signs) and follow the road to the clubhouse.

Puspa
Indian (Bengali)

1051 – 40 Avenue NW
Phone: 282·6444
Monday – Saturday 11:30 am – 2 pm, Monday – Thursday 5 pm – 10 pm
Friday & Saturday 5 pm – 10:30 pm
Reservations recommended — Fully licensed — Non-smoking
V, MC, AE, DC, Debit — $ – $$

PUSPA offers a unique dining experience with its Bengali cuisine from the northeast corner of India, and it has a unique location with its view of Northmount Drive. It's the only place in Calgary currently serving this style of food and one of the few Indian restaurants in the northwest.

Puspa—which means "flower" and is also a woman's name—is a fairly plain space with a subdued atmosphere. They don't go overboard with the red and brass gewgaws—the tables are set with burgundy cloths, and white linen napkins are folded into water glasses. The staff are a welcoming bunch, quick with menu suggestions yet appropriately unobtrusive with the service. And they seem to do a gangbuster business in takeout, with people constantly dropping by for their curries-to-go.

Food-wise, Puspa is very interesting. The dishes have names familiar to Indian food devotees but preparations that will taste a bit different than we get around town. The tandoor-roasted butter chicken is bathed in a creamy yogurt sauce, but it is sweeter than most Punjabi versions. And the bhoona shrimp is cooked in a thick sauce with tomatoes, peppers, onions, and spices, but it is less creamy here than in Kashmiri restaurants. Even the paratha—a fried white-flour bread—is done a bit differently; the dough is rolled flat, fried, and presented as a thick, cracker-like disc instead of as a thin, flaky bread.

Puspa does feature some dishes exclusive to Bengal. The shrimp patia comes in a hot and sour sauce fashioned on Persian spices. It is biting hot with a mouth-puckering sour edge, a dish that is deep in flavour. The chicken dhansak is a hot Persian curry cooked with lentils. To capsulize the style simply, Bengali food is very full bodied but not as complex in spicing as many of its neighbouring provinces. And though there may not be as many layers to it, there is usually plenty of intensity.

Price-wise, Puspa has broken the $10 barrier with some of their more intricate shrimp, lamb, and chicken dishes. But most things remain in the $6 to $10 range. The servings are not as big as at some places, but the value is still high.

Puspa presents an excellent package and enjoys strong support from the neighbourhood. It is great to see this kind of diversity in our city.

Rajdoot

Indian (Mughlai & Northern)

2424 – 4 Street SW
Phone: 245·0181
Monday – Friday 11:15 am – 2 pm, Daily 4:45 pm – last guest
Reservations recommended — Fully licensed — Patio — Non-smoking section
V, MC, AE, DC, Debit — $$

THE grand pasha of local Indian cuisine is the Rajdoot, a professional family-run operation. It's a room filled with Indian statues and tapestries and the warm welcome of the subcontinent. Rom and Sue Anand can usually be found tending the buffet, welcoming guests, or telling colourful stories about India. And in the background, a well-trained staff—including two sons—work diligently at the food and service.

It's easy to see the process here. There's a thick glass window into the kitchen through which customers can watch the tandoori chefs. They press balls of dough against the inside wall of the super-hot tandoor and pull out fully cooked naan only seconds later. They skewer brightly sauced chicken, lamb, and fish on long metal rods and drop them into the oven. Then they slide the breads and meats onto platters that come smoking hot to your table.

The Rajdoot does a lot of buffets for those who like to sample. Every weekday lunch, they lay out over two dozen hot and cold items, ranging from the cooling raita nazeen (a homemade yogurt with cucumber) to the blistering lamb vindaloo. In between, there are steaming trays of rice with saffron and peas, tandoori chicken, and dhal mukhani, a rich lentil dish. There are always spicy and cooling dishes, meat and vegetarian plates, and cooked and uncooked offerings. The food displays a rare complexity of spicing with a subtlety of touch. And for only $9.95, it's a buffet bargain.

On Sunday and Monday evenings, they offer buffets for an equally value-packed $14.95, but their biggest night of the week is Tuesday when they do their popular vegetarian buffet for $12.95. It is super.

The Rajdoot also offers a full menu of Northern Indian dishes developed during the Mogul Dynasties (the 1300s to 1600s). These dishes are typically richer and less intensely spiced than the central or southern ones and include more meats. But when you order off the menu, they will make the food as intense as you want, without losing the subtle flavours. Good Indian food should never be lost in the lust for heat.

One of our favourite dishes is the butter chicken mukhani—boneless tandoori chicken in a cream sauce. The cream smoothes out the spices, creating a complexly flavoured dish. Then there's the saag gosht Nepali, the rogan josh, and the surprisingly simple Delhi lentil dish, channa chandi chowk. The list goes on.

And we keep going back for more.

The Ranche
Contemporary Ranch Cuisine

Bow Valley Ranch, south end of Bow Bottom Trail SE
Phone: 225·3939
Monday – Thursday 11:30 am – 10 pm, Friday & Saturday 11:30 am – 11 pm
Sunday 10:30 am – 9 pm
Reservations recommended — Fully licensed — Veranda
Non-smoking dining room, smoking in lounge
V, MC, AE, DC, Debit — $$ – $$$

FIRST, a little history: In 1896, following a fire that destroyed the dwelling on his ranch near the confluence of the Bow River and Fish Creek, William Roper Hull built a new house. Rumoured to have cost almost $4,000, the huge brick home quickly became the centre of Calgary's splashier social events. But only six years later, Hull sold the property to Patrick Burns, and it remained in the Burns family's possession until 1973 when it was acquired by the Province as part of Fish Creek Provincial Park. Following extensive fundraising and planning, The Ranche opened as a restaurant in the summer of 1999. And it is gorgeous.

They converted two front rooms into a dining room and a lounge, and the old kitchen forms another dining area. But most customers are sat in what used to be a large family room, an addition from the '50s that is now tied into the rest of the house better than it ever was. A veranda sweeps around three sides of the house, adding depth and texture to the exterior. And on a non-mosquito evening, it is an elegant place to sip a Chardonnay or an iced tea while the sun sets across Fish Creek Park.

The menus have been created to update ranch cuisine. They are thoughtful collections of beef tenderloin with seared spinach ($30), venison chops with apricot perogies ($36), preserved lemon risotto with scallops, prawns, and mussels ($21), and lamb burgers with Ermite cheese ($10).

We started our dinner with a green salad plated with orange-infused smoked salmon and bison carpaccio with a honey, balsamic, and Dijon sauce. Both were fabulous. The thinly sliced bison was piqued by the mustard and honey while roasted garlic and orange balanced perfectly with the delicate smoked salmon.

Then for our main courses, we did something we rarely do—we ordered the same thing, the braised rabbit lasagna prepared with goat cheese, smoked mozzarella, and a saffron sauce. Such silky flavours and rich depth, the layers of rabbit slipping from between the pasta. Wonderful. (And our dinner companions loved their lemon- and shrimp-stuffed sockeye steaks.)

On a cautionary note, the main dining room can become very loud. Seating about 125, the tables are well spaced, but the noise level climbs quickly. So be prepared to absorb a few decibels along with your meal.

Overall, the setting is outstanding, the food is terrific, the service is professional—the whole package is unbeatable. And, it is gorgeous.

Restaurant Indonesia
Indonesian

1604 – 14 Street SW
Phone: 244·0645
Tuesday – Friday 11:30 am – 2:30 pm, 5 pm – 11 pm
Saturday 5 pm – 11 pm, Sunday 5 pm – 9 pm
Reservations recommended — Fully licensed — Non-smoking
V, MC, AE — $ – $$

SINCE RESTAURANT INDONESIA opened, it has been Calgary's best Indonesian restaurant. The fact that it is Calgary's only Indonesian restaurant should not diminish this accolade. It is one fine place.

They have often quoted me in their ads as saying that they have the best satay in town, so every time I go, I have to check to see if I still agree with myself. And every time, I reiterate my praise. Tender, juicy chunks of meat (chicken, beef, pork, or lamb) are tastily charbroiled on skewers and served with an excellent peanut sauce. Great stuff. Always a pain, though, to get the meat off those pointy little sticks without poking someone or flicking a bit across the room.

One evening we ordered some satay, the ayam saus Java, the gado gado, and the aduk aduk tempeh—all classic Indonesian dishes. Ayam is the word for chicken, and in this Java version, it was done in a creamy sauce with basil, pepper, and a few chilies. A marvelous dish that was rich, balanced, and intense. The gado gado— cooked vegetables, hard-boiled egg, and tofu in more peanut sauce—was excellent. But our favourite was the aduk aduk tempeh, a uniquely Indonesian dish. Tempeh is a fermented soybean cake that, in this preparation, was fried in a spicy sauce with shrimp. The texture was firmer than tofu and quite pleasant, the flavours savoury and exotic.

And this food will not do damage to your wallet. The above feast for two—with coconut rice—cost $39, including tax and a good tip. And there was plenty of food left over for lunch the next day. Their prices have changed little since the early '90s. (Note: They include the popular *rijsttafel*, or "rice table," on their menu, providing a sampling of Indonesian food in a multitude of small dishes for $22.50 per person.)

They serve a refined version of Indonesian cuisine here, reducing the fat, increasing the quality of ingredients, and creating dishes with flavours as intense as Thai food and as subtle as good Chinese cooking. So the rendang beef is lean and boneless, and the pork in lemon grass is aromatic with the herb. Few of the dishes are deep-fried, so the delicate nature of the fresh ingredients is preserved.

Restaurant Indonesia continues to impress. In spite of its singularity in the market, it has never reduced its quality of food or service. I suspect that even if they had direct competition, they would still be the best.

The Rimrock Room
Canadian & Fusion

133 – 9 Avenue SW (The Fairmont Palliser)
Phone: 260 · 1219
Monday – Saturday 6:30 am – 2 pm, 5:30 pm – 10 pm
Sunday 7 am – 2 pm, 5:30 pm – 10 pm
Reservations recommended — Fully licensed — Non-smoking section
V, MC, AE, DC, Debit — $$ – $$$

THE feeling of history is palpable in The Rimrock Room. The spacious lobby of the Fairmont Palliser Hotel takes you back to 1914, to the days of rail travel, the Great War, and the Turner Valley oil strike. The Rimrock is Calgary's oldest existing dining room, the scene of historic characters and activities, a room filled with the weight of memories.

Opened originally as a bar and cafe called the Grill Room, the restaurant came to be called The Rimrock in 1962. Charlie Beil, the Banff artist whose 38-foot Rimrock mural adorns the south wall, gave the name of his work to the room. Along with the ornate fireplace and the many pillars covered with hand-tooled leather panels, the mural lends an undeniable sense of the West to the restaurant.

You can find some pretty good food here, ranging from the always popular Palliser clam chowder in the house-made bread bowl to the more exotic dishes like cumin-crusted sablefish in a Zinfandel vinaigrette. The menus, which are adorned with historic Canadian Pacific photos, have been created to satisfy international tourists and local traditionalists alike. So they offer their share of beef, carved from prime rib roasts and served with Yorkshire puddings, grilled as strip loins and highlighted with a shallot and pearl onion sauce, or broiled as tenderloins accompanied by a portabello stew. There are multicultural tones too with jerk pork tenderloin, sea bass in a miso and sake marinade, and pappadams. And Contemporary items like the sablefish, a shrimp and pancetta wrap, and a daily vegetarian entree.

One of the favourite ways of enjoying The Rimrock is to indulge in the lunch buffet, set at $15.95. Covered in bowls of salads, tureens of soup, and gleaming hot trays, the buffet features AAA top sirloin roasts. This is outstandingly tender beef, with a variety of roasts available to ensure that you can have your beef cooked as you like it. The rest of the buffet provides an admirable supporting cast—the roast pork is glazed with a light gravy, the baked sole is tender and moist, and there is always the clam chowder. And the dessert buffet. It is filled with surprisingly tasty white-chocolate mousse concoctions, carrot cakes, and other chocolate and fruit creations. (And on Tuesday evenings, they have a Death by Chocolate dessert buffet.)

Calgary is fortunate to be home to a hotel with as much history as The Palliser, a dining room that respects that history, and a staff that honours the tradition. Charlie Beil would be proud.

River Café
Regional Wood-Fired Canadian Cuisine

Prince's Island Park
Phone: 261·7670
Monday – Friday 11 am – 11 pm, Saturday & Sunday 10 am – 11 pm
Closed in January
Reservations recommended — Fully licensed — Patio — Non-smoking, including patio
V, MC, AE, DC, Debit — $$ – $$$

THERE are few nicer places to be in Calgary than Prince's Island. Surrounded on one side by the Bow and on the other by an estuary created by the nineteenth century lumber magnate Peter Prince, the island is a carless bit of greenery in our downtown core. And the only business operating on it is the River Café.

The building at the core of the restaurant started out as a utilitarian Parks and Recreation structure. Over the years, a unique collaboration between the City of Calgary and some creative restaurateurs has transformed the rough-hewn concrete bunker into a stylishly rustic ninety-seat eatery.

The River Café has, hands down, Calgary's prettiest location. Huge, and at times fluffy, cottonwood poplars frame the view over the water, and geese and squirrels wander by on the green grounds of the park. With its fishing-lodge look and creative regional Canadian cuisine, this is one of the busiest restaurants in the city. It is very difficult to get last-minute reservations.

The food is adventurous without being pretentious, confident without being complacent. And outstandingly Canadian. Pasta and rice have been eliminated from the menu in favour of items like oat groat risotto and Great Northern white bean cassoulet. Buffalo hump is slow roasted and teamed with local barley in a rustic soup. And Alberta wild boar is served as scaloppine while halibut is crusted with fresh horseradish. If anyone wants to learn about Canadian cuisine, the River Café is the place to take them.

The house-cured salmon with wild boar bacon-wrapped shrimp and striped beets is a symphony of flavours, a crunchy blend of textures. And a spinach and pear salad with spiced pecans and goat cheese is delicate and tangy. I've had some pretty wonderful desserts here too, from a rich bread pudding to a dense lemon-curd and white-chocolate napoleon.

But these dishes do not come cheap. Salads are $7 to $10, with other appetizers in the $7 to $13 range. The buffalo pot-au-feu with the oat groat risotto is $17, and the horseradish halibut is $26. Beef tenderloin with potato cakes, a Leoni Parmesan butter, and a chanterelle sauce tops the list at $36.

The River Café has achieved a cuisine that is a tribute to its surroundings and worth these prices. I think they have become one of Calgary's very best restaurants.

www.river-cafe.com

Rococo

International

DOWN town
That's the Spot

125 Stephen Avenue Walk SW
Phone: 233·2265
Monday – Friday 11:30 am – last guest, Saturday 5:30 pm – last guest
Reservations recommended — Fully licensed — Patio — Non-smoking section
V, MC, AE, DC, Debit — $$ – $$$

THE old Bank of Nova Scotia building on Stephen Avenue Walk has adopted the florid rococo tones of eighteenth century Europe in an elaborate renovation. The large central room is bathed in natural light under a huge and original skylight. Marble floors are dotted with black-linened tables and oversized chairs. Plush burgundy-velvet banquettes jut into the room, creating quieter areas, and a huge Titanic-style staircase sweeps up one side to a mezzanine level. The room is immense to the point of creating intimacy with its shear size. It actually works. And aptly, it is named Rococo.

From a food perspective, Rococo is fairly understated. At lunch the menu is an appropriate collection of salads, pizzas, pastas, and sandwiches, with a few entrees like chili-roasted chicken and veal scaloppine with a Madeira reduction. The dinner menu is more upscale, with the priciest dishes being a $28 potato-crusted sea bass and a $37 ten-ounce tenderloin.

And the food is quite good. The only soup on the lunch menu is a blend of chickpeas, chard, and lima beans. If I were to name my 100 favourite ingredients, chickpeas, chard, and lima beans would be in the last ten. But this soup is rich with tomatoey flavours, and I find that lima beans taste much better these days than when I was eight.

The entrees contain similarly fine flavours. A lamb calzone special was filled with melted cheese and chunks of lamb, all folded into a good crust. The pizza with chicken, chorizo, and shiitake mushrooms was covered with tasty toppings and a great tomato sauce. It seemed odd to be eating with my hands in a place where the staff wear tuxedos, but it also felt pleasantly decadent.

The desserts, however, I ate with cutlery. A peach tart with crème anglaise was the only dish that I felt focused too much on look. The crème anglaise, swirled with a couple of other fruit sauces, was lost in the mix, though the tart itself was very good.

If Rococo has a difficulty, it is that the space can be intimidating—there is a sense that we should dress up. Though it is not a requirement, Rococo does present an elegant alternative if you want. Sometimes it's nice to spiff up.

Rose Garden
Thai

207 Stephen Avenue Walk SW
Phone: 263·1900
Monday – Saturday 11 am – 10 pm, Sunday 5 pm – 10 pm (closed Sundays in winter)
Reservations recommended — Fully Licensed — Patio — Non-smoking section
V, MC, AE, Debit — $ – $$

A lot of high-toned and flashy restaurants have opened on Stephen Avenue over the past few years. And many of them have great food and wonderful ambience. But in the middle of all the splashy places is an unassuming Thai restaurant that is packed every weekday for lunch. The Rose Garden offers a full lunch and dinner menu, but also sets out a great midday buffet of red curry beef, Thai barbecued chicken, and spring rolls that often has the restaurant full before noon. This is one of downtown's favourite hangouts, a place to meet friends and a place for good Thai food.

The lunch buffet is $11, a bargain compared to many of the neighbourhood menus. It's especially a good deal when you look at the quality of the food you are getting for your dollar. The buffet is constantly tended. Bowls of scorching hot calamari are delivered as quickly as they are devoured.

And devoured they are. Many fans of the Rose Garden are—to be charitable—hearty eaters. Big guys from oil companies tuck in and make numerous trips to the buffet. But many lighter eaters are here too, going more for the freshness of the food. Some dishes are deep-fried, but many are stir-fried and come across as quite light in a world of greasy buffets.

I've never found skimping on the quality. The tom yum goong soup is well structured and packed with shrimp and mushrooms. The cuts of meat used in the red curry beef and the ginger chicken are always good—you don't have to pick through bones and gristle here. And there is more than just broccoli and green peppers in the various vegetable dishes.

While customers are pillaging the buffet, Rose Garden staff swoop down on the tables, tidying them and bringing fresh water and napkins. It is unobtrusive, professional service that is always done with a smile.

The quality and care flow into the look and tone of the room. In spite of being a hectic lunch buffet place, it comes across as calm, even serene. Tables are spaced as well as possible in the long, narrow room, allowing almost everyone a certain amount of privacy. The decor is mildly Asian, and the room always strikes me as well maintained.

So the Rose Garden is not big and loud, and it's easy to miss with all the other distractions of Stephen Avenue. I think that's just the way its many fans want it.

Saigon
Vietnamese

1221 – 12 Avenue SW
Phone: 228·4200
Monday – Thursday 11 am – 10 pm, Friday & Saturday 11 am – 11 pm
Reservations recommended — Fully licensed — Non-smoking section
V, MC, AE, DC — $ – $$

WE have a ton of good Vietnamese eateries in Calgary. But few capture the nuances of the French influence on this cuisine as well as the Saigon.

It is an angular room filled with glass-topped tables. A small area around the back provides good separation for smokers, and north-facing windows offer a scenic view of 12th Avenue traffic. The Saigon will never win any awards for design, but it is clean, comfortable, and simple.

Which fits perfectly with the food. There is a huge list of dishes—170 in all—from the cha gio to the tamarind sautéed chicken, with great variety in between. Vietnamese cuisine is meant for sharing, unless you are indulging in what the Saigon calls "a meal in a soup," which we do frequently. This is a huge bowl of noodle soup filled with meats, fresh herbs, onions, sprouts, and lime and usually consumed as a quick lunch.

But it is worth going in a group to sample the amazing range of flavours. We never have a meal here without cha gio. (Catherine is often happy with just a couple of orders of them.) Rice paper is rolled around ground pork or chicken, shredded carrots, spices, egg, and vermicelli and is then deep-fried. You wrap these rolls in lettuce and mint at the table and dip into a fish-sauce vinaigrette. There are so many flavours and textures in this one dish. Also as a starter, the Saigon's salad rolls are unbeatable. Greens, sliced shrimp, and vermicelli arrive at the table wrapped in soft rice paper and you then dip in a savoury hoisin. They're marvelous.

Of the many main dishes, the satay sautéed shrimp and the la lot beef remain among my favourites. The shrimp are done to crunchiness in a peanut-chili sauce with slices of onion. The la lot beef is an unusual dish of meatballs wrapped in fragrant la lot leaves and charbroiled. The lemon grass chicken is always good, and then there is the caramel sautéed shrimp or the barbecued pork chop on rice. Excellent.

The most expensive single dishes hit $12.75, and the Vietnamese fondues or Genghis Khan grills are in the low $20s. Five cha gio cost $3.75, the la lot beef is $9.75, and the lemon grass chicken is still $8.75.

The Saigon is a family-run operation where there is a great deal of skill in the kitchen and friendliness out front. And the food offers you some of the best quality for your dollar in the city.

Saigon Y2K

Vietnamese

310 Centre Street S
Phone: 265·3035
Sunday, Monday, Wednesday & Thursday 11 am – 8 pm, Tuesday 11 am – 3 pm
Friday & Saturday 11 am – 10 pm
Reservations recommended — Fully licensed — Non-smoking section
V, MC, AE, DC — $

REMEMBER Y2K? What ever happened to that overblown scare? I haven't heard the much-used abbreviation for a long time now. But one cafe that has kept the memory alive is Saigon Y2K in Chinatown. A bright yellow and blue sign protruding onto Centre Street announces it boldly.

Inside, Y2K is a large square room seating about fifty at tables and booths. It is fairly nondescript aside from a few decorations. There are a couple of bright red neon signs, overhead fluorescents muted by red and blue coverings, and a really cool waterfall picture that moves gently, creating a visually soothing presence.

Service at Y2K is pleasant and speedy in the Vietnamese noodle-shop mold. If you want a quick meal, an eatery like this is the place. There isn't a lot of lingering—in and out in twenty minutes is quite doable.

Not that we were in a rush. My guest and I indulged in a plate of prawn and pork salad rolls—four of them for $5.25. I suspect they were made to order because they took more than the usual thirty seconds to be delivered. Excellent prawns. A little heavy on the noodles, but otherwise fresh, tight, and tasty.

Then we had a couple of bowls of bún, the ubiquitous noodle dish topped with greens, your selection of cooked meats, and nuoc mam, the Vietnamese fish sauce. My guest tried one with shredded pork and grilled pork, and I had one with the same meats plus some spring rolls. I guess you could say we pigged out.

Both bowls were in the $6.50 range—very good value. The basic bún were quite good with well-cooked, still-firm noodles, crunchy greens, and decent fish sauce. And the grilled pork was tasty. But both the shredded pork and the spring rolls were dry and not easily reconstituted with more sauce. Still, it was quick and cheap.

Saigon Y2K has over 100 other dishes on the menu, most of which are noodle or rice based. There are some fried noodles, some vegetarian dishes, and some specialties like prawn and crab-paste soup and sweet and sour prawn soup.

I think Saigon Y2K is an OK place for a quick lunch. The food is fresh and nicely prepared, and even if the Y2K computer scare itself was a bust, this cafe should have greater staying power.

St. James's Gate
Irish Pub

207 Wolf Street, Banff
Phone: 762•9355
Daily 11 am – 2 am
Reservations accepted seasonally — Fully licensed — No non-smoking section
V, MC, AE, DC, Debit — $$

THE Irish pub craze has hit Banff in the form of St. James's Gate. Seating 210, the Gate is filled with the cozy nooks and snugs that make Irish pubs popular. It is done in dark wood and Guinness memorabilia, and there is little natural light beyond the first bank of street-side tables. It's the kind of pub that could be in Calgary or Cleveland or County Cork.

St. James's Gate is the name of the ancient entrance to the suburbs of Dublin, and since 1772, it has been home to the Guinness brewery. Choosing this history-laden name is a major responsibility for the pub, and they have taken efforts to achieve their official Guinness certification.

The Gate provides a place for those of us with sensitive eardrums to relax over a draft and some good food without having to change out of our hiking boots or take out a second mortgage. It is comfortable enough for the après-ski crowd and presentable enough for suited conference-goers. In between, there is the multitude of Guinness fans.

The menu is typical pub fare of shepherd's pie, Irish stew, and fish and chips. But they upscale it with chili-glazed salmon, stuffed pork chops, and braised lamb shanks. We had a spinach salad and a steak and Guinness pie along with two cups of a corn and chicken chowder. The soup was excellent, filled with tender chunks of chicken and kernels of corn and prepared as a thickened broth with fragrant herbs. And it was an appropriate preamble to the steak and Guinness pie. This one had a nice crust—a little flaky, a little gooey—and a meaty filling with abundant gravy, mushrooms, and chunks of steak. Overall, a very fine meat pie. The spinach salad came in an orange-sesame vinaigrette with slices of orange-teriyaki chicken and canned mandarins (I hadn't seen those since the '70s). This salad has since disappeared from the menu. Perhaps it has gone back to the decade from whence it came.

Two cautions. First, emerging from the Gate on a sunny day can be damaging to the eyesight with the sudden transition from dark to light. Second, while squinting your way out the door, you may not notice the step that drops you down to the sidewalk. It can be very abrupt.

Regardless, if you too are trying to find a comfy spot in Banff for a beer and a plate of liver and onions, this is the place.

Sakana Grill

Japanese

116 – 2 Avenue SW (Harmonious Centre)
Phone: 290 • 1118
Daily 11 am – 2 pm, 5 pm – 11 pm
Reservations recommended — Fully licensed — Non-smoking section
V, MC, AE, DC, Debit — $$

THE SAKANA GRILL is a charming oasis amidst the bustle of downtown. Entering the restaurant, you cross a small bridge over a pond. A large open area features three teppan grills where meals are cooked to order. Along one wall, there is a row of tatami rooms with movable walls, and along the other, there is a row of booths. Towards the back is perhaps the most interesting feature, what they call the Water Floating Sushi Bar. This is a large, oval-shaped bar surrounded by a moat. An armada of lacquered sushi boats circles in the trough, pushed along by water jets.

On top of the boats are individual servings of sushi; if you see something that you like, you just pluck it off. Pricing is fairly simple: the sushi comes on plates of five different colours, and each colour indicates a price—anywhere from $1.70 for a light-coloured plate with a floral motif to $3.90 for a black plate. It may be just a gimmick, but it is a good one. Be forewarned though. Those little plates can pile up in an expensive hurry.

The sushi is of pretty good quality. The cuts are not huge and the variety is not the most extensive, but they taste fresh and clean. And the price is really not bad. Ordering off the menu, the medium sushi combo with five pieces of nigiri and six tekka rolls costs $9.50.

The Sakana is an entertaining place to lunch. The teppan cooks do the toss-the-knife-in-the-air-and-bang-the-salt-and-pepper-shakers-together thing. They cook the fresh meats and seafoods that customers have selected from a buffet, plus they add in some vegetables and sauces. It's like a Mr. Edo with entertainment. This style of Japanese cuisine is great for groups and a good introduction to the food for newcomers and kids. (If it is a special occasion, the chefs will have you dressed in plastic wigs and kimonos, singing Japanese songs.)

Also available at the Sakana Grill is a wide range of other Japanese dishes, from yakitori and kushiage (two different styles of skewered meats) to tempura vegetables, teriyaki chicken, and shabu shabu fondue. So it is a full-service Japanese restaurant.

The Sakana is a good location for a midday getaway—it's the kind of place that downtowners can walk to for lunch, eat an enjoyable meal, and walk back to the office, all in about an hour. But its popularity has made it a busy noon hour choice, so make sure to phone ahead.

Sandro
Italian & Pizza

431 – 41 Avenue NE
Phone: 230•7754
Monday – Friday 11:30 am – 2 pm, 5 pm – 10 pm, Saturday 5 pm – 10 pm
Reservations recommended — Fully licensed — Non-smoking section
V, MC, AE — $$

I'M old enough to remember when pizza was an exotic treat found only in small Italian cafes and hole-in-the-wall pizza joints. Then the fast-food chains got involved and pizza became one of the basic quick-meal options. When foodies came along with Gorgonzola, pine nuts, and pears on their pizzas, we forgot about the little Italian cafes with their basic traditional pizzas. Places like Sandro Pizzeria.

Sandro is on the second floor of a nondescript building above Calgary Lock & Safe and has an unbeatable view of the Greenview Industrial Park from its perch over Edmonton Trail. It has never been an upscale Italian restaurant. The room is basic and clean, though low ceilings tend to spread cigarette smoke through the room. There is a bar in one corner, green and white tablecloths top the closely packed tables, and a generally lively, pleasant feeling abounds.

Well-groomed waiters in vests and starched white shirts show you to your seats. They take their jobs seriously, in a casual Italian way, and they are good. The clientele is an eclectic bunch that ranges from high school students to business-suited regulars to couples wearing Harley-Davidson togs. All enjoying the food.

Sandro's menu includes a reasonable list of pastas, veals, and seafood. We've tried their Caesar salad and the lemon shrimp appetizer on past visits and found both to be good. Not stellar, but decent, benefiting from extra squirts with a lemon slice.

But pizza appears to be the top seller, and with good reason. The crust is perfect— crisp, not too thick, not too thin. The last pizza we had here, a simple fourteen-inch combo of mushrooms and pancetta, was a classic. The pancetta was thinly sliced and covered the pizza, the sauce provided a tangy balance, and the light coating of cheese highlighted the taste without drowning it. The Sandro Special with capicollo, mushrooms, olives, peppers, and prosciutto is a pizza that exceeds the sum of its parts. The prosciutto is thinly sliced and placed on top of the hot pie after it comes out of the oven. Smart.

Depending on the type of pizza ordered, the crust may go a bit soggy after a few minutes—the metal pizza plates used for serving sometimes subject them to the misfortune of a little steam. Just remember to order dryer ingredients or eat faster if you want to enjoy the crispness.

Santorini Taverna

Greek

1502 Centre Street N
Phone: 276·8363
Tuesday – Thursday 11 am – 10:30 pm, Friday 11 am – 11:30 pm
Saturday noon – 11:30 pm, Sunday 4 pm – 9:30 pm
Reservations recommended — Fully licensed — Patio — Non-smoking section
V, MC, AE, DC, Debit — $$

EVEN when Santorini first opened its doors, it looked ancient. The wood floors, white plaster walls, and ceramic tiles all appeared as though they had washed ashore from the Aegean Sea. Now, fifteen years later, Santorini feels as comfortable as a plate of moussaka, as relaxed as a Greek fisherman's cap. Partly, it's the requisite Greek restaurant look—white walls trimmed with azure and adorned with pictures of the Greek isles. Partly, it's the smell of suckling pig and flaming cheese, and partly it's the warmth of the owners and staff.

There are no huge surprises on the menu. The usual keftethes (meatballs), horiatiki (Greek salad), and souvlakia (kebabs) are all there, lined up with broiled swordfish, prawns with feta, and quails in red wine sauce. There are various combination platters, or you can dine as the Greeks do—on a dinner of mezethes, an array of appetizers. There's also marinated octopus, spanakopita (spinach pie), and dolmathes (stuffed vine leaves), plus artichoke hearts, soup of chicken broth and lemon, and terrific pastichio, a layered pasta and beef dish.

And then there's the ultimate house specialty—the arni kleftiko, or roast lamb. Why can't we make lamb like this at home? Take a decent cut, roast it with a few herbs in a covered pan, sprinkle with a little lemon, and serve with equally simple and delicious potatoes. Nothing to it. Hmmm. Oh well, just another reason to go back to Santorini.

Few places achieve the consistency that Santorini has over the years. They never waver in quality, and their prices remain moderate. (The top price is about $20 for the rack of lamb.) That's thanks to owners Andreas and Maria Nicolaides and their commitment to service and quality. Originally from the Greek side of Cyprus, they bring their personal warmth and generations of Greek hospitality to their work. Maria oversees the service staff, while Andreas supervises the kitchen. And in the tradition of Mediterranean restaurateurs, their kids take reservations, serve food, and help out in the kitchen. Their presence furthers the feeling that you're at a big family dinner as well as a professional restaurant.

Santorini is a treat. On a cool winter night, it's possible to think, if only for a few hours, that you're in an old Greek seaside cafe overlooking the water instead of Calgary's Centre Street. And afterwards, when you're standing in the parking lot with snowflakes drifting down, it can seem just a little bit warmer than it did before.

Savoir Fare

French-California

907 – 17 Avenue SW
Phone: 245·6040
Monday – Saturday 11 am – 2 pm, 5 pm – last guest
Reservations recommended — Fully licensed — Non-smoking
V, MC, AE, DC, Debit — $$$

S AVOIR FARE was the brainchild of three talented Calgarians—Octavia Malinowski, Peter Fraiberg, and Grayson Sherman. They built one of the premier catering organizations in the city and still had time to establish one of the most creative cafes of the '90s. But all things pass and eventually the trio moved on to other ventures, leaving Savoir Fare's catering operation and restaurant in the capable hands of Mark and Karen Massicotte. The new owners are no slouches themselves, having years of experience in the food and event planning industries.

At the time of the sale, Savoir Fare had just received a make-over. What was originally termed a 21st Century Diner had become a more upscale dinner club with table linens and a couple of banquettes. It's still a small space that seats just over thirty, but it is now a soft, demure enclosure, subdued somewhat from its brasher early days.

This maturity is reflected in the dinner menu with seared sea bass in a rice wine-butter sauce and grilled lobster with artichoke orzo, both for $28. And with the tiger shrimp dumplings and the grilled ostrich medallion, at $10 for each appetizer. They have placed their prices alongside the big players in the Calgary market. Even the wine list starts at $35 for a bottle of Tuscan red and ramps up quickly.

For the most part, the food justifies the price tag. A roast duck breast and leg on whipped brie potatoes with a blueberry compote ($26) is delicately complex, an of-the-moment look at duck and fruit. Underlying spices bring in the flavours of Asia, giving it an almost Peking duck tone. And the roasted chicken on apple-infused rice in a garlic, thyme, and double-smoked bacon sauce ($22) is robustly delicate, an expert balance of flavours.

Now, although dinner is up there in the price category, they do tone things down at lunch. They have kept a meat loaf on the menu for $10 (meat loaf was one of the previous owners' most popular dishes). There are also sandwiches of grilled portabellos and peppers at $9, blackened salmon at $11, and beef tenderloin tips at $13.

And whatever the meal, there is the Savoir Fare dessert menu. They are not quite as spectacular as before, but the list includes some nice chocolate offerings and good cheese and port pairings.

There's no doubt that Savoir Fare has changed, but it continues to be a fine restaurant—it's just not a 21st Century Diner anymore.

Savoury

Contemporary

322 – 11 Avenue SW
Phone: 205·4002
Monday – Friday 7:30 am – 4 pm
Reservations accepted — Beer & wine only — Non-smoking
V, MC, AE, DC, Debit — $

S AVOURY seats about twenty in an almost overdone brown and black decor inside the Vintage Building. One wall is brick, another is painted yellow, two others are covered in murals. Racks of jarred olives and tomato sauces snuggle against support pillars, and the floor is covered in a large checkerboard pattern. One end of the room is consumed by a couple of coolers and coffee and panini makers. There is nearly too much going on for such a small space.

There is a variety of panini, the Italian sandwiches on focaccia, plus some salads, cookies, muffins, a hot special of the day, and a soup. Fairly straightforward, but Savoury has an experienced chef running the show so the food is of high quality. Judy Wood worked with Sunterra Market for a long time and brought her skills here to her own cafe a few years ago.

On the floor below the eatery, a large kitchen produces the cafe food as well as that for their booming catering business. The cafe was really more of an afterthought to the catering, but it became instantly popular. The menu presents a taste of the catering breadth by offering a constantly changing selection from a lengthy list.

Back to the panini. My barbecued chicken version was filled with asparagus, roma tomatoes, aged cheddar, and an apple and sun-dried tomato barbecue sauce. That day, there was also a hot capicollo one with artichoke hearts and a roast turkey with pesto. At $4.75 each, these panini are not a bad deal.

Also on the positive side was the daily soup of cream of asparagus. It was thick and creamy, filled with asparagus, and a good deal at $3.25 for a big bowl.

All the cooking is impressive at Savoury, but it's the pastries that really take it over the top. Good old Prairie-based squares and cakes and cookies that are way better than any I ever had at a community hall or church event of my youth. The butter tarts are the pure definition of what they should be: flaky crusts, neither too thick nor too thin, filled with a buttery, sugary, almost frothy filling, with either raisins or toasted pecans suspended in the mix, the tops almost a brown sugar crust. Outstanding.

I like the quality of everything at Savoury, including the staff. It's uptown and down-home at the same time and in a good way.

www.savourycatering.com

Silver Dragon

Chinese (Cantonese)

106 – 3 Avenue SE
Phone: 264·5326
Monday – Friday 10 am – 11:30 pm
Saturday 10 am – 1:30 am, Sunday 9:30 am – 9:30 pm
Reservations recommended — Fully licensed — Non-smoking section
V, MC, AE, DC, Debit — $$

WAITING in line at the Silver Dragon, I was reminded of my first visits to this Chinatown classic almost thirty years ago. My roommate and I would come down here for dim sum, the Silver Dragon being only one of two restaurants serving it at that time. And back then, it was only on Sundays. The place was mostly red, and there were few other Occidental faces in the crowd. We enjoyed the experience and brought many people here over the next few years. In spite of dim sum's growing popularity, we never made a reservation, lining up only occasionally.

So when we dropped in on a recent Sunday evening, I didn't even think to reserve ahead. Wrong. We were added to a long list with an unlikely estimate of twenty minutes. So we waited and watched the goldfish swimming in the tank by the door.

The Silver Dragon looks different these days. The room still has a distinctive L-shape, and there's still a long staircase leading up to it, but they have redone the interior with natural wood, adding skylights and gold trim. It appears successful, a far cry from the utilitarian fluorescents and worn carpet of the early '70s.

But many long-lived restaurants survive on reputation rather than on current product, so I was interested to see how the Silver Dragon would fare. We were seated after only fifteen minutes and presented with the menu, a collection of 235 mostly Cantonese dishes. The prices have gone up a bit over the years, and they include a few non-Cantonese dishes, but most looked surprisingly familiar.

We ordered some grilled dumplings ($7.50), prawns in black-bean sauce ($15), spicy palace-style chicken ($9.75), and stir-fried vegetables ($8). And we were impressed. The dumplings were perhaps the best we've ever had, fat and flavourful, with a tasty pastry and two dipping sauces. The prawn dish featured at least a dozen and a half huge prawns, perfectly cooked, and the chicken was crunchy and crisp. (But spicy? Well, it was actually pretty mild.) Even the vegetables were excellent, a combo of baby corn, pea pods, bok choy, broccoli, and mushrooms.

All the flavours were gentle but sincere, allowing the natural taste of the ingredients to come through. On top of that, service was pleasant, brisk, and professional. Once seated, we were fully fed and on our way in about forty-five minutes.

Which made the next folks in line very happy.

Silver Inn

Chinese (Beijing/Peking)

2702 Centre Street N
Phone: 276·6711
Tuesday – Friday 11 am – 2 pm, Tuesday – Sunday 5 pm – 10:30 pm
Reservations recommended — Fully licensed — Non-smoking section
V, MC, AE, Debit — *$$*

W HEN I first started reviewing restaurants for CBC Radio in 1980, I began with some of my then-current favourites. Like the Silver Inn, at the time one of the most innovative and creative places in the city. I had been going to the Inn since it opened on 4th Street in 1974, and I had always loved it.

By the time I reviewed the Inn, it had moved to Centre Street. Which was probably good, because their original location was a dive. The building was rundown, the dishes were chipped and cracked, and the potholes in the lino were so big you could lose your chair in one. They have remained on Centre Street ever since—that's astounding stability.

Louise Chan established the Silver Inn, and her sister Alice opened the original Home Food Inn in 1978. Alice and her husband K.K. have had a number of restaurants over the years and have recently moved to White Rock. Louise has moved into the greenhouse business, and brother Kwong now runs the Inn. Of greater culinary importance is that this family popularized ginger beef, making Calgary the undenied capital of this Asian-Canadian delicacy.

In the '70s, the Silver Inn's grilled dumplings, chicken and cashews in yellow bean sauce, and prawns in garlic sauce were really adventurous for those whose most exotic dining experience had been chicken chow mein. So a good beef dish was an important draw for the Silver Inn. Their ginger beef, also known as chili beef, was one dish that was guaranteed to please everyone. It became a top seller and remains so to this day.

It is still a good, nicely balanced version. As is the ginger chicken. They are slightly chewy dishes with crisp coatings and glossy, sweet sauces that carry hints of ginger and chilies. The Silver Inn has always made a sweeter cuisine than many other Peking restaurants, and their ginger dishes are less strongly flavoured than those of the other places. They follow a middle-of-the-road style of seasoning, but the ingredients are high quality and there is nothing substandard in the preparation.

The Silver Inn remains a classic. They were among the first to sell hot and sour soup, chicken and cashews, and stuffed onion pancakes, and these dishes remain almost exactly as I remember them from the mid-'70s. They may not serve the most intense and exciting Chinese food in the city, but it is a comfort to still have them around.

Sino

Vietnamese Fusion

513 – 8 Avenue SW (Penny Lane)
Phone: 503·0474
Monday – Wednesday 11 am – 6 pm, Thursday – Saturday 11 am – 9 pm
Reservations recommended — Fully licensed — Non-smoking
V, MC, AE, Debit — $$

MOST restaurateurs can tell horror stories about things that went wrong during the first convulsive days of their food outlets. But few opening sagas are as chaotic as that of Sino, a new Vietnamese Fusion restaurant. Ken Nguyen, the chef-owner at Sino, is a charming, calm fellow who has amazing talent in both culinary and floral arts. (His food at Indochine was always superb, and his flower arrangements at his two Itinerant flower shops—Mount Royal Village and North Hill Shopping Centre—are stunning.) His new Sino is a tasty melding of these two passions—now that it's open.

Let's get to that story. Nguyen tried to open Sino for months. Construction shortages (his job was too small to interest many contractors) and inspection delays (inspectors are hugely busy too) left him weeks behind his projected opening. But he had booked a group that was unable to move their date. (It was my U of C Food & Culture program, so I'm taking responsibility for this.) The day before the event, everything was ready except for the final natural gas hookup. Nguyen left his restaurant that evening knowing that he had to meet the gas technician the next morning and then he would be set.

Unfortunately, the area around the gas hookup outside Penny Lane became a crime scene overnight. So the area was closed off with yellow police tape for the entire "opening" day, and the gas technician was unable to access the pipes.

Many other restaurateurs would have thrown up their hands and said, "Sorry, can't do it tonight." (And who would blame them?) But instead, Nguyen went out and bought a bunch of electric fry pans and deep fryers to cook a meal for my class of thirty-four. His staff did yeoman work. Sure there were a few technical glitches— no change for the bar, no credit card machine, even the brûlée blowtorch wouldn't work—but my class enjoyed the experience immensely.

And the meal? Simply a fabulous fusion of Vietnamese, Thai, French, and Contemporary food ideas. Prawns rolled in pepper and cloves, chicken lacquered with tamarind sauce, salmon deep-fried in rice paper and dipped in chili-lime vinaigrette, rice intensified with both shaved coconut and coconut milk. All served beautifully in a bronze and green bistro setting on plates accented with fresh orchids.

Sino is one of the hottest eateries on the market, with dishes that push well beyond the Vietnamese noodle-house style. Perhaps the struggles in birthing this restaurant helped create something truly exceptional.

Spolumbo's
Deli & Sausage Makers

1308 – 9 Avenue SE
Phone: 264·6452
Monday – Saturday 8 am – 5:30 pm
Reservations accepted for private room only — Beer & wine only — Non-smoking
V, MC, Debit — $

A few years ago, a group of retired football players got together and, with some family recipes and a sausage machine, opened Spolumbo's Deli. Before long, the meatball sandwiches became so popular they had to move into a big new building.

Mike Palumbo and the Spoletini brothers, Tom and Tony, are large, good-natured guys with a real eye for quality meat and a knack for strong lateral movement—I was always amazed at how they could move so gracefully in the confined quarters of their old location. All those years with the Stamps have come in handy.

They moved everything over from the original deli, including the chalkboard menu. They upgraded the coolers that showcase the meats for sale, installed an ice tub for self-serve drinks, and built a new sausage plant in the back. The eating area has a sparse, funky character with high ceilings and tables lined up in rows. It is totally non-smoking and filled with the bustle of people.

Spolumbo's is as good a sausage as I have had. I like the freshness, the comparatively low fat content for a sausage, and the absence of a chemical taste. The chicken with apple and the turkey with roasted peppers are particularly tasty. They make about sixteen kinds of sausage, the most popular of which is still the original spicy Italian.

Eating at Spolumbo's is not a grand, elegant experience, but rather a roll-up-your-sleeves-and-chow-down event. Construction workers, guys with ties tossed over their shoulders, and moms with strollers are all packed in and enjoying lunch. It is not quiet, and surprisingly, the lineups are just as long as at the old place. Even though it seats ninety as opposed to the old twenty-something, it is packed. But the line moves quickly, and the wait is usually under ten minutes.

The food is not delicate either. Big sausage or cold cut sandwiches are packed with flavour and dripping with sauce. The meat loaf sandwich is a serious, messy feed. These are usually six-napkin meals. Spolumbo's breads are OK too. They hold together well and provide a neutral backdrop for the meats. There are also a few good side dishes like a rich and creamy clam chowder, but they still don't serve dessert.

Regardless, it's the kind of food that will squelch any lineman's appetite and satisfy the most discerning sausage aficionado. And I'm not just saying that because any one of these guys could snap me like a twig.

www.spolumbos.com

Stranger's
Caribbean

2650–36 Street SE
Phone: 248·4012
Monday–Thursday 10 am–8:30 pm, Friday 10 am–10 pm
Saturday 9 am–10 pm, Sunday 9 am–6 pm
Reservations accepted — Fully licensed — Non-smoking
V — $

WE don't have a lot of restaurants in Dover. And we don't have a lot of Island food around town either. I have long been waiting for someone to do a more elaborate Caribbean cafe, at least since Jennifer's disappeared a number of years ago.

But Stranger's is coming closer than anyone else of late and is drawing fans to the east side of Deerfoot with some tasty food. It's still not anything fancy, but there are tablecloths and there is a pleasant comfort level in the bright orange and green room.

Stranger's offers the popular Island dishes of vegetable or curry beef rotis, brown stew fish, and jerk chicken, all served in large platefuls for under $10. I tried a combo of jerk chicken and brown stew chicken with rice and peas for $8.50.

And it was pretty good. Especially the brown chicken. It had a rich, mild flavour with none of the typical jerk burn. The jerk itself was pretty low on the spice-meter—they've kept it fairly mild, but have a potent hot sauce you can add for more zip. Both chicken dishes, however, showed the shortcomings of Caribbean cuisine. The chicken was not trimmed of excess fat and gristle and was chopped into small chunks, leaving bony bits. This necessitated careful chewing. And my jerk chicken was overcooked to dryness. But the rice and peas were as good as I've ever had, and a mango mousse was a great dessert—lightly tangy, not too heavy, though not terribly pretty (it looked like gelled pea soup).

They also do a weekend breakfast featuring that Island delicacy of salt cod and ackee fruit. Ackee, also known as vegetable brain, is an odd fruit that cooks up to look and taste like scrambled eggs. The mix of flaked salt cod and chunks of ackee has to be experienced to be appreciated—it is definitely an acquired taste.

All the food goes best with a drink from the Caribbean. Stranger's carries a full line of Carib beer, Ting, and a choice of ginger beers from either Jamaica or Trinidad. Ginger beer is a robust way of washing down the taste of salt cod and ackee.

I enjoy the service here—just about as friendly and laid-back as the Islands themselves. Don't expect speed at Stranger's, but do expect big smiles and a warm room. You won't be a stranger for long.

Sultan's Tent

Moroccan

909 – 17 Avenue SW
Phone: 244·2333
Monday – Thursday 5:30 pm – 10:30 pm, Friday & Saturday 5 pm – 11 pm
Reservations recommended — Fully licensed — Non-smoking
V, MC, AE, DC — $$

THE SULTAN'S TENT is the oldest of the two Moroccan restaurants in town, having served tasty North African tajines and couscous for over twelve years. The room is draped in tapestries and filled with the brass tables, wooden antiques, and leather hassocks of Morocco. With low, cushioned seating and an appropriate soundtrack, the Sultan's Tent provides an immediate cultural transition from the hubbub of Calgary to the dusty back streets of Casablanca.

The best way to enjoy the Sultan's Tent is to let the culture envelop you. Sink into the cushions, relax, wash your hands with rose water poured from an ornate silver urn, enjoy the leisurely pace of Moroccan dining. Don't plan any other activities; this is not a quick-bite-and-off-to-the-theatre place.

The food of the Sultan's Tent follows the desert history of the native Berber tribes and the visiting Arab traders. The stewy tajines combine chunks of lamb or chicken or spicy sausages with dried fruits and honey or preserved lemons and olives or prunes and almonds. The results are dishes of intense flavours, the tartness of lemons rolling against the richness of lamb, softened by North African spices.

In some dishes, like the harira soup, a little heat is introduced courtesy of the food cultures south of Morocco. Overall, Moroccan food is not particularly spicy, but watch out for the harissa sauce, a blend of peppers that will water many an eye. Most dishes remain in a savoury, meaty range, piqued by fruits.

On the lighter side of the Sultan's Tent is a selection of salads that always tantalizes our taste buds. The marinated carrots and beets are spritely tart, the delicate pickling enhanced with overtones of mint. The broiled peppers and tomatoes with cumin and cilantro in the felfla salad open up our appetites, making us yearn for the main courses.

Couscous dishes are a favourite at the Sultan's Tent. These feature the semolina-based pellets of couscous topped with more stewy concoctions of lamb sausages or vegetables or prawns or chicken.

Service is pleasantly understated in a desert-tent style. As the evening rolls along, the pacing of the meal helps remove the stresses of the day and we sink even lower into the cushions. After a few hours, we just don't want to return to the city. The Sultan's Tent feeds our bodies, delights our palates, and teases our desire to travel. We always leave with the feeling of being pampered like a sultan and fed like a king.

Sumo

Japanese

200 Barclay Parade SW (Eau Claire Market)
Phone: 290·1433
Sunday – Wednesday 11 am – 11 pm, Thursday 11 am – midnight
Friday & Saturday 11 am – 1 am
Reservations recommended — Fully licensed — Patio — Non-smoking section
V, MC, AE — $$

It seems that sushi is only partly about the food itself and a lot about the show. In some places it's trains, in others it's boats, and now Sumo has weighed in with the biggest fleet in the city. Sumo has twenty metal boats plying a large moat, delivering fresh sushi to customers clustered around the bar.

Sumo is owned by the same folks who originally built Sushi Ginza, and it shows a similar sense of style. But it has been created more for the downtown office crowd than for the suburban dwellers of the south. While the Ginza in Willow Park Village has a quiet and relaxing bamboo-and-waterfall theme, Sumo is quite over the top. Here they are competing with Joey Tomato's and Brewsters for that after-work crowd. So they have added a 100-seat patio and created a 140-seat restaurant with huge samurai swords piercing the ceiling and a big copper dragon dangling above the sushi bar. It's loud, lively, and fun.

One problem I have with Sumo is that the nigiri sushi comes without the telltale swab of wasabi, the green paste that goes between the fish and the rice. This little bite is essential to create the true flavour balance of nigiri sushi. The owner of Sumo feels that many of his customers are new to sushi and he doesn't want to scare them off. I think he is doing them and himself a disservice. Newcomers should learn the true style and then ask for the wasabi to be omitted if it bothers them. And serious sushi-izers won't take Sumo seriously.

Which is too bad, because the sushi is fundamentally good. The nigiri sushi deluxe is a nice plate of eight nigiri pieces and six inside-out tekka rolls. Not the cleanest cuts I've ever seen, but generally good quality ingredients. This package includes a decent tossed salad and a bland miso soup for $15.

Sumo offers more than sushi though. The menu includes a selection of appetizers, teriyaki and tempura dishes, soba noodles, and some other Asian choices like ginger beef and Thai-style vegetables with fried rice.

Sumo fits into the mid-range of good sushi bars and is one of the better eateries in Eau Claire. It stands to be popular with the sake happy-hour crowd, even if they do employ the Easy-Bake Oven style of sushi making.

Sushi Ginza

Japanese

10816 Macleod Trail S (Willow Park Village)
Phone: 271·9642
Monday – Wednesday 11:30 am – 10 pm, Thursday – Saturday 11:30 am – 11 pm
Sunday noon – 9:30 pm
Reservations recommended — Fully licensed — Non-smoking
V, MC, AE, Debit — $ – $$

I T is getting so that I don't have to go downtown anymore. Residents at the south end of the city are seeing the emergence of some interesting food establishments— bakeries, butcher shops, cafes—places of quality and free parking. Places like Sushi Ginza, a full-service Japanese restaurant in Willow Park Village.

The Ginza is arguably the prettiest Japanese restaurant in town with tatami rooms for shoeless dining, a floating sushi bar, and a little pond. Tables are well placed, and natural light flows into the front area.

The floating sushi bar is an oval-shaped metal moat with a fleet of small lacquered boats. The chefs stand inside the oval where they create the sushi and place it on little trays that then go onto the boats. Sushi fans sit on the outside of the oval and, as the trays go by, pluck off the ones that appeal to them. The sushi is priced by the tray: a flowered tray is $3; a tray with wavy blue lines is $2.50. Most trays carry two pieces of nigiri sushi or four or six pieces of sushi roll. It is quite easy, at least for me, to have those trays quickly add up to $20 or more.

They do pretty good sushi, the typical variety of tuna, salmon, scallop, and shrimp, with some California and rainbow rolls. There are also the hand-rolled cones and, like most Japanese places, their own signature cone—this one is tuna, salmon, shrimp, and smelt roe for $3.50. The sushi rice is well flavoured, and the cuts of fish are fairly clean and uniform. I have no real complaints with the quality, though they do omit the swab of wasabi on the nigiri sushi in an effort to appease the Western palate. It is available on request, but wasabi fans beware.

The Ginza also offers cooked Japanese food, such as yakitori chicken, tempura, various noodle dishes, and teriyaki salmon. Prices are reasonable with few plates pushing into the mid-teens. There are lunch combos in the $8 to $9 range that provide tempura or sushi or sashimi with salad and rice and a further choice like chicken kushiage or teriyaki steak—good value for what you get.

Service has become quite crisp over time and the sushi chefs are very friendly. And now that sushi has hit the south, there is one less reason to leave the neighbourhood. I like that.

Sushi Hiro

Japanese

727 – 5 Avenue SW
Phone: 233·0605
Monday – Friday 11:30 am – 2 pm, Monday – Saturday 5 pm – 10:30 pm
Reservations recommended — Fully licensed — Non-smoking section
V, MC, AE, DC — $$

SUSHI is all the rage these days. I don't think anyone actually cooks seafood anymore. And with this trend have come sushi trains and boats and sake bars and karaoke. But in all the smoke and mirrors, we sometimes lose sight of the classics, the older spots that served sushi long before it became so hot.

One of those is Sushi Hiro, a place hidden in the shadows of the Norcen Tower on 5th Avenue. It's been there for eons and remains popular with its loyal clientele. It is advisable to call ahead at lunch because it is always packed. Even the sushi bar is filled to capacity, and a battery of sushi chefs works diligently to keep up with the orders.

Customers keep coming back for the consistency and the quality. Things haven't changed a lot over the years. There are no trains or boats to deliver your sushi, and the decor has been the same pale green for decades. But that's OK. The sushi cuts are clean and thick, the rice is particularly tasty, and the rolls are plump and firm. They have put a lot of effort into the cones and rolls in recent years. There are scallop rolls, hotate rolls, negi hamachi cones, and even a Hiro cone. Issei Hiro, the owner and head sushi itamae, is very skilled and his talents come through in his work. He pays great attention to the quality of the sushi and it remains some of the best in the city.

I think one of the reasons it is among the best is that they do little else. They carry a short list of tempura, teriyaki, and a few specials such as tonkatsu and oyakodon—nothing too innovative. These items feel like they're there for those who get dragged along for lunch and don't want to partake of sushi.

For those who do indulge in the raw side, the special nigiri sushi combo makes a great lunch. Eight pieces of nigiri are served along with three slices of a tuna-filled roll. A nice blend of flavours and good variety of sushi. With a little pickled ginger and a lot of wasabi blended into the soya, it's the kind of combo that should satisfy most sushi cravings.

Sushi Hiro remains a classic in downtown, unknown to many but a pilgrimage for others. It is a cut above most in its class.

Sushi Kawa

Japanese

2204 – 4 Street SW
Phone: 802·0058
Monday – Friday 11:30 am – 2 pm, Sunday – Wednesday 5 pm – 9:30 pm
Thursday – Saturday 5 pm – 10:30 pm
Reservations recommended — Fully licensed — Patio — Non-smoking section
V, MC, AE, Debit — $$

ALTHOUGH SUSHI KAWA is the second sushi bar in the Mission area (the other being Sushi Hana), I think it has a pretty good chance of sticking around for a while. First, sushi and Japanese food are really popular right now, and second, Sushi Kawa does a pretty good job. (By the way, *kawa* means "river" in Japanese and is part of the owner's name.)

Former CBC Television guy Jordan Kawchuk told me about the dynamite sushi rolls they have at Sushi Kawa, and he was not just into hyperbole. They are actually called dynamite rolls. They are the inside-out variety where the rice is on the outside of the roll and the nori plus the cucumber, avocado, capelin roe, and mayonnaise are on the inside. But the key ingredient to the dynamite roll is tempura shrimp, which adds a crunchy texture to the centre. These are tasty but the nori on ours had toughened to the point where it was almost impossible to bite through. So all of the rolls—which are delicate enough to begin with—fell apart in our hands.

Other than that, most of the sushi we had was well made, with decent omelette and good tuna and snapper. But I wasn't impressed with our salmon sushi, which included a filament that was not possible to bite through. That showed some inexperience in the kitchen.

The prices at Sushi Kawa are competitive. The deluxe combo I had contained six nigiri sushi (those are the ones with the fish on top of the rice) and four pieces of maki (the round slices of rice and nori). For $11.25, that wasn't bad. Other sushi combos and individual pieces are available, ranging from $1.50 for a basic tuna to $16 for a sushi and sashimi combo. Sushi Kawa also runs a more complete menu of yakisobas and donburis and tempuras, all at reasonable prices, but the emphasis is strongly on the sushi.

We enjoyed the service at Sushi Kawa—that genteel and discreet Oriental style. And the room itself is pleasantly understated, with large windows and wooden floors. The tables are well spaced to allow for privacy, but there is an incongruously huge television in one corner where a major sumo match was being shown when we were there. I'll leave it to you to decide whether sumo is something you want to watch while having sushi.

Generally we liked Sushi Kawa. As my lunch partner said upon leaving, "Kawa-bunga dude."

Teatro

Seasonal Market Cuisine

200 Stephen Avenue Walk SE
Phone: 290·1012
Monday – Thursday 11:30 am – 11 pm, Friday 11:30 am – midnight
Saturday 5 pm – midnight, Sunday 5 pm – 10 pm
Reservations recommended — Fully licensed — Patio — Smoking at bar only
V, MC, AE, DC, Debit — $$ – $$$

OVER the last few years, Teatro has matured into one of Calgary's finest restaurants. It occupies a lovely space and has a talented chef and creative menu. It's one of those places that many people think of for special occasions or when someone else is paying the bill.

Teatro consumes the old Dominion Bank building on the edge of Olympic Plaza. It is sun brightened and white, an elegant room offset by an open kitchen at one end and a huge wrought-iron gate at the other. Seating about 110, it can become quite noisy, especially when the before- or after-dinner crowd piles in. Sound baffling on the ceiling has helped somewhat, but I find some areas still too loud. Regardless, this is a beautiful room.

Chef Michael Allemeier works with an ever-changing palate of local and international ingredients to create very fine food. A summer lunch had me scooping up a chickpea, clam, and rosemary soup garnished with the house olive oil. (The oil comes from the Italian estate of one of the owners.) This seemingly odd combination worked remarkably well, the chickpeas and clams blending into a chowdery thickness.

My main course—a special of grilled flank steak draped over romaine lettuce and roasted new potatoes—was just as good. The beef, from the well-respected T.K. Ranch, had been well aged and cooked perfectly rare. The vegetables were full of character: the potatoes had the freshness of early summer, and the romaine was crunchy and sweet. With a chanterelle cream over the greens, this plate was a simple symphony of flavours. So smartly conceived.

Don't expect anything cheap at Teatro. The soup was $8, the steak $18, and a dessert of banana cake and sour cream ice cream topped with pecan sauce was $8. (But boy, was it good!) At dinner, the menu slides up to $38 for grilled prawns with ginger- and chili-sautéed rapini, potato pancakes, and a lemon grass aïoli and $37 for rack of lamb with Parmesan scalloped potatoes. The most popular item on the menu remains the lobster and scallop lasagna, which is a rich and robust dish at $27. (Warning: don't plan on doing anything too serious after this dish. It's rich.)

Teatro also has one of the best wine lists in the city and some of the best service staff. It is a well-run operation from top to bottom. It surely deserves its rating as one of the best of the best.

Thai Sa-On
Thai

351 – 10 Avenue SW
Phone: 264·3526
Monday – Friday 11:30 am – 2 pm, Monday – Thursday 5 pm – 10 pm
Friday & Saturday 5 pm – 11 pm
Reservations recommended — Fully licensed — Non-smoking
V, MC — $$

MANY people find Thai food too daunting with names like kai tod ka tiam prik Thai (that's garlic chicken) or too hot with its multicoloured curries. That's unfortunate because it is one of the world's great cuisines. And it is also surprisingly user-friendly, especially at Thai Sa-On.

Thai food is one of the few Asian cuisines traditionally eaten with a fork and spoon, a custom that dates back to the mid-nineteenth century. Though Thailand was the only major Asian nation never to be occupied by a European power during the colonial era, King Mongkut borrowed much from his Euro-advisors, including cutlery.

And although Thai names are long and fun to pronounce, the dishes are well translated on the menu at Thai Sa-On: beef flavoured with lime juice, chili powder, and roasted rice; shrimp stir-fried with ginger root; or green curried chicken. The degree of spiciness is indicated by one, two, or three stars, and customers are welcome to add to or cut back on the levels. (An oil company group visits Thai Sa-On once a week and orders twelve-star dishes. Ouch.) But Thai food is not all hot. The cuisine balances hot dishes with cooling ones. So for every three-star curry, there's a no-star shrimp and broccoli stir-fry.

The Chanhao family—three sisters, two brothers, their mother, and various cousins—present consistently tasty, well-constructed food. The tom yam soup is a warming and cold-clearing soup. With a sweet and sour stock packed with lime leaves, chilies, and lemon, it is enough to push back a virus half a day. We enjoy the meat dishes stir-fried with chilies and basil leaves and the smooth dishes incorporating coconut milk, like the Panang kai (kai is chicken). And the vegetarian dishes are a hit with both vegetarians and meat eaters. Pad karee jay (yellow curried vegetables) or pad pag tua (vegetables with peanut sauce) are favourites.

The service is as gracious as anyone would want. The staff wear either traditional Thai or contemporary Western clothing as well as warm smiles, and they are experts at dealing with first-timers and regulars alike.

Then there are the prices. At Thai Sa-On, nothing costs over $12.95. And for that, you are looking at a whole fish cooked with ginger and lime or sweet and sour sauce. Most dishes are comfortably under $10.

Looking for flaws at Thai Sa-On, I really find none. The food is so good and the experience is so pleasant, I only wonder why there aren't more places like it in Calgary.

Thomsons
Canadian Grill

700 Centre Street S (Hyatt Regency)
Phone: 537·4449
Daily 6:30 am – 2 pm, 5 pm – 10 pm
Reservations recommended — Fully licensed — Patio — Non-smoking
V, MC, AE, DC, Debit — $$$

EVERY time I go into the new Convention Centre and the Hyatt hotel, I am impressed. I love the way they have integrated the old sandstone buildings and retained some of the names. Like Thomsons, named after the Thomson brothers who constructed a building on Stephen Avenue in 1893. That building has now become Thomsons Restaurant, the only dining room in the Hyatt.

I think the hotel has done a smart thing with this restaurant. It's a one-size-fits-all spot that is open daily for breakfast, lunch, and dinner. Following the current thinking in hotel food service, they have incorporated the concepts of a high-end evening dining room and a coffee shop, creating a multi-purpose facility.

The room is lovely. All the old brick and sandstone is highlighted by wrought-iron, Western-style lamps, and the arches of the former delivery doors are visible at the back of the restaurant. Tables are big enough to work on and are well spaced for the privacy needed for business meetings. Some of the chairs, however, have very uncomfortable backs.

I've tried both breakfast and lunch in Thomsons and have enjoyed much of what I've had. Once you're past the Hyatt prices, the food isn't bad. The Great Start breakfast features juice, pastries, preserves, and coffee. They'll add on cereal, fruit, and smoked salmon if the customer is so inclined (still at the $11.50 price tag). This is a huge breakfast with the supplements, but one shortcoming is the baking, which is not as good as it should be.

Lunch covers the basic territory of burgers and salads and sandwiches and includes a few higher-end items such as hickory-glazed salmon and Chilean sea bass on mashed sweet potatoes. The clubhouse sandwich is a more upscale version than what is found elsewhere—a grilled chicken breast is in there with a chipotle aïoli, replacing the usual sliced cold cuts and mayo.

Dinner moves into high gear with seafood cioppino at $31, maple-glazed duck breast at $32, and a sixteen-ounce Alberta ribeye with caramelized onions, chive mashed potatoes, and a veal reduction at $36. This is serious Hyatt dining.

I invariably find service in Thomsons to be excellent. The Hyatt hires well, trains well, and always has enough staff to support their activities.

But my biggest thrill so far has been the paper towels in the washroom. I think that's why they charge extra: they're really nice and soft. Very impressive. Love that Hyatt quality.

Ticino

Swiss-Italian

415 Banff Avenue (High Country Inn), Banff
Phone: 762·3848
Daily 7:30 am – 10:30 am, 5:30 pm – 10 pm
Reservations recommended — Fully licensed — Patio for drinks only
Non-smoking section
V, MC, AE, DC, JCB — $$ – $$$

TICINO has been one of Banff's most popular and consistent restaurants for many years. Their Swiss-Italian food fits well with the mountain setting and the Swiss Guide history of Banff.

It is a bright room seating about 110 in a comfortable Alpine setting, with another big room in the back for groups. An alpenhorn is mounted overhead, huge cowbells dangle from a rough-hewn roof, old cross-country skis hang on the wall, and stained glass candles dot each table.

They feature a classical turn on Swiss-Italian cuisine in dishes like the duck breast with chestnuts, cherries, and ginger in a sour cream and red wine sauce and the lamb loin breaded with figs, dates, and mint. Walking into the room, you'll likely be hit with the rich, mountainy smell of cheese fondue. This is the strong, sultry food of the southern Swiss canton of Ticino, where crossovers with Italy are significant. You will find linguine with veal and wild mushrooms and tortes with mascarpone. Abandon all diets, ye who enter here.

Many of the staff have worked at Ticino for years. That kind of consistency is unheard of in Banff. And it is easy to be comfortable with the service—skilled and reliable yet laid-back. Ticino does not try to be stuffy at all. It is simply a transplant of Swiss-Italian mountain elegance to Banff.

I tried the gnocchi with chicken and chestnuts in a creamy peppercorn sauce. This is a real Ticinese dish. The chicken was tender, the sauce was peppery, and the chestnuts added an interesting texture. The gnocchi were good, but I think my Sicilian friends would find them heavy. These seemed to lean more towards a Swiss spätzle. Suffice it to say that I could have skied to Canmore on a bowl of these and still not have been hungry. That could also have had something to do with my starter of the wild mushroom soup—thick, creamy, and porridge-like with chopped mushrooms. A wonderful soup.

Catherine's raclette cheese appetizer with potatoes and pickles was equally fine. The healthy slice of cheese was nicely melted, emitting that pungent raclette odour. Her chicken breast stuffed with goat cheese and crusted with crushed hazelnuts was a good choice too. And the potato dumplings, red cabbage, peas, and carrots presented a colourful and tasty arrangement on the plate.

So for a little Alpine flavour, Ticino is one of the best and certainly one of the most consistent eateries in the Rockies.

www.ticinorestaurant.com

Trocadero

Mediterranean

2215 – 33 Avenue SW
Phone: 249 • 1194
Monday – Friday 11:30 am – 2 pm, Daily 5:30 pm – 10 pm
Reservations recommended — Fully licensed — Non-smoking
V, MC, AE, DC, Debit — $$ – $$$

THE recently arrived Marda Loop Station houses various tenants, including Trocadero, a restaurant that serves what they call *Cuisine du Soleil*. That is a charming term, *Cuisine du Soleil*. This "food of the sun" is a collection of dishes from the south of both France and Spain and from the coast of Morocco: salade niçoise, mussels marinière, paella, couscous.

Trocadero is a suitably sunny location for lunch—although the entrance faces north, the restaurant extends the depth of the building with windows to the south and east. The interior is cozy, seating about forty in Mediterranean yellows and blues and in a decidedly non-Mediterranean clean-air atmosphere. With a ceramic tile floor, a small bar, an open kitchen, and linened tables, it sets up as a high-tone cafe or bistro rather than a formal restaurant.

The dinner menu follows suit. Though a rack of lamb Provençale and a roasted veal chop push over $20, most entrees remain in the teens. Appetizers run $6 to $12, and at lunch, there are $6 salads and soups, an $8 omelette du jour, a $13 seafood crepe, and a $14 chicken breast in cognac sauce. So this is not a quick drop-in spot.

Trocadero is a step in a new direction for Marda Loop. It's great to see a stylish place like this outside of the downtown and Beltline areas where these prices would not cause anyone to blink an eye. Trocadero is still quite a bargain compared to many places though, and the parking is free.

Quality-wise, Trocadero is well worth it. A mussel soup was a rich, well-balanced seafood broth packed with mussels, as good as any I have had in the south of France. And the paella Valenciana reminded me of the excellent paellas of Spain. Loaded with fresh shrimp, halibut, clams, more mussels, sausage, vegetables, and chicken, it was a savoury feast that defeated the appetites of two large-eating paella lovers. An eggplant soup was light on the eggplant flavour, but a rabbit casserole with mustard was highly received for its tenderness and taste.

On another visit, I tried a classic French dish of steak and frites, a simple ribeye with french fries. The steak itself was near-perfect, grilled medium rare in a red wine-peppercorn sauce. And the fries were beautifully crispy but just a bit undercooked on the inside.

Trocadero takes us close to the Mediterranean sun with its cuisine, setting, and service. That's something most Calgarians cannot get enough of.

Trong-Khanh
Vietnamese

1115 Centre Street N
Phone: 230·2408
Daily 11 am—9 pm
Reservations recommended — Fully licensed — Non-smoking
V, MC, Debit — $

THE TRONG-KHANH has been around since the late '80s when it was just a tiny hole in the wall on Centre Street with worn vinyl chairs, teetering tables, and young, earnest staff. It was one of the first places to serve Vietnamese noodle dishes—at the time a novelty, now a major food trend. Things have not changed all that much. The staff are a little older, fresh paint and carpets have spruced up the place, the tables seem a bit steadier, and the whole place is now non-smoking. But fundamentally it is the same small place, seating about forty, with almost the same menu and almost the same prices.

They have broken the $10 mark with dishes like barbecued pork and tiger prawns on steamed broken rice or dried salt and pepper shrimp, but most prices have remained startlingly low. Three shrimp salad rolls are only $4.50, while a couple of spring rolls with fresh lettuce and basil to wrap around them go for $3.50. The best bargains are the noodle dishes done as soups or as bowls of bún—rice vermicelli topped with other goodies. Almost all of these are under $6 and are a meal in themselves.

Like most of the other lunchers the day I dropped by, it was a full-bodied bowl of bún that I was after. The noodles were refreshingly light, the nuoc mam was just salty and fishy enough, and the aromatic chicken that topped my bowl, besides being crusted in peanuts and lemon grass, was tender, skinless, and boneless. I like a few more greens with my bún, but it was otherwise excellent.

I also tried the spring rolls and the salad rolls and found both to be quite reasonable and fresh. The spring rolls were particularly nice. Filled with ground meats and vegetables and deep-fried in their rice paper wraps, they were light and crisp. The salad rolls were a little loosely wrapped, but otherwise had all the right ingredients.

The Trong-Khanh presents the noodle-shop side of Vietnamese cuisine as well as any other restaurant and better than most. They have been at it longer and have built a loyal following that orders immediately by number without even looking at the menu. Those devotees helped them survive the lean years when their food was unknown, and now the cafe is packed every day. The Trong-Khanh deserves its success.

Tullamore
Irish Pub

124 – 10 Street NW
Phone: 270 • 3116
Monday – Saturday 11:30 am – 11:30 pm, Sunday noon – 10 pm
Reservations not accepted — Fully licensed — Deck — No non-smoking section
V, MC, AE, Debit — $ – $$

I've always liked Tullamore's space. It's very bright with windows facing west and south, and being upstairs, it perches you above the bustle of 10th Street. And it has a great deck for summer dining with a tree house feel. Plus they have free, though limited, parking in the alley just under the deck. The downside of the upstairs location is that it is easy to forget about Tullamore with its minimal street presence and long staircase leading up to it.

Fortunately, good Irish eateries can thrive in out-of-the-way spots thanks to their loyal fans. The sound of Guinness being pulled can attract its followers from miles around. Tullamore, which is named after an Irish city, has succeeded in this space since 1995.

But there is more to Tullamore than Guinness and Irish jigs. From the smoked salmon with soda bread through to the corned beef sandwiches and a Dublin coddle stew, Tullamore offers fare that matches up perfectly with the beer. And this is huge stuff. The lamb stew I had featured immense potatoes and carrots swimming in a meaty broth, with equally large chunks of tender lamb. I worked studiously on my plate until I was well past full and it still looked like I had hardly made a dent. My guest had the fish and chips—the one-piece-of-fish option—and it too was huge. Now a lot of that was the doughy Guinness and cornmeal batter on the fish itself— a good half-inch. But it was still one serious plate of food.

This is very traditional fare, perhaps too traditional for those of us looking for more flavour and less cooking. The word "rare" does not exist in the world of Irish pub food, and the word "spice" is just as uncommon. So the lamb stew, for example, is very cooked and very natural.

But I must compliment their soup of the day, a mix of Irish beans and French lentils. In a beefy stock, it was surprisingly loaded with a pleasant pepperiness. Quite a lovely soup. And it was served with a heavy soda bread, thick with grains. Nice bread if you like the dense, grainy kinds.

Service covers the friendly pub bases and delivers the food and brews quickly. Tullamore is a cozy place to spend some time with friends over a little Irish food and beer. And a good place to find a wee bit of free parking in Kensington.

Village Hearth

Bistro

1413 – 9 Avenue SE
Phone: 265·5739
Tuesday – Friday 11 am – 9 pm
Saturday 10 am – 5 pm, 7 pm – 11 pm, Sunday 10 am – 3 pm
Reservations recommended — Fully licensed — Patios — Smoking on 1 patio only
V, MC, AE, Debit — $ – $$

THE VILLAGE HEARTH is an eclectic place that fits the tone of Inglewood. It serves bistro-style lunches and dinners, does a basic Sunday brunch, and acts as a space for live performances, anything from magic shows to a screamingly popular drag show. In between, there is a collection of furniture that looks like it came from one of the antique shops down the street, some of the better pies in these parts, and two house birds, Dick and Bert. (The presence of these birds has caused some controversy in the past, but things are happily settled now.)

The Hearth is a rustic joint in a funky sort of way—it's part granola bar and part trendy cafe. There is a mix of posters and plants and some Christmas lights over the bar, plus tables and stools at varying heights. Totally non-smoking inside, smoking is only permitted on one of the two patios. The Hearth has a relaxed atmosphere that makes me want to have another pot of chamomile tea and sit for a while.

But on Saturday nights all the calmness goes out the window as Carly & Company take over the place for a full-tilt musical drag extravaganza called *Dine and Be Dazzled*. It's a dinner show with a difference, featuring Whitney, Dolly, Tallulah, and even Liza. (Evidently the Dolly-Whitney duo is a showstopper.) On those evenings, your $20 ticket includes the food and the show.

The rest of the time, the Hearth puts out a list of things like soups, salads, quesadillas, and wraps, with nothing over $10. The priciest item is the smoked salmon quesadilla with cream cheese and olive tapenade. And on Sundays, the Hearth is one of the quieter places for brunch. They don't do the bacon and egg thing, but rather, serve up sausage frittatas, fruit salads, and crustless quiches. The breakfast burrito is a big wrap of scrambled eggs with bacon, salsa, and cheese. Quite decent, but I could use more heat in the salsa.

Any time of day they offer their popular pies from a numerous selection baked in-house. The bumbleberry is a tart blend of rhubarb, strawberries, and raspberries, with a thin crust on top and bottom. The crust is not the flakiest I've ever had, but the overall production is quite nice.

The Village Hearth is an unusual place, as interesting to visit for its character and characters as it is for its food. And of course, to visit Dick and Bert.

Virginia's Market Cafe
Italian Diner

827 – 10 Avenue SW
Phone: 233·8155
Monday – Saturday 10 am – 7 pm
Reservations not accepted — Fully licensed — Non-smoking
Debit — $

IT seems that every time I go to Virginia's Market Cafe, they have changed the look. It started out as an Italian bakery with a huge table loaded with the daily baking. They made a few panini on the side, sold Italian ingredients, and had a few tables for eating. But over time, the concept has morphed into an Italian diner with more panini, glasses of red wine, and cedar booths filling the space. A recently installed gelato machine is now pumping out various flavours on a regular basis.

The prep area has been elevated into a new loft above the main floor, and various coolers and ovens crowd the room. The look is "eclectic garage" with stacks of plastic lids sharing wall space with Italian friezes and bottles of olive oil. The raw concrete floor barely shows beneath the booths and shelves of condiments, and in one corner—the only area that has not changed—the small open kitchen sizzles. It is a visual jumble of styles, a cacophony of looks, and somehow it works.

Not that it isn't confusing to the newcomer. To find the menu, look up, way up, to the stainless steel hood fan over the stove. Items are listed in felt pen on the fan— a short list of panini, burgers, and fries. Just stand around looking up long enough and someone will take your order.

Virginia's Market Cafe is the only place in town that always serves beet and sweet potato fries. And are these good. The regular fries are hand cut and tossed with sea salt and herbs. Fantastic. The real strength of the kitchen is the unique sandwiches. My favourite is the gourmet burger—two thin patties smothered in blue cheese and avocado on a very tasty roll. Delightful and slippery. A burger with a blue cheese bite. The rest of the panini and burgers are just as interesting.

The Market Cafe is a delightfully casual place where people lounge over a cappuccino or stuff down a quick lunch. Whatever your needs, it hits the spot, aided masterfully by the head cook, baker, bottle-washer, and owner—Mario. (Odd as it may sound, this Virginia's is owned by a Mario.) One of the friendliest guys in the restaurant business, he is also remarkably capable in the kitchen.

P.S. If you're wondering whatever happened to Virginia herself, at press time she was about to open the Palette Café in the Lorraine Building at 620 – 12 Avenue SW.

Waldhaus

German

Fairmont Banff Springs Hotel, Banff
Phone: 762·6860
Daily 6 pm – 10 pm
Reservations recommended — Fully licensed — Non-smoking section
V, MC, AE, DC, JCB — $$$

Most families have a restaurant or two that they like to frequent for special occasions. When I was a kid, it was the old Blue Willow Chinese restaurant in Edmonton. But for some strange reason, in recent years, it has become the Waldhaus at the Fairmont Banff Springs Hotel. I say strange because our family tree has no roots in Germany. (Not that we have any in China either.) But German cuisine is one style of food that most everyone in my family seems to enjoy, and the setting at the Waldhaus is unbeatable.

So we go there for big birthdays, anniversaries, and other major family gatherings. They graciously pull together enough tables to seat everyone and we have a grand time. We eat a lot of schnitzel, drink too much wine, and sing along to the lively oompahpah music. And when we have kids along who aren't quite up for the good German food, they kindly allow us to order nachos and such off the pub menu from downstairs.

The Waldhaus is one of the Springs' restaurants that is actually not in the Springs. It's located on the upper level of the old golf clubhouse just a short stroll down the mountain from the main hotel building. When the Springs built a new clubhouse in the early '90s, this high-ceilinged, rough-hewn room became the perfect location for a German restaurant. Seating about ninety, it has the full *gemütlichkeit*, or good times, feel. Banners fly overhead, a fire crackles in the huge fireplace, and the hearty German fare rolls out.

The jägerschnitzel is a hunger-stifling pork escalope covered in a mushroom and cream sauce. Sided with red cabbage and spätzle, it's as tasty as it is filling. And the roasted duck is a hearty Teutonic turn on classic cuisine with a cider sauce, caramelized apples, and grapes. And their fondues—both cheese and beef broth—are popular, especially with the après-ski crowd.

There are also rich appetizers such as a pheasant ragout in puff pastry and sautéed prawns done with garlic-herb butter, tomatoes, and Riesling. And, of course, there are the typical strudels and creamy tortes for dessert. There is a tomato and marinated onion salad, but generally, this is not a light menu, so be forewarned.

Service has always been excellent on our visits—no small task with a group as diverse as my family. So we will continue to return for our special occasions. At least until they suggest we don't.

Wildwood
Rocky Mountain Cuisine & Brew Pub

2417 – 4 Street SW
Phone: 228·0100
Monday – Thursday 11:30 am – 10 pm, Friday & Saturday 11:30 am – 11 pm
Sunday 5 pm – 10 pm
Reservations recommended — Fully licensed — Patio — Non-smoking section
V, MC, AE — $$ – $$$

IT is impossible to miss Wildwood. They redid the landmark Franzl's Gasthaus sign with their own corporate logo and it is visible for blocks. Stylized *W*'s are plastered tastefully on the doors and menus to reinforce the message that the place has changed from the days of Franzl's and the subsequent Mission Bridge Brewing Company.

Wildwood presents a fresh and light menu that leans to the current Rocky Mountain style. Hooked on local ingredients like buffalo, Spolumbo sausage, buckwheat honey, and Yukon Gold potatoes, the cuisine is heightened by Contemporary preparations and a global sensibility. You will find penne on the menu served with Spolumbo's whiskey-fennel sausage as well as pine nut-crusted mountain trout in a citrus-saffron sauce. There is elk steak, orange-glazed pheasant, caribou scaloppine, and wild boar-bacon flatbread. Very Rocky Mountain regional, yet very worldly at the same time.

On a beautiful spring day, we sat on the patio under one of the red umbrellas and enjoyed a lamb burger with Canadian brie, onion marmalade, and lingonberries. The rich lamb flavour was perfectly accented by the berries and the onions. Served with a side salad of greens in a raspberry vinaigrette, it was a delightful lunch. So was the daily sandwich special of back bacon with Swiss cheese and sautéed mushrooms. Slippery but nice.

Wildwood produces a line of beer in their basement brew pub that draws real ale fans from miles around. The serious imbibers tend to stay downstairs in the darkened confines, enjoying the brews and the various events Wildwood offers. At CAMRA's (Campaign For Real Ale) recent 3rd Annual Real Ale Festival, Wildwood's English bitter was named best all round beer.

Service has always been outstanding on our visits. Wildwood employs a professional staff who appear happy to work there. They know the food, they pace it well, and they create a pleasant atmosphere.

So whether you're dining in style on the main floor, kicked back on the patio catching rays, or buried in the basement with a brew, Wildwood is a delightful operation. I think Franzl's would be happy with the service and the *gemütlichkeit* that carry on their fine tradition.

www.wildwood@wildwoodgroup.net

Yuzuki

Japanese

510 – 9 Avenue SW
Phone: 261·7701
Monday – Friday 11:30 am – 2 pm, Monday – Wednesday 5 pm – 9 pm
Thursday – Saturday 5 pm – 10 pm
Reservations recommended — Fully licensed — Non-smoking section
V, MC, AE, DC, Debit — $$

M Y favourite place for sushi remains the rather obscure Yuzuki, a name that pops up on my Visa bill more often than any other restaurant. Located on an unpleasant stretch of 9th Avenue, its scruffy awning is lost on the traffic that buzzes by outside, and the small doorway is easy to miss, even for regulars.

Inside it is not much prettier, although it is usually filled with major sushi fans. The large space seats about sixty on two levels, and a toy train delivers sushi to some tables. But the chairs have been sat in a few times too often, the room screams for paint and repairs, and the washrooms—well, just avoid them if you can.

Once past the look, you can expect the best sushi available, prepared in a pristine environment. The cuts are sharp and clean and even, the nori is crisp to the teeth, the fish is as fresh as you'll find in town, and the flavours are rich and balanced. The rice itself is a pleasant blend; slightly sweet and vinegared, with a smear of wasabi, it is a perfect background for the fish. Fatty tuna, various roe, smoked eel, and more show up on one of the most extensive lists in the city.

There is also a lot of creativity at the Yuzuki. The chef wraps shrimp, salmon, and avocado around rice for the inside-out roll, and he fashions the sashimi into delicate flowers of freshly cut fish. The salmon-skin cone is unsurpassed—the best that I have had in Calgary. The skin is toasted with about a quarter inch of meat still on it. This gives it an oily, crispy texture that melds wonderfully with the rice, some greens, and the silky Japanese mayonnaise.

The Yuzuki offers other Japanese food too—the teriyaki and tempura and yakitori—and these dishes are also quite good. Catherine likes the oyakodon, a mixture of cooked chicken and rice topped with green onions and a raw egg that is cooked by the heat of the rice and chicken. It is a delicate and easy dish for those unfamiliar with Japanese food. They also serve combinations in lacquered bento boxes, those sectioned containers that have a compartment for each dish.

The food at the Yuzuki is excellent—good enough to keep me returning on a regular basis. But then, I am used to the hard chairs and leaky taps. Be prepared and you will be rewarded.

www.yuzuki.com

Purveyors

Auburn Saloon

712–1 Street SE, 266•6628

Located near the Epcor Centre for the Performing Arts, the Auburn remains the darling of the pre-theatre cocktail set and the post-theatre arts crowd. With a cocktail list of over seventy creations, from classic dry martinis through to zombies and Harvey Wallbangers and on to sidecars and golden cadillacs, the Auburn has a beverage for all palates—as long as those palates are alcohol friendly.

The Auburn also does a decent lunch in their airy, high-ceilinged room. There's no non-smoking area, but most days at lunch, the air isn't too bad. The same can't be said for later in the evening.

Bakerland

131–2 Avenue SE, 262•3388

Looking for a quick and cheap snack in Chinatown? Bakerland is a good Chinese bakery situated in the Far East Shopping Centre. It is a starkly empty room bathed in harsh fluorescents, but I like the pastries here, especially the ones filled with fresh fruit. The pineapple bun is rich and acidic and a perfect balance to their spicy beef satay bun. Bakerland has a decent dine-in area that continues the minimalist look. Try to get a table that has a view of the Bow. Not that it matters much—these pastries go down quickly.

The Better Butcher

New Location TBA, 252•7171

I am frequently asked where to find good, well-aged Alberta beef. My favourite place is The Better Butcher. They age it a minimum of twenty-one days, providing an outstanding level of taste and tenderness.

The folks here are highly proficient at their work. Between Randy (the Canadian) and Gerry (the Brit), they can cut meat pretty much any way you want. And they are astoundingly pleasant for a couple of guys who spend their days wielding big knives.

A while ago, I took two of their twelve-ounce tenderloin steaks to an old friend who now lives in London, and I think that much raw meat scared him when he first saw it. Living on a yoga diet and avoiding British beef like the plague, he had not eaten a steak like this in years. He figured there was no way he could consume it all in one sitting. Ten minutes later, he was mopping his plate and looking at the remainders of mine with a bloody eye. You can take the boy out of Alberta, but...

(Note: At press time, The Better Butcher was in the process of changing to a yet undetermined location.)

Blends & Central Blends*

637 – 10 Street, Canmore, 678 • 2688
1312 Edmonton Trail NE, 230 • 3226
*203 – 19 Street NW, 670 • 5665**

If you are looking for a good cup of coffee in Canmore, just follow the smell of roasting beans to Blends. It's a tiny coffee bar that acts as the epicentre of alpine culture in the area. It does have the annoying mountain trait of not opening until 9:30 a.m. and of being closed on Sundays. Wonderful for the staff, but we need our coffee early and certainly on Sundays. Oh well—kudos to them for placing their own sanity ahead of a bunch of caffeine-crazed visitors.

Fortunately, their Calgary locations indulge caffeinated city tastes with earlier hours and Sunday openings.

Boca Loca

1512 – 11 Street SW, 802 • 4600

Finding just the right chili for that mole or some fresh cactus paddles can be difficult in Cowtown, so Renette Kurtz opened Boca Loca. Fans of Central and South American foods flock to her store for tortillas, chipotles, and epazote. Each day she makes a couple of fresh salsas, such as the basic pico de gallo or her popular mango version. She also does enchilada sauces with tomatillos and roasted poblanos and carries tasty tamales from local chef Norma French. Look for cooking classes and cookbooks too, all focused on the warmer side of the Americas.

Brûlée Patisserie

722 – 11 Avenue SW, 261 • 3064

Brûlée resides just downstairs from The Cookbook Co. Cooks and is owned and operated by Rosemary Harbrecht, a talented baker. Harbrecht specializes in customized baking, with gorgeous blackberry dacquoise or chocolate ganache or carrot-butterscotch layered cakes. Citrus fans will love Catherine's favourites, the lemon soufflé and the lemon mascarpone tarts. Brûlée has a limited quantity of daily baking available—cream cheese brownies, blueberry-orange oatmeal squares, toasted nut slice, sugar cookies, and gingersnaps, to name just a few. Cookies run $6 to $10 per dozen, with cheesecakes and other desserts in the $12 to $30 range.

Caffè Beano

1613 – 9 Street SW, 229•1232

An expansion at Caffè Beano a few years back means there is more room for folks to lounge over their espressos and double lattes. (Not that there's any more room to order; that area is often congested.) One of Calgary's favourite independent coffee purveyors, Caffè Beano seems to be constantly busy with relaxing Mount Royalites, tired 17th Avenue strollers, and hip Beltline residents. But if you avoid the morning rush hour of drop-ins on the way to work, it is a terrific place to meet friends or while away an afternoon over a book.

The coffee here remains among the best. Sourcing great beans, they produce some of the thickest and darkest espressos on the market. Unlike staff at some of the corporate coffee conglomerates, those at Beano will make your brew just the way you like it, not to a preordained formula. They also make very good sandwiches and bake their own goodies on-site. Few things beat a double espresso with one of their biscotti, unless it is a double espresso with one of their muffins.

Beano is non-smoking, a major plus for its many fans, but there are some benches outside for those who just can't handle coffee without a smoke.

Caffè Mauro

805 – 1 Street SW, 262•9216

Caffè Mauro is a small and surprisingly quiet oasis just off Stephen Avenue. It serves one of the better espressos in the downtown core. Using Mauro coffee—hence the name—they do Italian espresso the way it's done in Italy: dark and with a serious crema. Just make sure you ask for a "short" pull. They use Kicking Horse beans for their drip coffee and whip up a few pizzas and panini on the side. Most ingredients come from the Italian Supermarket since Mauro is run by a member of the family who owns that popular store.

Chocolaterie Bernard Callebaut

1313 – 1 Street SE, 266•4300

It's been almost twenty years since Bernard Callebaut arrived in Calgary with the dream of making Cowtown a major chocolate centre. In 1982, he left his family chocolate operation in Belgium—now owned by Tobler and Suchard—and brought 130 years of experience to town. He kept a connection with the old plant by ensuring that they produce chocolate for him from a proprietary recipe. His first shop was in the space that is now Savoir Fare, and he immediately made the best chocolates I'd ever tasted.

He eventually outgrew the space and built a solid brick edifice just south of downtown. A visit here is a chocolatey pilgrimage for many aficionados and can include a self-guided factory tour on weekdays. The main showroom contains a mind-boggling display of chocolates in all their glory, with over seventy fillings and countless shapes.

There are thirty-seven Callebaut shops in Canada and the States, including eight in Calgary and Banff. And there are now two in Japan.

M. Callebaut and his products have won numerous awards, including the *Grand Prix International Artisan Chocolatier* in 1998 at the *Festival International du Chocolat* in Roanne, France. And they are still the best chocolates I've ever tasted.

Confetti Ice Cream Factory
4416 – 5 Street NE, 277 • 5731

I've never been sure just why Confetti is located in the Greenview Industrial Park. A more obscure location would be hard to imagine. Regardless, dedicated dessert fans flock to the place for house-made lemon sorbet, frozen fruit yogurts, and blueberry cheesecake and cookie dough ice creams.

Run by former Sidneysider Bob Pankhurst and his Calgarian wife Gail, Confetti supplies customized ices to many restaurants too. If you see a menu with cinnamon or red-bean ice creams or Bianco Blanco, a vanilla ice cream ball filled with raspberry mousse, your dessert is probably from Confetti.

The Cookbook Co. Cooks
722 – 11 Avenue SW, 265 • 6066 or 1 (800) 663 • 8532

The Cookbook Co. Cooks is a unique hybrid of cookbook store, cooking school, and food shop. The bookstore carries the largest and most varied collection of cookbooks for many miles around. The food shop boasts a huge range of sea salts, dried beans, handcrafted potato chips, ground chilies, and all those other ingredients that can be difficult to find. There are a couple of coolers for fresh herbs and frozen stock, another one for a small but well-chosen selection of cheeses, and a few baskets for breads and other foods-of-the-moment such as Hotchkiss tomatoes.

Downstairs is a well-equipped cooking school where guest chefs such as James Barber, Julian Bond, and Ted Reader show off their skills to avid foodies. In addition to the big name cooks, lots of local chefs teach here too. You'll find the likes of Rogelio Herrara, Peter Kinjo, and dee Hobsbawn-Smith instructing classes on Latin American, Japanese, and Canadian cuisines. Every once in a while they even let me teach a New Mexican or Southwestern session.

Along with its neighbours Brûlée Patisserie, Bodega, and the private wine shop MetroVino, the Cookbook Co. has helped make the Building Block a serious food and wine destination. It's one-stop shopping at its best.

Core Café & Juice Bar

105 Stephen Avenue Walk SW, 263·2673

The creation of Graden Sol and Darci Schapansky (literally—they did most of the construction themselves, with the help of family and friends), Core is a funky and very narrow cafe that seats about thirty. Their specialties are fresh juices and smoothies, with the addition of vegetarian chilis, daily soups, and salads. There are also smoked turkey wraps, tofu rice boats, and wheat grass quiches, covering the ground for vegans to carnivores.

In a move away from all their high-end neighbours, Core has kept prices for most items under $5. It's a welcome alternative for downtowners looking for something light, fresh, and fast.

Debaji's Fresh Market

Northland Village Shoppes, 202·3500
10233 Elbow Drive SW, 537·5700

I grew up in Wetaskiwin where my family shopped at Ray's Tomboy, the precursor of what is now Debaji's. It was run by Ray Debaji, and his entire family worked in the store. Ray's sons Nehad and Mazen learned their retail skills early, and they now run one of the most interesting grocery stores in Calgary. Debaji's Fresh Market is actually both a retail outlet and a cafe, located in Northland Village. (There is also a separate catering and cafe operation on Elbow Drive SW).

The retail store is big and bright and filled with classical music as well as colourful displays. They specialize in the freshest produce procured from contracted growers. You'll find key limes and mangosteens and fresh figs here in the best condition. The prices can be almost as amazing as the products (read high), but they carry things you'll find nowhere else. They also have a huge cheese selection, an abundance of organic products, and a broad range of meats and seafoods. The in-house bakery produces good fruit pies, and the deli counter generates decent take-home dishes (the rotisserie chicken is excellent).

Both cafes are casual and lively and constantly buzz with customers. And the food is light and fresh, created from the best of the market.

Decadent Desserts

914 – 16 Avenue NW, 245·5535

One of the finer custom bakeries in Calgary is Decadent Desserts, owned by Pam Fortier. Her repertoire includes a Lemon Hazelnut Crunch cake and a strawberry-rhubarb pie as well as oatmeal-raisin cookies and biscotti. There is an abundance of chocolate, from the Chocolate Overdose cake with over a pound of Callebaut chocolate to the Fantasy Fudge cake accented with chocolate leaves. And if nuptials are in your future, ask about the elegant wedding cakes.

Decadent Desserts is not a drop-in-for-a-piece-of-cake spot. It's a place to pick up dessert orders of whole cakes or pies or cookies by the dozen. Quality and execution are exceptional and creativity is stellar.

Dutch Cash & Carry

3815 – 16 Street SE, 290 • 1838

This place wins the award for hardest-to-find location in the book. Just off Ogden Road and down a string of unpaved roads in Bonnybrook, DC & C shares a warehouse-type building with other tenants. There's a small sign out front, but it may take a few passes to find.

Popular with the local Dutch community, DC & C carries Dutch licorice, cheese croquettes, dark coffee, cured horse meat, and aged Gouda among their 400 imported products. In the late fall, they bring in alphabet letters made with Dutch chocolate, a popular gift for Christmas. And there's more than food—there are also pots, pot scrubbers, and dish towels to complete your kitchen.

Edelweiss Village

1921 – 20 Avenue NW, 282 • 6722

The Edelweiss Village is a German gift shop, grocery store, and cafe that can answer all your Teutonic needs. The cabbage roll lunch comes with piles of sauerkraut and potato salad and your choice of wurst. It's enough to feed three people. The rouladen is a thick and tasty roll of beef, and the decadent hazelnut torte is nutty and creamy. If you're looking for German cheeses, mustards, kitchen wares, and beer steins, this is the place. Plus, their selection includes goods from countries such as Holland, Switzerland, and Austria.

Eiffel Tower Bakery

1013 – 17 Avenue SW, 244 • 0103
502 – 25 Avenue NW, 282 • 0788

In an area known as the "breadbasket of the world," it can be awfully hard to find a good loaf of bread. And meanwhile in France, it can be difficult to find good flour for the talented bakers there to make into bread. So the Eiffel Tower offers a great solution: French bakers running their own shop in Calgary. The result? Impressive bread, flaky chocolate croissants, and decadently creamy desserts. It's wonderful stuff. Not cheap, but they have to cover the costs of all that butter and cream and top-notch flour, as well as the high-tech ovens.

The Eiffel Tower produces a wide range of items, from crusty loaves to crunchy meringues to buttery brioches. Bakers roll baguettes and create outstanding cakes. The Royale is a multi-layered treat of cream and chocolate and some crunchy thing we just love. It's possible to hurt oneself with this cake—at least it is for us. A little piece goes a long way.

All the baking is done at the 17th Avenue location, with distribution from there to the other outlet. This means that there is typically more selection at the Mount Royal store, but parking is easier at 25th Avenue.

Evelyn's Coffee Bar

201 Banff Avenue, Banff, 762·0352
249 Bear Street, Banff, 762·0330

It's difficult to get a good cup of coffee in Banff. Mostly it's the hardness of the water, but when you combine that with the inexperience of most Banff baristas and the varying demands of global tourists, you have a recipe for caffeinated disaster. Two of the few places to make something drinkable are Evelyn's and her second cafe, Evelyn's Too.

I prefer the more relaxed tone of Evelyn's Too on Bear Street. The original Evelyn's is packed with the masses of people that pass by on Banff Avenue. Too is in the atrium of a small mall, so the tables have more space around them. And oddly, the coffee seems better at Too. Maybe it's the calmer atmosphere.

They sell large cookies, scones, cakes, and such—the type of baking that is typically mass-produced and tasteless. But at Evelyn's, the food actually tastes as good as it looks. An apple coffee cake oozes with stewed apples, and an oatmeal-cranberry cookie crumbles with yummy bits. A cheese scone had Catherine and I fighting over the crispy, cheesy crust as we sipped our double espressos. And then there are Evelyn's roast chicken sandwiches, a Banff legend.

There are many places to kick back with a paper and a coffee in Banff, but few are better than Evelyn's.

Gianni Java's

743 Railway Avenue, Canmore, 609·4362

Many places in Canmore have nice views, but I think the best belongs to Gianni Java's with its two-sided panorama of the Bow Valley. On the second floor of a new building, the room is brightly contemporary and almost all windows, allowing a great vista.

The coffee they brew using Custom Gourmet beans usually lives up to the setting too. They also carry a short list of sandwiches and salads, and a big cooler is always filled with carrot cakes and cheesecakes and cookies. It doesn't get much better than lounging on their deck with an espresso on a sunny day.

Golden Happiness

III – 2 Avenue SE, 263•4882

With its ornate and bright decorations, Golden Happiness is one of the most elegant bakeries in Chinatown. There is even a tankful of swimming carp in front of the display cases. Golden Happiness offers the widest range of baked goods in the neighborhood, including moon cakes, and they are the Chinatown favourite for wedding cakes and other baked fancies. Most of their offerings are excellent, but I find the ham and egg buns and the barbecued pork buns too oily. Service here is perfunctory—little time is allowed for questions. Know what you want and order it quickly.

Janice Beaton Fine Cheese

1708 – 8 Street SW, 229•0900

The sharpest cheese shop to arrive on the scene lately is Janice Beaton Fine Cheese, located under the big brown awning at the corner of 8th Street and 17th Avenue SW. Beaton, the original owner of Caffè Beano, has gone full tilt into the cheese biz with a few hundred personally chosen blocks and rounds in her showcase. A visit to her tiny shop is a fragrant trip down the cheese trail, from French bleu de Bresse to Portuguese St. Jorges to Norwegian gjetost. Great local cheeses such as Natricia's various goat creations, Sylvan Star's Goudas, Leoni's Parmesans, and Rocky Mountain's Camemberts are lined up beside their foreign counterparts. And they show very well.

Beaton's shop also carries Valbella meats, olives, pâtés from Quebec, and breads from some of our best bakeries. When requested, they can whip up a tasty cheese sandwich on the spot. And in addition to retail, they put together cheese tables for parties and offer skilled advice on how to deal with runny brie or how long to age that ash-encrusted fromage. The service is friendly and knowledgeable, and the cheese is excellent.

JK Bakery

1514 Railway Avenue, Canmore, 609•2381

JK Bakery in Canmore supplies the Bow Valley with exceptional breads. Some loaves take a couple of days to create because the bakers follow traditional European recipes.

There's a small outlet at the bakery, which is hidden in a strip mall on Railway Avenue. Here you can find Mediterranean loaves, Barcelona bread, ciabatta, and baguettes, among others, and they are the tastiest in the mountains. (Crazyweed uses their bread to make superlative sandwiches.) There are also dense and fruity scones and display counters filled with the day's pastries. There is no mass production so the breads aren't available in Calgary. Yet another reason to drive out to Canmore.

Joshua Tree

805 Edmonton Trail NE, 230•9228

In these days of corporate, look-alike coffee cafes, it is heartening to see a few independents making their own way. Joshua Tree gets lost among the video shops and vacuum cleaner stores nearby, but once inside, you can barely hear the traffic.

They do not roast their own coffee, but glean the best from roasters such as The Planet. As a result, they have the capability to produce as good a cup of Joe (or perhaps Josh?) as can be had in these parts. They also feature a limited list of panini and quesadillas. On the sweet side, there are cakes, cookies, banana bread, and biscotti.

Jugo Juice

Eau Claire Market, 205•3300

Jugo is a full-tilt juice, smoothie, and wrap concept with eight Calgary locations and another dozen across Canada. (Eau Claire is their flagship shop.) The smoothies range from combos of strawberries, banana, and orange juice to blends of peach, pineapple, blueberries, mango sorbet, cranberry juice, and thermogenic herbs purported to stimulate the metabolism and burn fat. And on a daily basis, health-seeking regulars belly up to the bar for syrupy shots of wheat grass juice.

Firmly rolled into twelve-inch tortillas, their wraps of smoked chicken or turkey with greens and jellies are tasty. Less heavily loaded than some wraps (that's a good thing), they're a light complement to the smoothies.

Juiced

2015 – 4 Street SW, 209•6552
North Hill Shopping Centre, 220•1846
Calgary International Airport, 503•8925
Cascade Plaza, Banff, 760•3889

Modelled after the juice bars of Southern California, Juiced is a fully liquified, totally healthy and holistic operation that has popped up in malls and on trendy 4th Street. They offer a variety of smoothies, fresh juices, and boosts. You can get a Peach Passion smoothie with peaches, bananas, and peach sorbet. Or a Cranberry Crush with cranberry juice, strawberries, and raspberry sorbet. Poured into large, low environmental impact styrofoam cups (their use is justified on lengthy posters), these smoothies are very good.

I also like the fresh juices, twelve-ounce squeezes of combos such as tomato, carrot, beet, pepper, parsley, and celery or carrot, apple, beet, and ginger. They squeeze a lot of wheat grass juice too. Served in shot glasses or espresso cups, wheat grass is the beverage of choice for many healthy types.

Juiced also offers a brief list of sandwiches (in the Calgary locations only), including roast turkey, honey-cured ham, and vegetarian. These are filled with tomatoes, green peppers, and sprouts, but are not so huge that they fall apart. The bread is quite nice, so they're good—not earth-shaking, but good.

Manuel Latruwe Belgian Patisserie
1333–1 Street SE, 261·1092

Manuel Latruwe is a lovely bakery in the Callebaut mall showcasing skilled Belgian baking that tastes as good as it looks. And it looks great. The use of cream, butter, and eggs to create patisserie masterpieces is high here. A multi-layered caramel cake is a combination of seven separate recipes: there's a ganache, a caramel, a vanilla cream, a glaze, some caramelized pecans, the chocolate decorations, and the cake itself. These are not mass-produced, preserved sweets, and they are not cheap. Yet the strawberry and passion fruit mousse with dacquoise sponge cake, the crunchy meringues, and the lemon tarts are worth every cent.

They also make one of the best baguettes in the city. It is lightly crusty on the outside and slightly chewy on the inside, a perfect baguette for making into a sandwich or simply eating by itself. They produce other elegant and more rustic breads, and their multi-grain is a sandwich staple in our house.

Manuel Latruwe is also the name of the talented fellow who creates the breads and pastries. Latruwe and his wife and partner Lieve are young Belgian bakers who have found instant fans in their new Canadian homeland.

My Favorite Ice Cream Shoppe
2048–42 Avenue SW, 287·3839

My Favorite Ice Cream Shoppe is an unusual place. You go in thinking that you will have a cone or a shake, and by the time you leave, you have listened to young artists playing the grand piano, engaged a city alderman in discussion on local politics, and endured an endless stream of one-liners from the owner. "Our maple-walnut has more nuts than the Alliance Party," says Rork Hilford, the head scooper.

You can choose from over seventy-two flavours of ice cream, ones like mocha fudge, jaffa orange-chocolate, Rolo-Rolo, and cookie dough. Many are made solely for Hilford through special arrangements with various makers. Single-scoop cones are $2.75, and it is the biggest scoop (seven ounces!) of ice cream I've ever seen.

I often order a milkshake. At $4, it's not the cheapest in the city, but you are paying for quality. If you'd like it double-thick or malted, the price goes up $1. (The addition of powdered malt has become very popular lately.) Also big are freezes. These are milkshakes made from ice cream with pop instead of milk, the bubbles in the pop giving the concoction a real fizz.

So, with its cones, shakes, bad jokes, and all, MFICS is always a hoot.

The Planet

DOWN town
That's the Spot

2212 – 4 Street SW, 541•0960
101 Bowridge Drive NW, 288•2233
PanCanadian Plaza, 290•2200
3605 Manchester Road SE, 243•9992

In her most Yogi Berra mood, Catherine once said to me, "The Planet has the best coffee in the world." But then if you pump a perfectly pulled double espresso with a little steamed milk into her, the buzz will make her say almost anything. I don't know about the whole world, but for our taste, The Planet makes the best coffee and roasts the best beans in the city.

The original Planet on 4th Street is a smoky joint filled with caffeine fiends of all stripes. One summer Saturday afternoon, we arrived to find an entire wedding party—tuxedos, gowns, and all—enjoying some post-vow espressos. It is probably the only time anyone has worn that much white in The Planet. At press time, this location was expanding next door, and there should be a non-smoking side open by now.

The various locations offer a number of nibblies to go along with the coffee, but they do not pretend to be full-service restaurants. They are content to bring the best coffee possible to those of us with serious caffeine cravings.

Prairie Mill Bread Co.

4820 Northland Drive NW, 282•6455
7337 Sierra Morena Boulevard SW, 686•2500
919 Centre Street N, 277•1137

Prairie Mill has carved out a tasty niche with its retro-pioneer bakery concept. The shops have the appearance of age, of a time when bakers ground their own grains to make rustic breads. Big cutting boards are covered with samples, and wooden racks hold the baked goods. Quite the juxtaposition from their high-tech ovens.

The breads are decent too—the sourdough has a real bite, the sunflower-whole wheat toasts beautifully, and the cinnamon buns are the size of wagon wheels. It all has the rich flavour of organic grains and the freshness that comes from daily flour grinding.

The Roasterie

314 – 10 Street NW, 270•3304
227 – 10 Street NW, 283•8131

Most days, the sidewalks around 10th Street are filled with the aroma of roasting coffee emanating from the original Roasterie. It's a small place on the east side of 10th where the roaster takes up almost half the room, pushing coffee drinkers to the small plaza outside. The coffee is fresh and robust, from the ever-popular espresso through to the Danish Breakfast Blend and the Montana Grizzly. They'll make it as strong and dark and heavy as you want.

To offer a little more room and to provide a non-smoking section, The Roasterie has a second outlet almost across the street. Same coffee, but no smoke.

Valbella Meats

104 Elk Run Boulevard, Canmore, 678•4109

Many of the restaurants in this book carry the products of Valbella Meats on their menus. And rightly so: they are uniformly excellent. This Swiss-run shop smokes goose breast and venison, cures wild boar and buffalo, and makes a terrific bünderfleisch, or air-dried beef. Their retail outlet sells all these meats, plus fresh cuts and a line of cured sausages. And they have opened a small cafe on-site for those who just can't wait to take the meats home. Look for Valbella in the Elk Run Industrial Park—that's just to the right of the Trans-Canada as you come to Canmore from Calgary. Vegetarians beware.

Venus Cafe

610 – 8 Avenue SW, 264•3717

The Venus Cafe answers the crying need for caffeine from workers in the west end of downtown. Squeezed next to the Uptown theatre, it is a quietly funky place that pumps out high quality Planet coffee and dandy muffins and cookies that are baked on-site. They also sell Uptown special event tickets when the box office is closed.

There are five tables for those who like to sip-in and plentiful insulated containers for those who want to sip and stroll. With casual service and a homemade style, Venus is anything but a corporate cookie-cutter coffee house.

Wayne's Bagels

328 – 10 Street NW, 270•7090

Wayne makes bagels by the traditional method. Up to twelve flavours, they are hand-rolled, boiled lightly, and placed two-by-two on long wooden planks. They are then slipped off the planks to bake in a sixteen-ton, brick, wood-burning oven. This produces a chewy bagel that is not too tough, has a light crust, and tastes slightly smoky.

Wayne does the typical poppy seed, sesame seed, whole wheat, garlic, and onion styles of savoury bagels. What he does not do are the trendy and sweet styles, like blueberry or chocolate chip. He just does good bagels and that's fine by me.

Wild Sage

Dany Lamote's Wild Sage is a combination food outlet that offers takeout sandwiches, soups, and salads; meals to take home; house-made condiments to purchase such as chipotle horseradish and rhubarb-raisin chutney; and catering services. A lot of things for a small Eau Claire shop.

Lamote is one of the most experienced chefs in town, having opened Divino, Mescalero, Cilantro, Teatro, and other top-notch restaurants. His commitment is to local producers and processors and to organic whenever possible. So you will find him roasting organic beef on his huge rotisserie, slicing it into Manuel Latruwe bread, and topping it with aged cheddar and his horseradish mayo. On his take-home menu, there's lobster lasagna, lamb loin on rosemary skewers, and grain risotto with cranberries.

Lamote will also assist in accessing muskox or emu or racks of wild boar for your next gourmet cook-off. Even better, he will help with ideas on how to prepare these items. (Poached eel anyone?) Wild Sage is creating an important connection for the consumer with this service. These are ingredients that have been the exclusive domain of restaurants. Now we can cook venison ourselves—or better yet, have Lamote and his crew do it for us in our homes.

The Lists

The following lists will guide you to various food styles and geographic areas. Entries are in alphabetical order in the "Restaurant Reviews" section of the book unless otherwise indicated. (P) after the name of an establishment means the entry is in alphabetical order in the "Purveyors" section. All establishments are in Calgary unless stated otherwise.

Baked Goods

Bakerland (P)
Brûlée Patisserie (P)
Caffè Beano (P)
Decadent Desserts (P)
Eiffel Tower Bakery (P)
Evelyn's Coffee Bar (Banff) (P)
Golden Happiness (P)
Heartland Cafe
JK Bakery (Canmore) (P)
Laggan's (Lake Louise)
Lazy Loaf & Kettle
Manuel Latruwe Belgian Patisserie (P)
Pies Plus (Calgary & Bragg Creek)
Prairie Mill Bread Co. (P)
Venus Cafe (P)
Wayne's Bagels (P)

Banff

Banffshire Club
Barpa Bill's Souvlaki
Buffalo Mountain Lodge
Chocolaterie Bernard Callebaut (P)
Cilantro Mountain Café (see Buffalo Mountain Lodge)
Coyotes
Evelyn's Coffee Bar (P)
Juiced (P)
Kootenay Park Lodge (Kootenay Park)
Le Beaujolais
Maple Leaf
The Pines

St. James's Gate
Ticino
Waldhaus

Breakfast/Brunch

Buffalo Mountain Lodge (Banff)
Chez François (Canmore)
Coyotes (Banff)
Galaxie Diner
Il Sogno
Indulge
The Joyce on 4th (see James Joyce)
Kane's Harley Diner
Louisiana
The Mecca
Nellie's
Nellie's Breaks the Fast
Priddis Greens (Priddis)
Stranger's
Thomsons
Village Hearth

Canadian

Buffalo Mountain Lodge (Banff)
Deer Lodge (Lake Louise)
Maple Leaf (Banff)
Oh! Canada
The Ranche
The Rimrock Room
River Café
Thomsons
Wild Sage (P)

Canmore

Blends (P)
Chez François
Crazyweed Kitchen
Des Alpes
Gianni Java's (P)
JK Bakery (P)
Valbella Meats (P)

Caribbean

Dutchie's
Stranger's

Chinese

Bakerland (P)
Buddha's Veggie
Golden Happiness (P)
Golden Inn
Harbour City
Leo Fu's
Lok Tao
Silver Dragon
Silver Inn

Coffee Bars

Blends (Calgary & Canmore) (P)
Caffè Beano (P)
Caffè Mauro (P)
Central Blends (see Blends) (P)
Evelyn's Coffee Bar (Banff) (P)
Gianni Java's (Canmore) (P)
Heartland Cafe
Joshua Tree (P)
Lazy Loaf & Kettle
The Planet (P)
The Roasterie (P)
Venus Cafe (P)

Contemporary

The Belvedere
Big Rock Grill
Blonde
Blue Rock
Bonterra
Brava Bistro
Buffalo Mountain Lodge (Banff)
Cafe Divine (Okotoks)
Cilantro
Cilantro Mountain Café (Banff, see
    Buffalo Mountain Lodge)
Coyotes (Banff)
Dante's
Deer Lodge (Lake Louise)
Divino
Escoba
Florentine
Indochine
Indulge
The Living Room
Mescalero
Pau Hana Grille
The Pines (Banff)
Piq Niq
River Café
Savoir Fare
Savoury
Sino
Teatro
Thomsons
Wild Sage (P)
Wildwood

Diners

Boogie's Burgers
Galaxie Diner
Kane's Harley Diner
La Cantina
Lion's Den
The Mecca

Spolumbo's
Virginia's Market Cafe

Drinks

Auburn Saloon (P)
Big Rock Grill
Buzzards
James Joyce
The Joyce on 4th (see James Joyce)
St. James's Gate (Banff)
Tullamore
Wildwood

French/Continental

Chez François (Canmore)
The Cross House
Fleur de Sel
JoJo Bistro
La Chaumière
La P'tite Table (Okotoks)
Le Beaujolais (Banff)
Owl's Nest
Plunkett's

German

Edelweiss Village (P)
Kensington Berliner
Waldhaus (Banff)

High Tone

Banffshire Club (Banff)
The Belvedere
Blonde
Carver's
Da Paolo
Des Alpes (Canmore)
Il Girasole
La Chaumière
Le Beaujolais (Banff)
Owl's Nest

The Pines (Banff)
Post Hotel (Lake Louise)
The Rimrock Room
Rococo
Teatro

Historic Setting

Annie's
Auburn Saloon (P)
Banffshire Club (Banff)
The Belvedere
Cilantro
The Cross House
Deer Lodge (Lake Louise)
Divino
Heartland Cafe
James Joyce
Kootenay Park Lodge (Kootenay Park)
Lake Louise Station (Lake Louise)
Latin Corner
Murrieta's
Piq Niq
Post Hotel (Lake Louise)
The Ranche
The Rimrock Room
Rococo
Teatro
Thomsons

Indian

Anpurna
Clay Oven
Kashmir
Maurya
Puspa
Rajdoot

Interesting Ambience

Bodega
Da Salvatore
Galaxie Diner

The Highwood
Kane's Harley Diner
Lion's Den
The Living Room
Mescalero
Moroccan Castle
River Café
Sakana Grill
Santorini Taverna
Sultan's Tent
Sushi Ginza
Waldhaus (Banff)

Irish

James Joyce
The Joyce on 4th (*see* James Joyce)
St. James's Gate (Banff)
Tullamore

Italian

Bonterra
Da Paolo
Da Salvatore
Il Girasole
Il Sogno
La Brezza
Lina's Italian Market
Mamma's
Sandro
Virginia's Market Cafe

Japanese

Cafe de Tokyo
Misai
Sakana Grill
Sumo
Sushi Ginza
Sushi Hiro
Sushi Kawa
Yuzuki

Lake Louise

Deer Lodge
Laggan's
Lake Louise Station
Post Hotel

Latin American

Boca Loca (P)
Casa de la Salsa
El Sombrero
Juan's
Las Palmeras (Red Deer)
Latin Corner

Mediterranean

Barpa Bill's Souvlaki (Greek, Banff)
Bodega (Tapas & Spanish)
La Tasca (Tapas & Spanish)
Mimo (Portuguese)
Moroccan Castle (Moroccan)
Santorini Taverna (Greek)
Sultan's Tent (Moroccan)
Trocadero (Moroccan, Spanish &
    French)

Middle Eastern

Aida's (Lebanese)
Ali Baba (Syrian)
Cedars Deli Cafe (Lebanese)
Istanbul (Turkish)
Pita's Plus Donair (Lebanese)

Most Obscure

Anpurna
Casa de la Salsa
Dutch Cash & Carry (P)
Dutchie's
Il Girasole
Jonas'

Marathon
Mimo
Pau Hana Grille
Puspa
Savoury
Stranger's

Noodles

Cafe de Tokyo
The King & I
Oriental Phoenix
Rose Garden
Saigon
Saigon Y2K
Thai Sa-On
Trong-Khanh

Okotoks

Cafe Divine
La P'tite Table

One of a Kind (Almost)

Café Metro (Smoked Meat)
The Cookbook Co. Cooks
    (Cookbooks & Ingredients) (P)
Dutch Cash & Carry (Dutch) (P)
The Highwood (Culinary School)
Janice Beaton Fine Cheese
    (Cheese) (P)
Jonas' (Hungarian)
Little Chef (Family)
Louisiana (Cajun & Creole)
Marathon (Ethiopian)
The Mecca (Southern Barbecue)
Mimo (Portuguese)
Pfanntastic Pannenkoek Haus
    (Dutch Pancakes)
Restaurant Indonesia (Indonesian)

Pizza

Calzoni's
Sandro

Red Meat

The Better Butcher (P)
Buchanan's
Buzzards
Café Metro
Carver's
Debaji's Fresh Market (Northland
    Village location) (P)
James Joyce
The Joyce on 4th (see James Joyce)
Kensington Berliner
Little Chef
The Rimrock Room
Spolumbo's
Valbella Meats (Canmore) (P)
Waldhaus (Banff)
Wild Sage (P)

Romantic

Bonterra
Florentine
The Living Room
Owl's Nest
Rococo
Teatro

Seafood

Boyd's
Misai
Murrieta's
Pelican Pier
Sakana Grill
Sumo
Sushi Ginza
Sushi Hiro

Sushi Kawa
Yuzuki

Smoothies

Core Café & Juice Bar (P)
Jugo Juice (P)
Juiced (Calgary & Banff) (P)

Sweets

Chocolaterie Bernard Callebaut
   (Calgary & Banff) (P)
Confetti Ice Cream Factory (P)
My Favorite Ice Cream Shoppe (P)

Thai

Chili Club
The King & I
Rose Garden
Thai Sa-On

Vegetarian

Aida's
Ali Baba
Anpurna

Bodega
Buddha's Veggie
Cedars Deli Cafe
Clay Oven
Core Café & Juice Bar (P)
Debaji's Fresh Market (Northland
   Village location) (P)
Jugo Juice (P)
Juiced (Calgary & Banff) (P)
Kashmir
Marathon
Maurya
Moroccan Castle
Puspa
Rajdoot
Restaurant Indonesia
Sultan's Tent
Thai Sa-On

Vietnamese

Indochine (French-Vietnamese
   Fusion)
Oriental Phoenix
Saigon
Saigon Y2K
Sino (Vietnamese Fusion)
Trong-Khanh

The Best of the Best

The following will guide you to the best of the best. As in "The Lists," entries are in alphabetical order in the "Restaurant Reviews" section of the book unless otherwise indicated. (P) after the name of an establishment means the entry is in alphabetical order in the "Purveyors" section. All establishments are in Calgary unless stated otherwise.

Best Bang for the Buck

Aida's
Ali Baba
Anpurna
Barpa Bill's Souvlaki (Banff)
Boogie's Burgers
Boyd's
Cafe de Tokyo
Cafe Divine (Okotoks)
Cedars Deli Cafe
Core Café & Juice Bar (P)
Coyotes (Banff)
The Highwood
Kane's Harley Diner
Lion's Den
Louisiana
The Mecca
My Favorite Ice Cream Shoppe (P)
Nellie's
Nellie's Breaks the Fast
Pita's Plus Donair
Puspa
Restaurant Indonesia
Rose Garden
Saigon
Saigon Y2K
Sandro
Trong-Khanh
Yuzuki

Best Business Lunch

If someone else is paying:
Blonde
Buchanan's
Da Paolo
Dante's
Il Girasole
Il Sogno
Murrieta's
The Rimrock Room
Teatro
Thomsons
Wildwood

If you are paying:
Café Metro
Da Salvatore
Escoba
Indochine
Indulge
Jonas'
Piq Niq
Rose Garden
Saigon
Sino
Spolumbo's
Yuzuki

Best Patios

Big Rock Grill
Blue Rock
Bonterra
Buchanan's
Buzzards
Cilantro
Cilantro Mountain Café (Banff, *see* Buffalo Mountain Lodge)
The Cross House
Deer Lodge (Lake Louise)
La Cantina
La Chaumière
The Living Room
Mescalero
Nellie's (17th Avenue location)
Nellie's Breaks the Fast
Oriental Phoenix (58th Avenue location)
Priddis Greens (Priddis)
The Ranche
River Café
Teatro
Tullamore

Best People Watching

Auburn Saloon (P)
The Belvedere
Bodega
Brava Bistro
Cilantro
Crazyweed Kitchen (Canmore)
James Joyce
Kane's Harley Diner
Laggan's (Lake Louise)
Latin Corner
The Living Room
Mescalero
My Favorite Ice Cream Shoppe (P)

River Café
Sandro
Teatro

Best Service

Banffshire Club (Banff)
Boogie's Burgers
Da Paolo
Fleur de Sel
Florentine
The Highwood
Il Girasole
JoJo Bistro
La Chaumière
La P'tite Table (Okotoks)
Little Chef
Mescalero
Owl's Nest
The Pines (Banff)
Plunkett's
Priddis Greens (Priddis)
Rajdoot
Restaurant Indonesia
Santorini Taverna
Thai Sa-On
Ticino (Banff)
Waldhaus (Banff)

Best View

Annie's
Buffalo Mountain Lodge (Banff)
Deer Lodge (Lake Louise)
Kootenay Park Lodge (Kootenay Park)
La Cantina
Post Hotel (Lake Louise)
Priddis Greens (Priddis)
The Ranche
River Café
Waldhaus (Banff)

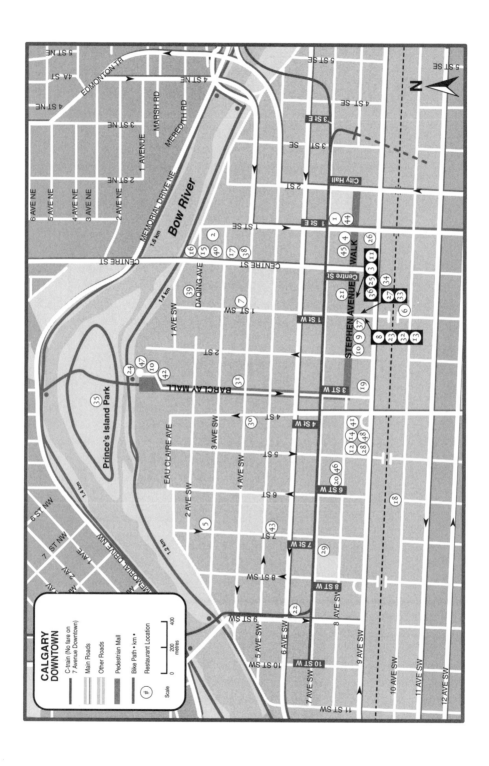